GEORGE
RAFT

Also by Lewis Yablonsky

THE VIOLENT GANG
SYNANON: THE TUNNEL BACK
THE HIPPIE TRIP
ROBOPATHS: PEOPLE AS MACHINES

GEORGE RAFT

Lewis Yablonsky

McGraw-Hill Book Company

New York   St. Louis   San Francisco
Düsseldorf   London
Mexico   Sydney   Toronto

Book designed by Marcy J. Katz

GEORGE RAFT

23456789 BPBP7987654

Library of Congress Cataloging in Publication Data

Yablonsky, Lewis.
  George Raft.

  Bibliography: p.
  1. Raft, George.
PN2287.R22Y3   791.43 '028 '0924 [B]   73-21842
ISBN 0-07-072235-8

Acknowledgment is made to the following for their kind permission to publish or reprint material from copyright or otherwise controlled sources:

Pete Hamill, "The Last Caper," *New York Post*, March 4,
1967.

Clifford Odets, *Six Plays* (Random House, 1933, 1962), p. 430.
Commentary by Harold Clurman used with permission.

Frances Farmer, *Will There Really Be a Morning?* (New York,
G. P. Putnam, 1972), pp. 127–128. Used with permission.

CONTENTS

PREFACE

Let me confess at the outset that I am an enormous admirer of George Raft. Raft — the movie star of the thirties and forties — had an effect on my life in the same way he has had on millions of people around the world. Many of my early heroic images of manhood were shaped by the immense figure of Raft on the giant screen. To me he was "the man": as a gangster (and he was a magnificent hood), a detective, a dancer, a spy, or a man trying to correct an injustice who fought against big odds; whether he won or lost, he did so with poise and style.

George Raft has always struck me as a more interesting personality than many of his contemporaries in Hollywood, because his personal life had an intrinsic and peculiar link with the consistent image he projected from the screen, no matter the part he played. An intriguing aspect of the man was his diversity. Indeed, there were and are many George Rafts: the world-famous dancer, ex-fighter, movie star, sportsman, alleged friend of the underworld, gambler, and fabulous "ladies' man."

My principal motivation in undertaking his biography was to capture the man in all his roles, to trace a life which touched so many areas of American life and encompassed several landmark decades. In addition to George's story, the book touches other themes: the making and meaning of a "star" or public personality; the studio system and behind-the-scene battles; the complex relationship between a star's personal life and his screen image; and a portrait and assessment of the powerful impact the golden years of Hollywood have had on American society.

George Raft — the man and the movie star — gave a new style to American masculinity: coolness to mask the heat of emotions and control the drives that demand raging release. There is evidence that many of America's most outrageous business entrepreneurs, the gangsters, emulated the coolness of Raft. Some, like "Crazy" Joe Gallo and Benny Siegel, had tragic gangland endings. Gallo, an eminent Brooklyn *mafioso*, was shot to death in New York in a Little Italy restaurant in 1972. A neighbor who knew Gallo in his earlier days commented: "Joey was the kind of guy who wanted to grow up to be like George Raft. He would stand on the corner when he was fifteen flipping a half dollar, and practiced talking without moving his lips."

George Raft's cool facade masked a man plagued by phobias, nervous habits and hidden fears. His feelings about himself were sometimes so negative that he looked into a mirror only when he combed his hair, and then he rushed the process. Since his earliest movies, Raft has consistently refused to view himself on the screen. After George saw his first movies he refused to see the rushes, rough cuts or even the final print of any of his subsequent films. In an appearance on the Johnny Carson Show, Carson showed an old film clip of Raft's movie *Bolero* and was amazed to see George turn away. When Carson questioned him, Raft replied, "I'm afraid to look, because I'm probably awful."

Awful—the man in this and other scenes was notable for his cool assurance and absolute confidence in his strength. These were the hallmarks of his screen personality, which at its best reflects a recent comment made by the great French actor of *Z* and other marvelous films, Jean-Louis Trintignant. "The best actors in the world," he observed, "are those who feel the most and show the least."

Raft recalls that many directors ordered him not to smile because friendliness diminished his toughness. The cool look, no matter the situation or its tension, has always been George Raft's salient characteristic. George Burns' comment about Raft and one of his costars, Gary Cooper, in his speech at a testimonial dinner given by the Friars Club in honor of George Raft is surely the definitive statement: "Raft and Gary Cooper once played a scene in front of a cigar store, and it looked like the wooden Indian was overacting."

In every respect George is a full partner in this book. George and I spent many months in intensive discussion of his life, experiences and his reactions to success and adversity. Over the past two years we also socialized, dined and went together to a variety of Hollywood events. He personally arranged many meetings for me related to the book and secured the cooperation of men and women who seldom if ever grant interviews. Their affection for George Raft was amply demonstrated by their generous gift of their time and reminiscences.

Among those who gave interviews or provided special data for the book are: Fred Astaire, Lucille Ball, Joan Bennett, Milton Berle, Harry Brand, Marlene Dietrich, Leo Durocher, Robert Ellenstein, Robert Evans, Howard Hawks, William Holden, Kirk Kerkorian, Jack Lemmon, Mervyn LeRoy, Dean Martin, Walter Matthau, Swifty Morgan, Pat O'Brien, Al Parvin, Edward G. Robinson, Gilbert Roland, Rosalind Russell, Frank Sinatra, Sylvia Sydney, Raoul Walsh, Mae West, Darryl F. Zanuck, Richard Zanuck. Mack Grey, George's personal friend, confidant, and assistant during his early Hollywood years, provided a host of valuable insights.

George wishes to acknowledge his great appreciation to two special friends, Danny Goodman and Sidney Korshak. Danny gave unsparingly of his time, arranged many important interviews, and drew upon his own twenty-year friendship with George to provide a wealth of useful observations that have enriched this biography. Sidney Korshak has generously helped George through many difficult periods in recent years; without his compassionate support and wise counsel this book might never have been completed. We are both enormously grateful to all of these people for their cooperation and encouragement.

Finally, we want to thank Irving Shulman for reading the first draft of the manuscript and making many useful suggestions, Bob Cornfield for his valuable assistance and knowledge of film history, Kathleen Matthews for detailed editorial work, Clive Miller for reading the final draft, and Fred Hills for his keen insights and editorial guidance throughout several stages of the manuscript.

A number of other people, film personalities among them, provided information anonymously. We of course have respected their decision and right to maintain their confidentiality.

A man of eminent discretion, George was never a "kiss and tell" lover or a confidant who later revealed private information. Significant sections of the book are derived from sources other than George Raft, and there are many incidents and anecdotes that George felt should not be included. In certain instances I have nevertheless retained material that seemed to me pertinent to the social and professional dimensions of his personal history. As the author of this authorized biography I must therefore assume final responsibility for its content.

Lewis Yablonsky
Santa Monica

1

FROM HELL'S
KITCHEN

George Raft was a tough kid; he had to be. Growing up in Hell's Kitchen in the early 1900s meant learning the authority of the clenched fist and the open blade. "Hanging out" was a perfected art and self-defense a necessity. It was a world in which street savvy and quick reflexes spelled survival, and the model for success might more easily come from the underworld than from polite society. This was the neighborhood whose cast of famous and infamous characters included Vincent, later known as "Mad Dog," Coll; Gene Tunney, one of the great heavyweight champions; Mike Jacobs, the Madison Square Garden promoter; and an older kid, an immigrant from Liverpool, England, named Owney Madden, or Duke, as they knew him on the streets, who became one of New York's most powerful gang bosses. In this world one learned early that success would not be lightly granted; it must be seized, and only the toughest and most agile could do so.

George Raft was born on September 26, 1895, in a ten-family tenement on New York's 41st Street between Ninth and Tenth Avenues. Three blocks west was the entertainment capital of the world, Broadway, where some thirty years later, as headline dancer at the Palace Theater, he would be a "star." That tenement was also a short distance from the later sites of the Paramount and the Strand movie theaters where in the thirties and forties almost a hundred films starring George Raft played.

George's grandfather, Martin Ranft—who introduced the merry-go-round and other amusement park rides to the United States—had emigrated from Germany to Boston in 1875. When his business prospered, he moved his family to New York City. Conrad, Martin's eldest son, was slated to inherit the family's growing business. With his light blond hair, blue eyes, and solid muscular physique, Conrad was the embodiment of the handsome, stolid, Germanic type. But—lured by the Mediterranean beauty of a girl from Little Italy—he proved to be a disappointment to his parents. Eva Ranft was a strikingly beautiful girl, with jet black hair. olive complexion, and full figure. Her family had a modest produce business, and Eva often helped her mother hawk vegetables from a horsedrawn wagon. When Conrad and Eva married, he was disowned by his parents and the young couple moved to 41st Street to escape the disapproval of their

3

families. Catholicism was their only common cultural heritage, but they shared the experiences and ambitions of most second-generation immigrants.

Cut off from his father's business, Conrad Ranft went to work at the John Wanamaker department store as a delivery man. He spent twenty-seven years with the firm, eventually working his way up to a small managerial position as route supervisor in the company's warehouse.

Conrad and Eva Ranft had ten children, nine boys and one girl; their daughter was born three years after George, their eldest son. As the years passed and the small apartment became increasingly crowded, George spent more and more time on the streets.

Hell's Kitchen was one of the toughest neighborhoods in New York, and the children quickly became street smart. Because of the poverty, the prevalence of violence, and the size of his family, George had to develop self-reliance and physical strength to survive. His mother and father worked long and hard to provide for their family and had little time to attend to any but the most basic needs of their children.

Raft's brothers were light complected, but he had his mother's dark, swarthy, Italian looks and he felt this made him his mother's favorite. His physical distinctiveness, together with the growing size of the family, helped to estrange him at an early age from his younger brothers. The streets became his home. It wasn't until his late teens, however, that he would abbreviate the family name to Raft and thus widen the gap between himself and his family.

Like many self-made men growing up in that era, George began to measure himself against other kids at an early age. Intellectual ability and gentleness were foreign criteria for measuring character in his neighborhood.

He and his friends climbed rooftops and bombed passing policemen with flowerpots, milk bottles, or bricks. A kid without a knife wasn't fully equipped to go out. Few of them could afford brass knuckles, but a roll of coins or a gaspipe coupling inside a fist was just as good. They would wait for a passing streetcar to muffle the noise, then crack store windows with bricks wrapped in newspapers, and steal whatever they could use or fence. The roughest among them was George's friend Owney Madden.

George's later life was to be greatly affected by their boyhood association.

Madden once told George why he went into the rackets. Simply, one day he was walking home with his mother, who carried a shopping bag filled with food bought from the street pushcarts. A young neighborhood thief came up from behind, cut the strings on her shopping bag, and took off with the groceries. "You know, Georgie," Owney said, "he did it with a pair of scissors. When I saw what that kid'd got away with and how easy it was, right then and there I decided I was a fool not to do it myself." He became a member of the Gopher Gang and was tough enough to become a leader.

Street ethics demanded a continual defensive stance, and George had a quick temper. It didn't take much more than a word or a challenging look and his fists would be up or a weapon improvised. Once he cut the leather fingers from a pair of his mother's best gloves to make them into a powerful pair of boxing gloves. When George's mother saw what he had done with her gloves, she didn't scold, she tried to understand. In the midst of this cold world of violence she was a gentle influence. The forces outside his home were, however, too tough to be softened by his mother's indulgence.

At times, unwittingly, Eva Ranft's love for her son and her preoccupation with his appearance forced him into more than his share of street battles. She was an orderly woman who dressed impeccably, and kept the Ranft flat as immaculate as a hospital suite. Her preoccupation with cleanliness and neatness extended to her children. According to George, "A lot of the time my mother wouldn't let me leave the house without wearing a Buster Brown suit with a starched collar. I loved my mother and I dressed up to please her, but you can imagine the fights I had. An especially bad day for me was my birthday, because it came during the Jewish New Year holidays. On my birthday my Mom would make me get all dressed up, and the local gangs would really be on the lookout to beat up a Jew. Well, there I'd be, dressed like I'm going to synagogue. Five or six of them would jump me. I learned the hard way what it's like to be a Jew, and maybe that's why I later always had a special feeling for my Jewish friends."

George's father, in contrast to his sympathetic and almost

fawning mother, was cold, distant, and seldom seemed interested in his son. Conrad Ranft stressed independence and encouraged his son to fight his own battles. George recalls one particular day when his father, returning from work, saw him in a fight with another boy. Instead of stopping the brawl, his father intervened only to tell his son: "If you don't win, I'll take care of you later myself."

It soon became clear that George was having more than his share of boyish escapades. At the age of nine he was on his way to becoming a young hood: unmanageable, truant, continually in fights. George's parents were alarmed: the streets of Hell's Kitchen were crowded with living testimony to the futility and bleakness of that lifestyle. They tried a time-honored solution: "They put me to work in my Uncle George's barber shop. I had to sweep up the hair, shine shoes, and keep the place clean. He was really strict and belted me if I didn't do my work right. I hated the place. I felt confined."

It was the most menial of positions for the young boy, but it eventually proved to be a turning point in his life. The strict demands of his uncle and the boredom of his situation encouraged George to investigate the bright lights and glamorous life of nearby Broadway. The gossip of his uncle's clients whetted his appetite for a more exciting life and hinted at thrills and pleasures foreign to his own neighborhood.

Makeshift theaters called nickelodeons, in which flickering images gave a semblance of reality on a screen, began to appear up and down Broadway. Spectators gasped when George Barnes fired a gun right at the camera in one of the first story-films, *The Great Train Robbery* (1903). In plusher Broadway theaters, stage productions such as *The Wizard of Oz* (1903), *Babes in Toyland* (1903), *Little Johnny Jones* with George M. Cohan (1904), and *The Squaw Man* (1905) were playing. George and his pals would walk three blocks over to the Great White Way and look in awe at the brilliant marquees which announced such stars as Eva Tanquay, Otis Skinner, Weber and Fields, and Sarah Bernhardt. When they could raise a few cents they would spend several hours in the dark interior of a nickelodeon watching the marvel of human figures on the screen.

While authorities differ in assigning dates to the birth of film, it is probable that the first major showing of a movie in the

From Hell's Kitchen

United States was the opening of the very first "Kinetoscope Parlor" on April 14, 1894, in a onetime New York shoe store at 1155 Broadway. The kinetoscope, which was to pave the way for the establishment of the film industry in this country, was invented by Thomas Alva Edison in association with W. K. L. Dickson, his assistant. The films, fifty feet in length and running less than a minute, moved continuously over a series of rollers and the frames were exposed through a revolving shutter and an electric light. By looking into an eyehole at the top of a wooden cabinet, one could see pictures move. But each showing, by the very nature of the machine, was short and could only be seen by one person at a time. What was needed was to project the images on a screen. Thomas Armat developed a machine that projected a series of successive still photographs with enough rapidity and of sufficient length to give the effect of motion and of reality. He called his invention the "Vitascope."

Anything and everything was put on film, with no attempt at a storyline. Then in 1903 Edwin S. Porter, a cameraman working for the Edison Company, made *The Life of an American Fireman.* It was an early example of scenes put together in a narrative form. Porter next set his sights on an even more ambitious production—*The Great Train Robbery*, a film that young Raft saw at least ten times. In addition to becoming the most famous of all the early movies, it provided the format for westerns as we know them today. The 1903 film, which Porter wrote, photographed, and directed, starred G. M. Anderson, who was later to win fame as "Broncho Billy."

The first permanent theater, probably Thomas L. Tally's Electric Theatre in Los Angeles, opened in 1902. In 1905 John P. Harris opened a plush motion picture theater enlivened by piano music, and called it the "nickelodeon" (a nickel being the admission charge; -odeon from the Greek word for theater). The initial attraction was *The Great Train Robbery*. The receipts for the first day's business totaled $22.50, but they more than tripled the next. Within a short space of time, the theater was grossing nearly $1000 a week and the daily shows were now running continuously from eight o'clock in the morning until after midnight.

When George Raft was thirteen there were more than 8000 "nickelodeons" in the United States, and it was estimated that over ten million fans saw nickelodeon movies in 1908.

7

Young George Raft became an enthusiastic "fan" of the nickelodeons; he saw *The Count of Monte Cristo* with James O'Neill; and most of the early films of D. W. Griffith, including Mary Pickford, America's darling, in *The Lonely Villa*, *The Adventures of Dollie*, *An Unseen Enemy*, *The Musketeers of Pig Alley*, and countless others.

George once recalled an experience that made him "look bad to the guys." On one excursion to a nickelodeon he was spellbound by the silent film version of *Les Misérables* (1912). Jean Valjean, the hero of Victor Hugo's classic, reached his greatest dilemma in the film when he had to decide whether or not he would save the life of a young boy pinned under the wheels of a carriage. Saving the boy meant revealing his identity (by exhibiting his strength) to the police and returning to prison. Of course, he chose to lift the carriage.

George could not contain his emotions and began to sob. His tough pals roared with laughter at George's sentimentality, and the experience taught him to conceal his emotions and maintain an impenetrable exterior.

When George returned from his Broadway adventures, his mother would scold him mildly for wandering too far from home. Then she would sit him down in the kitchen, feed him, and listen with rapt attention to his detailed description of the awesome fantasyland three blocks east. George enjoyed telling her the plot of every movie, which was usually the story of a triumphant hero who overcame insurmountable obstacles. And one night, after he had snuck into the backstage of a musical and watched a vaudeville dancer, he ran home to show his mother a new dance.

George loved his mother, and responded to her strong affection for her first son. She shared with him a sense of the romance and glamour of Broadway, and together they listened to a victrola and danced the popular steps of that era. "Even when I was a kid I had a sense of rhythm. Mom and I would dance together for hours. In fact, later on when I became a dancer and entered a lot of dance contests, my mother would sometimes be my partner. One time we won a flatfoot waltz dance contest. You put a dime under your heel and try to dance without losing the dime. We were a great team." But by the time George was ten, there were five other children and it was difficult for the young boy to adjust to the loss of his mother's undivided attention.

George loved baseball. When he was about eleven he proudly held the job of mascot for the New York Highlanders, who later on became the Yankees. "I used to bring the bats out in a wheelbarrow, take the players' uniforms over to a woman to be washed and generally help out.

"I played a lot of hookey in those days—in fact I hardly ever saw the inside of a classroom." He hung out mainly with the other guys on corners and stoops talking about sports, gang battles, and mostly invented tales of sexual prowess.

George's introduction to sex came at the age of twelve. He used to sit on his stoop at night "with the guys and goof around. When we would see a gal going by, like kids do we would yell or flirt with her." George noticed that late in the evening a very pretty nurse of about eighteen would pass his house, and he eventually made a point of being around when she walked by. She gave him a smile, and he suspected a hint of sensuality in her look. "One night I was sitting alone on the stoop. It was almost midnight. This nurse came over and began to talk with me. I really liked her. She began to kid around, and then she kissed me. It was a feeling I never had in my life. I suppose I was aware of sex from what some of the older guys said, but I really didn't know much. Before I could figure it out, the two of us, hand in hand, went down under the stoop into the cellar. There was an old beat-up sofa in one of the spaces down there.

"I was a big talker with the guys for a twelve-year-old—but I really didn't know anything about sex; but she certainly knew what she was doing. She had both our pants off in a hurry and we did it. Even though I was clumsy, I was very excited and found a new thrill in life. She must have liked it, because for a few months we would meet almost regularly when she got off work.

"She wasn't at all shy about sex; in fact she took her time, and I remember she saw to it that I learned to take my time and please her. She was a pretty good teacher, and I must have been a good student."

Despite their basically tolerant attitude toward George during his youth, his mother and father, prompted by his uncle, decided to confront him one evening. At thirteen he seldom went to school, refused to work in the barbershop any more, roamed the streets, and disappeared for days at a time without explanation. "The argument got so wild that I stuffed paper wads deep into my ears. Later I had to go to an emergency hospital to have them removed." That one experience was so traumatic that George attempted to avoid noisy arguments all of his life. He still scrupulously avoids them.

George had developed a fierce independence, which excluded anyone's interference with his activities. From that time, he virtually drifted away from his family, seldom to return except for brief visits to his mother. At thirteen, he was on his own. It seemed that his parents' fears were realized.

George spent a few years sleeping in subways, pool halls, empty lofts, and occasionally in one of the "mission homes" available to indigent youths. Once in a while, he might be put up by an older person in a room or apartment. To survive he worked as a helper in stores, delivered orders, shoveled snow, or carried bats for the Highlanders.

During this bleak and lonely period George felt the lure of romance more than ever. His imagination was filled with the bright and flashing marquees of Broadway. Every kind of entertainment from vaudeville to drama was presented on the stages beyond the chandeliered and thick-carpeted lobbies of these mysterious and palatial showplaces; but the only entertainment he could afford were the more stark nickelodeons. The five-cent admission was a tremendous bargain for George because sometimes it included a night's lodging. He would hide himself in a convenient closet or doorway and when the theater closed he would sleep peacefully in the warm deserted lobby or, when there was one, on the theater manager's sofa.

His interest in the making of movies led him to take the 129th Street ferry across the Hudson to Fort Lee, New Jersey, where many of the early silents were filmed. Although the studios were off limits to observers, it was easy for an agile young Raft to get into the makeshift studios of that era, where he could watch the magic camera record the exaggerated movements of the actors.

One day he was caught by a studio guard, and was roughly being escorted toward the front gate when in true movie fashion a leading lady—silent screen star Virginia Pearson—intervened. She told the guard she would be responsible for George, whom she thought was "a cute young man." That day he watched the filming from the luxury of the orchestra, ate lunch with the actors, and, when the day's shooting was complete, rode back to New York with the beautiful star in the studio's limousine.

In spite of such episodes, New York was a harsh city to an alienated and uneducated young man. To escape the pressures of his unfocused life he sometimes rode the rails to work in the orchards of upstate counties. On one of his cherry-picking adventures he was locked up in Troy, New York, after a railroad cop collared him in a freight car. Thereafter George flirted with jail many times but was never locked up again—except in the movies he made with Bogart, Robinson, and Cagney. His only touch with a "real" prison was later in life when he visited his childhood friend, Owney Madden, who was spending "time" in the most famous big house in the world, in Ossining, New York, popularly known as Sing Sing.

During these early years, Madden was becoming prominent in New York's underworld as a gang leader. When Owney could spare a few bucks he would hand his boyhood chum a five or a ten—enough, in those days, to keep George going for a week or more.

The extremes of rich and poor in the Manhattan of the early twentieth century were dramatically evident. The flow of immigrants into New York was unchecked, and many were starving in the tenements on the Lower East Side, while on the Upper East Side fashionable brownstones were being built for business and industry tycoons. George would look longingly at the horse-drawn—and later, horseless—carriages of New York's financial and social elite. These tantalizing sights of the luxuries that great wealth afforded gave George a sense of helplessness, envy, and frustration. Estranged from his family, without education, he could not imagine any possibility of social or economic achievement. This painful time created a sense of tremendous awe for the successful and powerful and, by contrast with his bleak poverty, low self-esteem. His own life seemed drab and aimless, and he developed an exaggerated respect for "class" and "society people." For a young boy growing up in Hell's Kitchen, with a disdain for education, athletes were the great and enviable heroes. They could achieve positions of wealth and respect without education or years of drudgery. Fighters like James J. Cor-

11

bett, John L. Sullivan, Sam Langford, and Jim Jeffries and baseball players like Ty Cobb and Honus Wagner were the big sports stars; and their names made headlines in the tabloids on the social as well as the sports page. For young George the power and wealth of the world of sports temporarily eclipsed the bright lights of Broadway.

The National and American Leagues were established by 1903, and the first World Series took place in 1903. Poolroom and streetcorner conversations inevitably drifted to batting averages, the introduction of the forward pass in 1906, or Jack Johnson's fight with Jim Jeffries in 1910. Young George Raft had a phenomenal memory for sports statistics, and this kind of recall served to give him a degree of status among his friends—and later served of inestimable value in memorizing his lines when he was a film star.

He had some talent as an athlete, for he could fight pretty well and played ball on Bronx sandlots. He would have given anything for a chance to play professional baseball, so he "fooled around" with several semi-pro teams on the Upper West Side. His ambition, however, exceeded his ability. At sixteen, passing for eighteen, he talked his way into a minor league club, and was given a tryout in Springfield, Massachusetts. After two days, playing in the outfield, the manager told him, "You can field pretty good, kid, but you can't bat. I don't think you'll make it."

Though George never made it as a ballplayer, his enthusiasm for the sport lasted all of his life. Like thousands of others, he would sit up on Coogan's Bluff in the Bronx, far from the action, squinting to see the big league teams in the stadium far below. After he became a star, he seldom missed a World Series, and luxuriated in the ability to sit in a first-class box seat. He never forgot those years when he hungered for the admission price to a real ball game.

Having had to defend himself while living on the New York streets, George tried to capitalize on his ability as a streetfighter, and when he was sixteen he became a professional boxer. He had his first fight at the new Polo Athletic Club on 129th Street and Park Avenue. "I always used to pal around with fellows who were older than I was. One night we crashed the gate at this A.C. The guy I was with knew a fighter and we were in the dressing room. Some kid didn't show up. The guy I was with had a lot of moxie and he bullied his way up to the promoter and told him, 'This kid here'—meaning me—'is a hundred-and-sixteen pound killer.' I became the substitute fighter and climbed through the ropes half scared to death. Somehow I dazzled the other kid with my footwork. And much to his surprise, mine, and everyone else's, I won the decision."

Although he had about seventeen fights at the Polo A.C. for a few dollars each—which was big money for a young man on his own—his undistinguished record included being knocked out seven times. But he decided his fight career was at an end when he was punched out by a fighter named Dougherty, who later made it as Frankie Jerome. When the fight was over George was left with a broken nose, two black eyes, and a puffed-up jaw. His left ear hung by a thread of flesh and required twenty-two stitches to sew it back in place. His reward for this was the loser's purse of five dollars.

Raft then decided to take up a less physically hazardous sport. He began to hang out regularly at pool halls up and down Broadway, most often a place called Crenshaw's, where he soon became something of a virtuoso with a cue stick. When he stayed in his league he could usually hustle the right games and win enough to pay for food and rent. One night, after the usual bantering challenge, he played several games with a slight, loud-mouthed young man named Billy Rosenberg who couldn't hold his stick correctly and had all the appearances of an easy mark. Somehow the youngster, a sidewinder, managed to win each game by just a few points. By the end of the evening George was broke and he knew he had been taken by an expert.

George, not one to bear a grudge, had learned the hard way to benefit from his losses, and he teamed up with Billy. Together they formed a slick combination: George was a good pool player and looked the part; Billy shot pool like a stumblebum, but when the money was right invariably he would win. Between them they beat many a sucker for his money.

When they caught the right mark and made a good score, they would celebrate at Lindy's, a fancy delicatessen for the "in" people on Broadway between 49th and 50th Streets. They would stuff themselves on the house specialties—pastrami sandwiches heaped with cole slaw and finish off with extra helpings of Lindy's famous cheesecake. They also enjoyed gawking at the show of

13

celebrities, hoods, and Damon Runyon characters who ate at Lindy's after hours.

After midnight, Lindy's was the place to be. Show business people like Al Jolson or Ben Bernie would be in booths adjacent to those of gangsters like Arnold Rothstein and Waxey Gordon. Writers and columnists like Mark Hellinger, Walter Winchell, and Damon Runyon found their basic material by observing this mixed swirl of exciting personalities.

Leonard Spigelgass, in his eulogy of Damon Runyon in *Screen Writer* (March 1947), recalled working with Runyon:

> Actually, he wasn't making up plots at all; he was re-modeling things and people he knew, and rearranging them, in better order. . . . His eyes were always open, his ears were always alert, his senses were always sharp. He became the instrument whereby the core of Broadway was articulated and brought to life . . . in Lindy's.

For George, the experience of being at Lindy's was comparable to working in his uncle's barber shop. He was an outsider, a hanger-on dazzled by people and conversations around him. But Billy Rosenberg, who had now shortened his name to Billy Rose, had chutzpah. He never hesitated to introduce himself and engage in conversation with the luminaries in Lindy's. Through Billy's aggressive promptings, George began to get a taste of the pleasures of recognition and fame.

George recalled one night when they sat next to a large table that was reserved for song writers, the denizens of New York's famous Tin Pan Alley. Billy, usually ebullient and a kidder, fell silent as two famous songwriters, Con Conrad and Ray Henderson, entered the restaurant and were escorted by a fawning maître d' to their special table. "George, what do you figure those guys make a year?" George estimated, "Maybe seventy-five or a hundred grand." George remembered Billy's response: "I don't see any fire coming out of their heads. If they can do it, I can do it." It was a momentous evening, immediately for Billy, and eventually for George as well.

Soon after, George lost his partner because Billy no longer

showed up at the poolroom. Billy Rose had written lyrics he thought were good enough to show some of the people he had met at Lindy's. Most of the early ones were bad, but Raft remembered Billy singing a song to him on Broadway one night that made George believe his old friend was "nuts." The song was "Barney Google with the Goo Goo Googley Eyes." Rose later wrote, with Con Conrad, "You Gotta See Mama Every Night," and topped these early hits later on with "Me and My Shadow" (Ted Lewis's theme song), "That Old Gang of Mine," "More Than You Know," "Mm Mm Mm, Would You Like to Take a Walk?" and "It's Only a Paper Moon." And Billy Rose went on to become a legendary show-business producer. Perhaps in part because of his association with this talented and aggressive man, George began to work on his incipient career as a dancer with greater determination. Like Billy Rose, Raft thought to himself, "If they can do it, I can do it."

George's mother had always encouraged his interest in dancing, and he spent endless hours outside the many clubs that lined Broadway listening to the music. Consequently, when he wasn't hanging out in the poolroom or making a quick buck at an odd job, he could be seen dancing around the Audubon Dance Hall or the Manhattan Casino. He had stamina and a consuming motivation to become expert, and he danced for hours on end. He had a good sense of rhythm and could quickly pick up a dance step. This natural ability gave him the enthusiasm to practice harder. He was well aware of the new acclaim achieved by good dancers. Vernon and Irene Castle had brought ballroom dancing to a higher degree of artistry and public acclaim. Vaudeville, the Ziegfeld Follies, and the early Kern, Berlin, and Gershwin musicals on Broadway had elevated popular dancing to a new importance.

George entered and began to win ballroom contests, and the prize money enabled him to move into a cellar room apartment that he decorated with college and baseball pennants. "It wasn't very expensive, and if I was hard-up I could always get money from my mother. I'd go see her, listen to a lecture, and get maybe a couple of bucks, which was enough for coffee and cakes for a few nights at Lindy's or another place called Freeman's, where all the actors used to hang out." Other than his mother, George had little to do with his family. He wanted to make his mother proud of him and this fired his ambition as a dancer, an activity that she understood and approved.

In time, George's long hours of hard practice as a dancer began to pay off. "There was a dance hall up in Washington Heights, the Audubon Ballroom, and I began to hang out there. I did dances like *Jada* and a thing called *I'll Say She Does.* Finally I became an instructor and used to get seven cents a dance. That and the contests I won made me a fair living."

An old friend of Raft's recalled a "Joe Frisco Dance Contest" that George won. Frisco, heralded as the creator of the jazz dance, wore a bright checked suit, a derby over one eye, and played with a cigar. "An all-around championship dance contest for good money was held at the St. Nicholas Garden on 66th Street. You could enter the one-step, tango, foxtrot, waltz, or the Frisco Dance Contest.

"I was lucky enough to win first prize in the tango. When George Raft came out to do an imitation of Joe Frisco, the hall was dark. Suddenly there's a spotlight on George. He had a jaunty look. Jet black hair, wearing a black suit with flare trousers. Over one eye is a sharp derby. He got a tremendous ovation even before he began his dance because he looked so perfect.

"Then he did a great impersonation of Joe Frisco dancing while he worked this cigar in his mouth. Even at that early stage in his career his dancing was professional caliber. He won the contest walking—or let's say dancing—away. After that there was no real competition for George."

The same friend told of another evening, when Raft was almost killed by a gang:

"About ten of us went up to this dance hall in Yonkers. George was just unbelievable with the women. This one attached herself to George—a beautiful girl. Then three tough guys came up to me. One said, 'Your friend's dancing with my girl.' Next he pulled a knife and said, 'I'm going to get him. Not now. In a little while.' Then they walked away. I told George and he said, '— him.' He was just carried away with dancing with this girl. Finally, the last thing I remember is the whole crowd of us running down the street trying to catch the streetcar for New York City. The guy with the knife and his gang were after us. We just about made it onto the rear of the streetcar. It scared the hell out of us and I felt certain that George, and all of us, had just escaped with our lives."

It was at this time that Milton Berle met George. "The first time I heard about George Raft was through my brother Phil, who was a pretty good ballroom dancer. I was then a thirteen-year-old kid actor. Phil, who rarely spoke of anyone but himself, got to raving one day about the greatest dancer he had ever seen. Somehow he lured me into this ballroom to see George dance. He was the sensation of the dancehalls in that era. No one had his class or ability.

"A few years later I met him when we were both doing vaudeville in Detroit. He told my mother, 'This kid's got something.' Being a wise guy I said something like, 'Yeah, and I know the girl that gave it to me.' In spite of my nasty brat crack, George said 'No, I'm not fooling. This kid's going to be a star.' I never forgot his saying that."

Now established as a polished dancer, George began to work in what were then called "tea rooms"—dark, well-appointed cafés which women frequented in the afternoons. Idle housewives, high-class prostitutes, and wealthy dowagers were the main clientele. Long before women's liberation, these establishments reversed the notion of which sex is the aggressor. Attractive men like George and Rudolph Valentino, who also worked in these places, were the sought-after companions. The female patron would be seated at a table, place her order for tea or coffee, and then at her leisure select one of the tea-room gigolos seated conspicuously at one end of the room. As in a dime-a-dance hall, the woman would discreetly tell the hostess her selection. The hostess would then tell the always-available young man that "the lady at table X wants you." He would then go over, chat, and dance with the lady. In some cases the introduction would lead to a more intimate relationship. In a tea room such as Churchill's, Raft would be paid two dollars for an afternoon's work in addition to tips from the ladies.

Raft emphasized his dark looks by slicking down his jet black hair with a whole jar of Vaseline—the hair style was later known as the patent-leather look—and wore tight, form-fitting clothes, a style which came to be associated with the great Valentino. At that time Valentino's name was Rodolpho Guglielmo.

"Valentino and I didn't have much time to talk to each other.

We'd just be sitting there and the hostess would come over to say, 'Go over to that table and dance with that woman.' We never asked anyone to dance, we were always *told* who to dance with. The hostess would say, 'George, you go over to table number seven.' The popular dances were the foxtrot and the one-step and the waltz."

George worked Churchill's in the early afternoon. At three o'clock he would go to the Sunken Galleries, another tea room on 95th Street, where he would dance until five-thirty.

"I was never a big eater of any kind, so I could keep going day and night. My whole life then was dancing. Of course, my dancing often led to my getting laid. I suppose I got into a happy rut. I would dance all day and practically every night sleep with a different broad. Maybe that's why I became such a sexy dancer. The two things—dancing and sex—would blend into each other.

"In those days the women would proposition me. After all, I was alone, and I had my rent to pay."

Not all beds were roses for George. "This one girl, Marilyn, who started to hang around the tea room, insisted I wear this tight collar that raised a vein in my forehead until it stuck out. She thought this vein was very sexy. Marilyn was twenty-three and though I looked older I was only seventeen.

"I had affairs and slept with a lot of women in those days. I never considered Marilyn special, but I went home with her pretty regularly. She was good looking and I enjoyed being with her. But I never really meant much when I told her, 'I'm in love with you.'

"One Saturday night, she came to the dance hall and she was mad as hell because I danced, as usual, with different women. Saturday was always a big night at the dance hall. Finally, she rushed up to me and screamed, 'You son-of-a-bitch! You've been cheating on me!'

"I was dancing with another girl. But it was obvious that Marilyn was going half nuts. I took her aside and I said, 'Look, take it easy. We can settle this,' She said, 'There's only one way to settle a son-of-a-bitch like you.' Then she took a long hat pin out of her hair and plunged it right into my chest.

"I was absolutely stunned with pain as I slid to the floor. All hell broke loose. She's yelling, crying, 'I didn't mean it. I love you. Please forgive me.'

"Finally a couple of friends got me to the hospital. Fortunately it went into my body in a place that didn't cause any real damage. A doctor cauterized the wound and in a few days I was okay. The doctor said that if it had gone a few inches to the right I would have been stabbed in the heart and died.

"I was just a kid then, but that experience taught me something about women. I never realized how possessive they could be or that I was, I guess you might say, that attractive.

"Up to then I never thought I was handsome. I felt I was the black sheep and the ugliest kid in my family. But I realized then that women really could go for me."

George had flirted with a number of professions. Eager for acclaim and wealth he had tried his hand at pool, boxing, and baseball. But he had only been second rate. It now seemed that dancing was to be his career. It was fast and fun and it came easily. He had served his apprenticeship in the minor leagues. He was now ready for the big time. An agent saw him dance in a ballroom contest and signed him up to dance, for the first time, in a legitimate theater, the Union Square Theater on 14th Street. "I'll never forget the night I broke into vaudeville on a real stage. I was very nervous, but once I heard the music and began to dance everything was okay. During this fast dance I just got carried away with the rhythm. When I finished they applauded wildly and I came back for five curtain calls. I was so excited I didn't know what happened."

Inspired by the heady recognition he was earning, he worked even harder at his dancing. No aspiring professional athlete, scientist, or teacher trained any harder than George to achieve success. He went to Harlem clubs and sat for hours studying the dance steps performed by the great black hoofers, whose most famous exponent was the legendary Bojangles. When Raft did these same dances downtown, he was hailed as sensational.

Around 1920, Broadway was a small cohesive community and George Raft's prominence and reputation as a dancer grew as his billing moved up to headline status. It was then that Stanley Burns, a show-biz entrepreneur, caught George's act. Burns, once an acrobatic dancer himself, now booked acts for a big touring show called *The Lilies of the Fields.* The show was owned by Harry and Elsie Pilcer. Harry himself used to dance with Gaby Deslys, a French music hall star who became a sensation in the United States. A star of Gaby Deslys's stature received $5,000 per week and it was apparent that Harry Pilcer dealt only with top performers. Pilcer's interest in George was gratifying and an important milestone in his career.

Burns was looking for somebody to dance with Elsie Pilcer and Dudley Douglas. Raft passed his tryout with Elsie Pilcer and was booked into the Orpheum and the B. F. Keith Circuits. He had made bigtime vaudeville. With Pilcer and Douglas, Raft—now a top professional, well-paid dancer—traveled from coast to coast and after a tour had no problem in getting bookings in top Broadway clubs.

George had many girlfriends, but there was no special steady, for Raft had no inclination for any relationship beyond one-night stands. After five years of running the streets hustling a few dollars to live, he was now luxuriating in his newfound wealth, and he was not at all interested in losing his freedom or sharing his prosperity with a partner. But it was not merely selfishness that kept him single. "When you work from one o'clock in the afternoon until six o'clock in the morning, you don't get a chance to see anybody permanently. Sometimes I might fall into bed for some sleep at around eight o'clock in the morning, and then get up at noon to go to work again. Once in a while I'd take a nap in my dressing room between shows."

His rapid dance movements were phenomenal and soon became his trademark. In theaters and clubs he received feature billing as "The Fastest Dancer in the World." George would become so carried away during a dance that he had to develop a way of dealing with the possibility of unwittingly injuring himself. "When I danced I used to move so fast that sometimes I'd hit the footlights. They'd hurt my feet so bad I would have to stop dancing because of the pain. So instead of shoelaces I used wire in my dancing shoes to numb my feet by cutting off the circulation—sort of like binding them. By using these laces I felt no pain and would be able to finish the number. Once, because my feet were so deadened I didn't know I had broken my toe until the next day."

"You know," he continued, "I could've been the first X-rated dancer. I was very erotic. I used to caress myself as I danced. I never felt I was a great dancer. I was more of a stylist, unique.

I was never a Fred Astaire or a Gene Kelly, but I was sensuous—
at least for those days.

"When I was doing my act with this five-piece band and Elsie
Pilcer, toward the end of the dance I'd start to quiver—shake all
over." One night the manager of a theater where George played
came backstage and told him his dance was indecent. He told him,
"It's no good for the children at the matinee. But," he added,
"I don't mind if you do it in the evening."

"Women liked it. They would say, 'Oh, man, the rhythm you
got.' Later when I made pictures like *Bolero* (1934), I used the
same sexy movements. In our dance act, Elsie used to smile at
the audience but I was told to look directly at her, and not to
smile. That made it . . . sultry. That no-smile deadpan expression
had the same effect when I used it in the movies."

George had not been drafted during the First World War
because two of his brothers had enlisted. Both were lost in action.
Another brother, a laborer, died in a fall from a scaffold, and in
1920 his sister contracted tuberculosis. The last time he saw her
was on a visit to her hospital in Liberty, New York, where, frail
and weak, she could hardly talk. She died a few weeks later.

His mother was still his biggest fan, and his success enabled
him to give her some money every month. Eva Ranft was still
a beautiful woman, with a lovely complexion and a trim figure.
With her son's support she was able to indulge herself with a
weekly trip to the hairdresser.

Now in his late twenties, Raft was doing better with each booking. His mother, who had worried about his future for many
years, saw evidences of success in her errant son and was clearly
proud of him. But like so many mothers Eva felt her son's success
was incomplete unless it was shared with the right woman.
Getting married at that time was the farthest thing from
George's mind. He had all the women he cared to have; moreover, he was concerned with his rising career. Yet one girl,
Grayce Mulrooney, did appeal to him. Grayce had been one of the
girls who had been his ballroom partners and he had dated her
a number of times.

Since then Grayce had become a social worker on Welfare
Island. Her mother was a probation officer, her uncle a ranking

police officer who later, under Mayor Jimmy Walker, became the Police Commissioner of New York City. A devout Catholic, chaste, and from a fine family, Grayce stood out in sharp contrast to the girls George usually spent his time with. "In those days," he recalled, "there were two kinds of girls, those who did and those who didn't; and Grayce definitely didn't."

Seeing George only when he was in New York wasn't enough for Grayce. When George was to tour the Keith Vaudeville Circuit with Pilcer and Douglas and would be gone for almost four months, Grayce, who was on vacation at the time, asked if she could travel with them for three or four days. George agreed. It was a fateful decision and one that would have a tragic effect on the rest of his life.

"We played Scranton first. Grayce had her hotel room and I had mine. I never said anything to Pilcer and Douglas but they probably thought that if a girl went away with a guy there was something between us. You know how people think. But they were way off in this case. I felt that Grayce would be mine someday, but as my wife."

After the late show in Scranton, the troupe of Pilcer, Douglas, Raft, and Mulrooney drove to Wilkes-Barre. They arrived around two in the morning. In those days a reservation at a hotel was not an absolute necessity. But this time Douglas, after booking their rooms, told the couple, "There's a convention here and I can't get three separate rooms but I can get two. So we're all set." George offered to sleep in the car, but Grayce and the others persuaded George to double up with her.

"I didn't want to tell Douglas that I had never gone to bed with Grayce. Anyway, he booked a single for us and we took one room, with twin beds. We were, of course, planning to sleep separately. After we had unpacked and settled down Grayce said, 'George, I want to tell you something.' I was really tired and wanted to go to sleep, but I tried to listen."

Grayce told George a long story about how she loved him very much. Reluctantly, she revealed that when he was on the road she had gone out with an older man prominent in New York business circles who was extremely jealous and followed her everywhere. She couldn't get rid of him and was frightened because he'd threatened to follow her on this trip.

George asked her if she had slept with him. Grayce became furious, cried, and said, "What do you think I am?"

George consoled her, told her to forget it. He was exhausted and told her they would work it all out when they got back to New York. He wanted her that night—but his pattern with women was never to make an advance unless he was sure it would be accepted. After kissing good-night, they went off to sleep in separate beds.

"I'm sound asleep. Suddenly the phone starts ringing. It's four in the morning!

"I got up, answered the phone, and I hear this angry man shouting, 'I want to talk to Grayce!' I don't know who it is. I thought it might be her father. Anyway I wake up Grayce, and she gets on the phone.

"She says, 'Hello,' then puts her hand over the phone and says it's this guy she went with. Then she says, 'He's having me followed. What should I do?'

"Some question to ask when I'm groggy and half asleep.

"While she's talking to him and crying at the same time, he's yelling through the phone so loud I can hear him. Things like, 'I'm going to get that son-of-a-bitch Raft for white slavery. You bitch, you, what are you doing with him? I'm going to get you, too.'

"Grayce is hysterical. 'Please Joe,' she's pleading, 'we didn't do anything. George didn't do anything. Don't do that to him. He's innocent.'

"Finally she just hangs the phone up on him.

"I don't understand any of it. I said to her, 'Grayce, what the hell's going on? What's it all about? What's he going to do to me?' She's sobbing and finally she calms down.

"She says, 'I have to admit something to you, George. I began to go with him because I was lonely. You were gone so much. He was nice to me at first—we'd go to dinner or a show and have fun. Then one night we were having dinner in this private room at this place and he made advances to me. He tried to rape me. But nothing happened.'

"I said, 'Did you go out with him again?'

"She began to cry hysterically. 'A few times. He forced me to and I was afraid of him. Now he says he's going to get you in trouble on the Mann Act. You know, it's white slavery to take a minor across the state line. I know the law and you could get twenty years in prison.'"

Since Grayce's uncle was a police officer, and she a social worker, George felt she did indeed know the law, at least better than he did. He felt sorry for her, but he was also worried about his own interests. He thought that he might get locked up.

"She's talking about my going to jail, and how she really loves me. I'm exhausted, you know, doing three shows a day. Well, anyway, it's dawn and we had wrangled about the thing almost all night.

"Finally I proposed. I said, 'Let's get married. That will solve everything.'

"She looked surprised and happy for a minute but then she starts crying again. 'Georgie, only if you really love me.'

"Finally, I said, 'Look, I really love you, okay?'

"I didn't mean it. What did I know about love, except that girls liked to hear it? But I felt sorry for her and frankly I was really afraid of what this man might do—like put me in jail.

"We had breakfast, went down to the City Hall in Wilkes-Barre. And by four that afternoon I was a married man.

"That night I did two shows, so by the time we get back to the hotel I was knocked out.

"I went through so much that day and night I didn't know what happened to me. Or really what the hell was going on. We're now back in the room alone sitting, kind of nervous. Finally I figure, this is it, my wedding night. I took a bath. I was always a perfume nut—so I put some perfume on. Then I put on soft silk pajamas and my robe.

"Grayce goes into the bathroom and I'm waiting with great anticipation.

"I'm thinking to myself, 'Well, this isn't too bad. Maybe fate had stepped in.' I began to think it might be nice to have a family. I liked kids. I was tired of one-night stands and the kind of girls I had been running around with, and Grayce looked good.

"It's now two o'clock. I've been waiting over an hour, and I've smoked almost a whole pack of cigarettes. What the hell could she be doing?

"I figure she wants to look her best and she's bathing and all that. A half-hour later I'm getting groggy again and really need sleep. Finally, finally—she comes out, eyes all red, and I see she's been crying. I thought to myself, 'Oh shit—what next?' She says, 'George, I got something to tell you. I can't lie to you. That man raped me, and then I began to go with him. We slept with each other almost every night. You were away. I'm no virgin!'

"I sat there shocked. She gets real hysterical and goes into this sobbing jag again. What can I do? I'm disappointed in her. I had been taking her out for a year and hadn't touched her. Why didn't she tell me before? I thought she was completely different. My wife was like any other broad I had been with. I felt tricked.

"At the same time I felt sorry for her—she couldn't stop crying. Finally I put my arms around her and she stiffened. She said, 'I'm too upset to make love tonight.'

"I felt very rejected and depressed. But what could I do? We were both wiped out from the emotion of that day. We each got into our own bed.

"I remember thinking to myself, 'Here's George Raft, the big Broadway ladies' man, on his wedding night, and nothing happened.' I had really made a mistake.

"I remember the next day I was even more convinced I had made a big mistake. I got paid, I was writing my Mom a letter, and I was putting a hundred-dollar bill in the envelope.

"Grayce looks surprised and says, 'What are you doing?'

"I told her I was sending my mother some money, something I always did. She starts a long argument about how we're married now and need the money to furnish an apartment and all that.

"I told her flat out, 'My mother comes first.' She keeps at me. I knew then for sure we weren't going to make it.

"We always had Sundays off. Grayce wanted to go back to the city and tell some people we were married. So the next night, Saturday, we drove back to New York after the show. I had to leave the same day, Sunday, for my next booking on Monday evening. I took Grayce to her home, kissed her good-bye, and we agreed to work it all out after I got back. I didn't want to get involved with her family at that time—because I wasn't even sure I wanted to be married to her."

When George returned to New York he went to see his parents

and told them he was married. At first they didn't believe it, but by this time they were not surprised at anything George did.

George went on to Ohio, to continue his vaudeville tour. A few days later, when he was in Dayton, he received a letter from his mother telling him that his wife was seen by a friend in a place called The Long Beach Club drinking with two men. George was furious. For him, that letter was the final blow.

A few weeks later, he was finishing the tour in Philadelphia. "I was still full of anger about my supposed wife out with some other guys. I called her from Philly and accused her. She told me to calm down since she could explain everything better in person. We agreed she would get on the train and come to Philly.

"After my late show we went to a speakeasy. She began to explain that the two guys she was with were old friends—crap like that. In the meanwhile she's belting the bottle pretty good, while all the time she's telling me how she loves me, junk like that.

"I wasn't a drinker at all, and I ordered a soda. I'd had one or two drinks in my life to see what it tasted like, but I was really disgusted with her, my wife, acting like a drunken floozy. We're arguing back and forth. In the confusion of our yelling I'm drinking this soda. It tastes awful, but I'm gulping it down because I'm thirsty. When the waiter comes over for a reorder I said to him, 'What the hell kind of soda is this?' The creep smiles and tells me that I've been drinking their finest home brew! If I wasn't so involved with Grayce I would have killed the son-of-a-bitch. I said it was time to leave. We went back to my hotel room. I couldn't believe what was happening to me. I actually went blind from that rotten home brew. I couldn't see!

"Anyway, she put on this negligee. I couldn't see it but I could feel it. One thing led to another and we began to make—let's call it—love. It was ridiculous. The first and last time I made love to my so-called wife I was blind drunk."

Some weeks after that night, Raft clearly ended his relationship with Grayce. She accepted the separation and went her own way; but—whether out of vindictiveness, obstinacy or, as she claimed, her devout Catholicism—she refused from 1923 until her death in 1970 to grant George a divorce.

Years later, when George became a success in Hollywood, Grayce, as his wife, demanded a share of his income. Without quibbling, because he recoiled from legal hassles, George signed over to Grayce ten percent of his earnings. Over forty-seven years Grayce's ten percent amounted to well over a million dollars. But the financial burden was the least substantial loss for Raft. He had lost a measure of his freedom, a beginning of the consequences of his success.

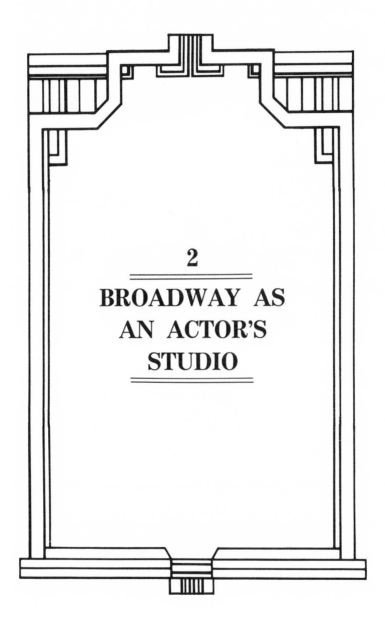

2
BROADWAY AS AN ACTOR'S STUDIO

In the early twenties the motion picture theaters began to attract larger audiences than live entertainment. Thousands of new movie palaces were opened and filled with fascinated audiences all over the country. The star system emerged in full force: Mae Marsh, Richard Barthelmess, John Barrymore, Mary Pickford, Charlie Chaplin, Lon Chaney, Douglas Fairbanks, Gloria Swanson, Rudolph Valentino, and Lillian and Dorothy Gish were all stars whose films earned millions of dollars. The range of films was exciting and varied: D. W. Griffiths' *Broken Blossoms*, *America* (1924), and *Orphans of the Storm; The Four Horsemen of the Apocalypse* (1921); *The Hunchback of Notre Dame* (1923) with Lon Chaney; Douglas Fairbanks as *The Thief of Bagdad* (1924). Audiences gasped at the parting of the Red Sea in Cecil B. DeMille's *The Ten Commandments* (1923), and laughed and cried hysterically at Charlie Chaplin's *Soldier Arms* (1918), *The Kid* (1921), and *The Gold Rush.*

In New York, vaudeville and theater still flourished. Such diverse entertainers as the Barrymores, Alfred Lunt and Lynn Fontanne, Marilyn Miller, Ed Wynn, the Marx Brothers, Nora Bayes, Sophie Tucker, and Al Jolson were among Broadway's most illustrious stars. Alongside the legitimate showplaces were the illegal and more exotic cabarets and theaters on and off Broadway. These garish establishments attracted those who on a night on the town would drop in for some after-theater fun, food, and drink. Among the patrons were gangsters whose company appealed to businessmen, politicians, famous entertainers, and visiting royalty. In those days, as Raft said, "A well-known gangster was respected as much as any movie star or politician." Certainly these men had an aura of wealth and power that made itself felt.

Prohibition linked booze with big money and George, from the privileged vantage point of his own success, was eager to be included both financially and socially in all the bigtime activities. The action and excitement of gambling, hustling and racketeering could be found in the luxurious and oftentimes seedy gambling establishments around Broadway and on the West Side.

Raft frequented a club located beneath Jimmy Durante's Club Durant in a small basement garage just off Broadway. A private staircase led to a back room filled with the dice tables of Arnold

31

Rothstein, who banked the game. A regular high roller seen at Rothstein's was George McManus, who several years later was tried and acquitted for the murder of his host.

The cast of gangsters who enjoyed Rothstein's crap game included men who were later to become legendary heroes of American crime: Al Capone, then known as Al Brown, was a regular; huge Waxey Gordon, another notorious hood from the lower East Side; Lucky Luciano; and Larry Fay, a local rum-runner. Large sums changed hands rapidly. One night Lou Clayton, Jimmy Durante's partner and a serious gambler, pawned his wife's diamond ring and managed to win a hundred thousand from Rothstein. Happy and excited with his big score, Lou came to George's dressing room in the club he was working and threw him a fifty-dollar bill. A few days later, he lost every cent at the same game. Broke again, he came to George to borrow a few hundred to stake his "getting even."

Many nights a big crap game was warned in advance from police headquarters to fold because the cops were on their way to raid the place. Bigshots would vanish through a rear exit and lesser lights were left behind to be arrested and give the raid some authenticity. Once George was trapped in a raid and, along with the others, was taken to the police station. Raft did not use his own name, was neither fingerprinted nor booked, and the charges were dismissed.

The prototype gangster–gambling king that Raft later played on film and in glamorous casinos around the world was not born full blown from his imagination. Arnold Rothstein, perhaps more than any other gambling king on Broadway, was the model for the tone and style of George's portraits and thousands of others that appeared on stage and screen. George studied Rothstein's movements with the same diligence that he had previously studied the steps of the uptown dancers.

Arnold Rothstein was born in 1882 on West 47th Street, a few blocks away from the hotel where he was to be fatally shot in 1928. His pale good looks, suaveness, and intelligence were the raw materials that he later parlayed into the role of consummate gambling king of New York. He began with corner dice and card games and later helped to pioneer rum-running, a narcotics sales syndicate, and posh gambling casinos that included showgirls as shills. By the age of twenty-five, Rothstein was known on Broadway as "the mastermind."

The inspiration for many of Damon Runyon's stories, he blended the cunning of a pawnbroker with the business sense of a top Wall Street financier. He would bet on the cut of a deck of cards or the color of the suit of the next man to walk into Lindy's. He would be as excited about a ten-dollar bet on whether the next horseless carriage coming around the corner had an odd or even license plate as a ten-thousand-dollar bet on a horse.

Rothstein worked hard at his profession to put together what was known in gambler's parlance as the big bankroll. The score that threw Rothstein into the big time was his "gamble" on the 1919 World Series when the Cincinnati Reds beat the Chicago White Sox. Rothstein won several hundred thousand dollars. It was determined through an investigation that eight men on the Chicago team, caustically renamed the "Black Sox," received $100,000 to throw the game. Rothstein was never found guilty of this gambling crime of the century; but the word around town was that he was the behind-the-scenes money man who put in the fix. It was a bad day for the national pastime and led to the appointment of Judge Kenesaw M. Landis as Commissioner of Baseball to insure that this would never happen again.

A restless and unrelenting gambler, it was reported that later, on July 4, 1921, Rothstein—who had by then amassed a bankroll of several hundred thousand dollars—let it all ride on a horse named Sideral at Acquaduct, and collected $850,000.

In the few years from 1921 to 1925, Rothstein parlayed the underground dive George sometimes frequented into the classiest gambling houses anywhere in the world. He operated the Partridge Club in New York, a casino on Long Island and one in Saratoga. He employed beautiful showgirls to lure customers his way. At the club in Saratoga, known as "The Brook," an oil magnate was reputed to have lost $500,000 in two nights of non-stop action.

Rothstein's exploits were notorious and held a disreputable glamour, appealing both to the twenties "jet set" and to the socially deprived. Here was a different and distinctively American kind of success. It is easy to see why such a figure would appeal to the great American novelist F. Scott Fitzgerald, who reputedly met Rothstein on one occasion. Some critics suggest that Rothstein was the model for Jay Gatsby and his confused idealism in Fitzgerald's *The Great Gatsby.*

In 1928, Rothstein found himself on a downhill path when he lost a sizable sum to a politically well-connected racketeer, George McManus, in a two-day marathon poker game. Rothstein, short of cash, paid most of his debts with a verbal IOU. He later welched on the debt, claiming the game was crooked.

He was shot in a meeting he had with McManus to discuss the debt at the Park Central, now the Park-Sheraton Hotel, on 56th Street, and died later at the hospital. In true gangland style, he never talked. McManus was tried in a fast, coverup trial, at which he was exonerated. It was alleged that McManus was given quick justice because he might have mentioned the acquaintanceship of Mayor Jimmy Walker and Police Commissioner Edward Mulrooney (Raft's wife's uncle) with Rothstein.

A few days before he died on November 4, 1928, Rothstein had bet on Herbert Hoover to win the presidency and Franklin Roosevelt to become Governor of New York. Had he lived, he would have collected both bets.

Men like Rothstein and Owney Madden were important heroes in that era and were considered by many as enviable and successful as any business man, tycoon, or politician. To survive in the competitive world of gangdom in the twenties was the social equivalent of achieving top status as an industry magnate, oil tycoon, or show-biz celebrity. Raft felt pride, therefore, when a gang overlord would compliment him on his dancing by patting him on the back and saying, "George, you're an okay guy." And an invitation to join the gangster's party was similar to attaining a place at King Arthur's Round Table. A group of these men could be found in fancy bistros like The Colony and Delmonico's or less elegant restaurants like Reuben's or Lindy's. George knew them all and often contributed to their animated conversations about sports, gambling, women, or clothes.

In contrast with Raft, Owney Madden was drawn to delinquent gangs and at an early age entered wholeheartedly into the subculture of crime. By the turn of the century, gangs were a permanent fixture in New York. The Hudson "Dusters," the Five Points Gang, and other groups with equally picturesque names controlled turf and crime in specific areas of the city. Pitched street battles between rival gangs were often too violent for the police to control. As a matter of record, gangs often kept the police out of certain neighborhoods.

Madden loved the gang way of life and rapidly fought his way up to the leadership of the notorious Gopher Gang. It was then that Madden became a favorite of Jimmy Hines, a popular Democratic party wardheeler who later achieved top political power in New York City. At election time Madden and his gang always managed to get out the right vote, and the Tammany political machine showed its appreciation.

Madden organized the Winona Club in Hell's Kitchen, which was raided by police during an all-night brawl that included out-the-window pistol practice. Madden barricaded the doors and over the piled furniture yelled a warning at the cops, "We'll shoot any bull who tries to bust in here." Policemen finally broke into the club, but Madden went scot free because he knew Hines, and Jimmy "owed him."

Early in his career Owney found it necessary to squelch an upstart gang member named Patsy Doyle, who wanted to take over. One night Doyle was found alone in a saloon by a thug name Willie "the Sailor" Mott. After they were seated at a table, Patsy Doyle was called up to the bar by two men who, after making sure he was Doyle, shot him six times. Mortally wounded, Doyle managed to stagger into the street and fell dead in the snow.

Owney Madden and two of his henchmen were arrested for the Doyle shooting. Initially charged with first degree murder, Madden was only convicted of manslaughter, since he had merely set up the killing, not participated in it. Later most of the witnesses against Madden said that they had been lying and that he didn't have anything to do with the Doyle killing. Nobody listened to them, and in 1915 Madden was sentenced to serve from ten to twenty years in Sing Sing. As a result of this homicide, Madden acquired the nickname of "Owney the Killer." George visited Madden in the penitentiary several times, and these visits served him to advantage when he played a convict in films like *Each Dawn I Die* (1939) with James Cagney and *Invisible Stripes* (1939) with William Holden and Humphrey Bogart.

Madden was released in 1923 and during his imprisonment

Prohibition had altered the make-up of the criminal world. Racketeers setting up efficient organizations and networks, merging and delimiting territories of control, strengthening their ties with politicians and policemen. But Madden quickly adjusted to these new conditions and honed himself into a cordial and smooth gangster. Despite his prison record and present activities, he numbered among his friends Walter Winchell, Damon Runyon, and Mark Hellinger. He also knew almost every ranking cop and politician in town, including Mayor Jimmy Walker.

By 1925, Madden had acquired the Phoenix Brewery on Tenth Avenue between 25th and 26th Streets. Prohibition agents often closed the plant; but, time and again, like the legendary bird, it reopened for production. From this plant Madden's gang supplied the East Coast with several hundred thousand gallons of beer which bore the personalized name of *Madden's #1*. Allegedly, Madden had such good protection that when federal agents once tried to raid the Phoenix the building was protected by a squad of city cops.

Not only had he his own brewery, but he owned several nightclubs, including Harlem's Cotton Club, and held substantial interests in Broadway shows, such as Mae West's *Diamond Lil* (1928), of which he held over fifty percent. In sports he later masterminded the complex career of Primo Carnera, who through devious means became Heavyweight Champion of the World and reputedly earned his backers almost a million dollars. His position had been diligently attained through hard years of violence and crime.

Madden and other gangster racketeers headquartered their business activities in the Publicity Building on the corner of Broadway and 47th Street. The building also held the offices of many other enterprises, including vaudeville booking agents, lawyers, and boxing promoters. At almost any time of the day or night, fight managers, pugs, hoofers, out-of-work actors, and smalltime gangsters would mingle together in front of the building. One of the regulars, Maxie Greenberg (later to be known as Mack Grey), an aspiring fight manager, vividly remembers George Raft at that time.

"There wasn't a sharper dresser or a nicer guy on Broadway. George's suits were always the latest style. Wide lapels, high trousers, spats, and you could cut your finger on the crease in

George's pants. He was one of the first guys to wear a black shirt with a white tie. He wore long collars. A pearl gray hat was pulled down over one eye. Come wintertime he'd either be in a black form-fitted coat with a velvet collar or a sporty brown camel wrap-around. He wore fifty-buck shoes with pointy toes, shined so bright you could see your face in them.

"Everyone said he was one of the best dancers in town. George knew everyone, so all of the guys on the corner figured he was into a lot of action other than dancing.

"In spite of his great appearance and reputation, I remember what a nice, friendly guy he was. Sometimes when he pulled up in Owney's big black Packard I'd open the door for him. He'd always slip me a few bucks and we might talk some about sports, especially boxing."

Broadway and Hollywood producer Mark Hellinger hung out with George on Broadway and knew a great deal about George's experiences with gangsters. When Hellinger became a producer at Warner's, where George was under contract, they spent hours reminiscing over New York in the twenties. Hellinger knew that there were times George filled in as a driver of a car that either lead or followed a fleet of Madden's beer trucks as protection from the hijacking by other gangs.

George got this assignment after another employee, "Feets" Edson, taught him how to drive a big car gangland style. This involved learning to get away fast, round a corner on two wheels, and go swiftly through dark, narrow streets where triggermen might be lying in wait. A natural training course was under the Third Avenue El where the trick was to avoid the tornup pavement and stay on the trolley car tracks from 59th to 110th Street.

Some nights Raft would leave one of the nightclubs where he worked as a dancer at dawn and, still in his tuxedo, pick up the loaded trucks at Madden's brewery on 26th Street and ride shotgun ahead or behind the trucks, until they reached 110th Street. There he would turn the fleet over to Dutch Schultz or another mobster, who would take the load to its final destination.

In addition to driving booze, George sometimes ran errands for Madden. One such activity involved regularly picking up the receipts of *Diamond Lil.* Knowing Mae West then led to their appearing together in the 1932 film, *Night after Night.* Mae West says of her first meeting with Raft, "I liked his style and dark good looks and wanted to use him in a new play I was writing called *Sex* (1926). But somehow he seemed nervous and felt he really couldn't do any serious acting."

Although he denies it, Raft reputedly did another favor for Madden. A show business promoter, Leon See, discovered a young Italian giant named Primo Carnera who was traveling with a circus through Southern France as its strong man. Carnera was six foot six, weighed 270 pounds, and was a gentle person although he looked fierce. See brought Carnera to the United States and began to promote him, with some success, as a boxer. Unfortunately, he was totally incompetent in the ring. He was clumsy and lacked a punch, but he looked tough and fight fans were impressed with his gigantic build.

With some partners Owney Madden took over Carnera, eased See out of the action and began a vigorous promotion of the Italian fighter. With great hoopla and fanfare they sent Carnera on tour around the country, to be matched against fighters who'd been paid to dive after they were tagged by one of the giant's awkward swipes. Carnera, poor clown, really began to believe he could fight.

After his whirlwind national tour and over twenty "victories," Carnera was set for his first big fight in Madison Square Garden against a pretty good fighter, "Big Boy" Eddie Peterson. Peterson was untrustworthy as a setup, especially after he let it be known that he felt he wasn't being paid enough. Owney wanted no slipups. If Peterson got lucky, the potential million-dollar proposition with Carnera could go down the drain.

One report alleges that several hours before the fight on January 24, 1930, Raft, as a favor to Owney, called on "Big Boy" Peterson at the Claridge Hotel. George carried a bottle of champagne and suggested that a few drinks would help Peterson calm down. There is no record of how much "Big Boy" drank, but Peterson seemed to be feeling no pain when he went to Madison Square Garden that night. Primo Carnera knocked him out in the first round and began his climb to the Heavyweight Championship of the World.

Owney Madden and his group had a pretty good run with Carnera. The pathetic giant was reputed to have earned Owney's combine three million dollars before the duped fighter, a man broken physically, emotionally, and financially, was finally told to go home after he was almost killed in the ring by a vicious slugger and honest champion, Max Baer. Budd Schulberg used this real-life tragedy of Carnera as the basis for his novel, *The Harder They Fall*, which was published in 1947 and made into a movie in 1956 with Rod Steiger and Humphrey Bogart.

In the mid-thirties, Madden, by then a wealthy man, voluntarily retired in Hot Springs, Arkansas, a favorite retreat for former racketeers. There Madden totally changed his life style and married a local girl, the Postmaster's daughter, and even joined the Chamber of Commerce.

Owney had often and without hesitancy loaned George money when Raft needed it—and Raft always repaid his debts, with interest.

Swifty Morgan, a popular Broadway entrepreneur, character, and old pal of show biz people like Frank Sinatra, recalls, "I was on vacation in Hot Springs taking the waters. I was sitting on the veranda of this hotel lazily enjoying the hot sun. I squinted because at first I did not believe what I saw. A guy pulls up in a truck in front of the hotel, hauling a large Chris-Craft boat on a trailer. He tells me he's looking for Owney Madden, and asks me where he can find him. The guy says, 'The boat is a gift to Madden from George Raft, the actor.' That boat had to be worth six grand!"

George saw Madden only one more time, when Madden and his close friend Frenchy DeMange came to Raft's mother's funeral in New York in 1937. Madden died at the age of seventy-three in 1965 in Hot Springs from a respiratory ailment.

George's relationships with Madden and other notorious friends during the early twenties was a crucial part of his life, but he never let it interfere with his show business career. By the mid-twenties he was a top Broadway entertainer, and, though he worked many clubs and theaters, much of his fame was attained as the featured dancer at Texas Guinan's club.

Texas Guinan was a fairly good singer who became the most famous cabaret hostess of the decade. Her life has been the subject of a forties Broadway revue, *Billion Dollar Baby* (1945), and a Betty Hutton film, *Incendiary Blonde* (1945). At her speakeasy, the El Fey Club, she opened the nightly entertainment with her famous greeting of "Hello, suckers." The Fey came from the name of her partner, Larry Fay, a friend of Madden's and a racketeer involved in numerous gangland activities.

In 1919 Jimmy Durante and Raft worked together in a Coney Island dive, the College Arms, on the boardwalk. Durante played the piano and Raft did his Charleston—eight times a day for $20 a week plus meals. A year later Durante opened his club. George interested Texas the first time she saw him dance at Jimmy Durante's Club Durant. She promptly offered him a job and two nights later he started at the El Fey at $150 a week.

Fred Astaire remembers Raft's performances there. "I went there several times to see George dance. I believe it was George Gershwin who first took us. He was a sensation in those days and we went especially to see George. The El Fey Club was the 'in' place to go. It was handsomely decorated in a gaudy red and gold but in many ways it was a dive. George was the main attraction, and Ruby Keeler and others who later became stars danced there also.

"They served terrible champagne and booze in coffee cups, but it was mainly the entertainment that packed the place, and George did the fastest, and most exciting, Charleston I ever saw. I thought he was an extraordinary dancer and later I heartily recommended him to a club owner I knew in London."

At the El Fey Club the clientele was a gossip-column amalgam of the social register and well-dressed hoodlums from Brooklyn, Jersey, Harlem, and the Lower East Side. When the millionaires and bluebloods discovered how exciting the entertainment was, and how interesting lawless men and women could be, the club was filled to capacity.

Not only did the El Fey Club audience include mobsters like Rothstein and Lepke, but it also attracted a special breed of high-class criminal, skilled operators who, even when they were not well-known gangsters, had a certain social polish and a professional (if not legal) stature. A good burglar served a lengthy apprenticeship and learned his trade well. Expert safecrackers and bankrobbers blueprinted their targets as if they were architects and military strategists. Their success was evidenced by their incomes and how lavishly they entertained in restaurants, theaters, cabarets, and speakeasies. Being with such people, talking to them night after night as George often did, made him privy to criminal habits and attitudes that no Hollywood writer or director could ever provide when he later played similar characters in movies.

"Texas would arrive at the club around midnight and say 'Hello, suckers.' This always brought the house down. Then she'd get up on two chairs and, from one o'clock until five o'clock in the morning, the show never stopped. The finest people in the world came there. Royalty and society people: the Vanderbilts, the Astors, the Whitneys, kings, queens. Of course, we also attracted some top mobsters. Ruby Keeler was in the show at Tex's, kids like that. She was only about fourteen years old and was working illegally. One night I put Milton Berle on to do a little act."

Visiting celebrities often specifically requested that Raft entertain when they came. "I had finished my act around five in the morning, went to my room at the Palace Hotel, and was just going to bed when Tommy, Tex's brother, phoned me. He says, 'We got a big Hollywood personality here, Adolph Menjou. Will you come over and dance?'

"He was very big then, so I got up, went over, and danced for him and his party. In those days I expected somebody to hand me something after I danced. That was the style then for paying performers. In San Francisco, way before this, they used to throw money at Blossom Seeley when she sang. I danced for Menjou and got nothing. When we met in Hollywood later, I didn't forget to remind him he still owed me."

Night after night George saw the top-drawer names of New York's café society throwing away their money. When George sensed an opportunity, he was not averse to grabbing a few extra dollars for himself—especially if the mark was someone obnoxious to George, and he could rationalize their being a victim.

One night during George's performance, he was heckled by two drunken, wealthy patrons who were at a ringside table. When the show ended, one of them wobbled into the men's room. George was furious and followed him. He noticed the big bulge in the drunk's pocket and got even with him by lifting his wallet, which contained $300. When he went backstage he said to Texas, "Did you catch those two slobs giving me the business from ringside?"

Those two "slobs" happened to be friends of hers. One was a comedian and writer named Wilson Mizner and the other was San Francisco Mayor James Rolph.

The next night, when Mizner and Rolph reappeared, George confessed to Mizner what he had done, returned the lifted cash, and apologized. Mizner roared with laughter. He told Rolph, "Any guy that can beat me for three hundred bucks deserves the dough." With that he returned the money to George. "Sunny Jim" Rolph became Governor of California, Mizner became a top screenwriter, and both were close friends of Raft's in Hollywood.

Since George had acquired some talents when he was associated with Madden, he sometimes helped out Fay with a few activities that were outside the range of his duties as a dancer, such as helping Fay hijack a rum-running ship anchored in the harbor. Certainly, Raft knew he was risking a federal arrest, and with his success he began tapering off some of the illegal activities. As a dancer, he was earning over $500 a week and no longer had an urgency to supplement his income. After one late show at the El Fey Club, George was having dinner with a friend in a Third Avenue speakeasy. At the next table sat Arthur Flegenheimer, better known as Dutch Schultz, with two of his gunmen.

"Dutch knew me from around town and had nodded to me when he came in. I was enjoying my meal when a buzzer sounded near the door. In those days everyone knew the buzzer was a police raid warning. But I was clean and didn't have to worry. Schultz collected two guns from his triggermen. Then, without a word, because I guess he assumed I was a right guy, he stashed three pistols under my overcoat which was on a chair at my table. Nonchalantly, he went back to his table and continued eating. The bulls frisked Dutch and were surprised when he came up clean. I sat there nervous as a cat, scared to death that I would wind up in jail.

"After they finished searching Schultz, the cops looked around the room, then left. Without even a thank you, Schultz collected his guns, went back to his table, and quietly finished his dinner."

Although he had not seen Grayce for several years, the pain of his attempt at marriage lingered on. He was content to stay free and easy, with a certain reluctance, though he began to associate with some of the wealthy women who were El Fey regulars. His reputed sexual prowess became common gossip in the club's powder room.

"For some reason I was leery of society women. Texas would point out some glamorous society broad. 'She's crazy about you,' she'd say, 'and wants to take you home.' I'd say, 'Christ, no, I'd much rather pick somebody myself.' I preferred a chorus girl, or a girl from the five-and-ten. I figured that, if I picked up somebody who didn't know who I was, whatever happened was happening because we both liked each other as people. Where with these society women who used to come into the club, it was more like 'Here's a different piece of candy, a brand new treat, this guy George Raft.' And, because the customer was always right in Texas's place, like it or not, I became like a male whore. These rich bitches, when they were feeling good, a little tight, they would have me. Then two nights later they might come in and never even say hello or let on that they knew me. There was little human feeling in it at all. Just sex. Sometimes it was like another performance for me."

The romantic type that George embodied was a sort that Valentino had made the raging fad. Rudolph Valentino made box-office history in films like *The Sheik* (1921) and *The Son of the Sheik* (1926) where he rode over the Arabian desert, luring women into his tent; in *Blood and Sand* (1922) he was the tragic bullfighter torn between duty and a siren; in his early success *The Four Horsemen of the Apocalypse* he danced the tango and dashed over the pampas; and *The Eagle* (1925) was set in Imperial Russia. His image of the smoldering, passionate Latin lover seemed a consummate ideal to women all over the world. George's dance hall co-employee, Rodolpho Guglielmo, was a box-office sensation in an entertainment medium that had a greater impact than any that had come before it. While Valentino exuded an air of mystery, of strangeness, of the foreign and the distinctly unattainable, Raft was to bring this romantic image closer to a familiar world and to add the allure of the underworld. He was handsome and erotic, but, most important, he was approachable. His sensuality appealed to women, his

43

tough-guy-on-the-make-in-a-tough-world aura appealed to men — and the combination proved devastating.

His natural good looks already gave him an edge. When he appeared on stage he was aware that the smooth Latin tango he performed, usually after his now-famous Charleston, had an additional wallop. He capitalized on the American female's erotic response to Valentino.

In real life, Valentino's first wife, Jean Acker, locked Valentino out of her bedroom on their wedding night. And the real love of his life, Natasha Rambova, his second wife, treated him like a fool. Moreover, Valentino's preoccupation with his personal romantic dilemmas and failures apparently sidetracked him from enjoying the fruits of the enormous appeal he had for a mass fantasizing female public. Although Valentino did not enjoy the sexual rewards that his image stimulated, George Raft profited handsomely from what he inspired.

Raft renewed his friendship with Valentino when the star came to the Playground nightclub where Raft was performing. "At the Playground on Sundays we used to have celebrity night. There was a guy named Rahman Bay who stuck needles in people without hurting them. Then it was considered a miracle, now it's Chinese medical practice. I was the emcee and brought Valentino up on the stage. It was a great treat for me to introduce Valentino. Then this mystical guy put a needle through the sheik's arm. The women in the audience went absolutely nuts! I thought they were going to rape the two of us.

"When women heard that I knew Valentino, they used to plead, 'Introduce me!' But I never imposed on him in that way.

"He had just separated from Jean Acker and he was on this tour, dancing with Natasha Rambova. Women were throwing panties and diamond rings at him. They would beg him for just one hour of love. Yet I only knew him as a depressed and lonely man."

Just before Valentino died in August 1926, he had talked with Raft for a long time at the El Fey Club and invited him to a Long Island Mansion he was renting. "We drove out in his limousine. He looked pretty bad, and I remember as we pulled up to this fabulous home he told me, 'Look how far I've gone since the days we worked together. It's all been great, but I am a lonely man.' A few weeks later he was dead from the results of an oper-

ation for appendicitis and peritonitis; and he was only thirty-
one."

With the passing of Valentino, George received many offers
to go on tour with some of Valentino's former dancing partners.
Jean Acker's agent made George an offer to tour with Acker,
but he would not have it. Although he admired Valentino, George
Raft, as always, was independent and wanted to make it his
own way. He therefore continued at the Guinan club, but he
branched out and definitely into the bigtime. In 1925, he went
into a major Broadway show produced by Charles B. Dillingham,
The City Chap, which played at the still existing Liberty Theatre
on 42nd Street. In addition to his Charleston, he performed a
new dance called the Black Bottom and took second billing only
to Skeets Gallagher, an established star.

On 42nd Street Raft saw a little colored boy dancing for pennies in front of the theater. The ten-year-old was homeless, thin,
and pathetic looking. "The kid reminded me of the days and
nights I had roamed the streets hungry. I took him with me
to a restaurant and bought him a meal that he quickly polished
off. I felt the kid had talent.

"I took him home with me that night and cleaned him up. I
bought him some clothes, got him a room, and gave him a few
bucks. For a year or so he worked as part of my act. I'd bring
him out to do a little dance with me, and the audience loved it."

George's schedule was enough for four men. But for a man
who had so recently made it there was always the specter of
quick oblivion. There were many shooting stars on Broadway—
acts and entertainers who were big for a while and then vanished. Compulsively, George took every booking he could possibly handle.

"I was the only one working in both nightclubs and theaters.
Sometimes I was working in four places in one day. First, I had
to be at the Rivoli Theater from one-ten until three in the afternoon for a matinee. Then I'd rush to the Liberty Theatre where
The City Chap was alternating with a movie. Then I went to
the Parody Club where I was working with Ted Lewis and was
through *there* around midnight. Then on to Texas Guinan's club
from around midnight until dawn. What a life! But I loved it."

Among the women in his life at this time was the popular
singer Helen Morgan, who worked at The Playground nightclub

with singer Morton Downey. In addition to dancing at the club, George often acted as M.C. and introduced the acts. "Helen was a great singer and a beautiful gal—but she often drank too much. Part of the reason she sat up on the piano when she sang her songs like 'Tea for Two' was that she was too loaded to stand up. Some nights we would have to black-out the lights. I would take her hand and walk her onto the stage and lift her up on the piano. After she was introduced and the spotlight came on, she would always come alive and sing beautifully."

Another girl George was fond of at this time was Hilda Ferguson, who was considered by Florenz Ziegfeld to be one of the most beautiful girls he ever booked into his Follies. George claimed he wasn't in love with her, but there was an undeniable attraction, and they would often rendezvous at one another's apartment. "Hilda was considered the most beautiful girl on Broadway and she was an exciting lover. We had one problem— she was Nucky Johnson's girlfriend."

Enoch Johnson, a good friend of Al Capone's, was the overlord of vice and gambling in Atlantic City, and one of the top ten racketeers in the country. His nickname "Nucky" was derived from brass knuckles, one of his favorite weapons.

George knew Johnson personally and was aware of his fierce reputation. He feared that his clandestine relationship with Hilda would be discovered and that her boyfriend would put George on his enemy hit-list, as he had many other people for lesser offenses. George didn't want any trouble with Nucky. He was a man George admired and respected. "I met him at his Silver Slipper Club in Atlantic City where I sometimes danced at special shows. I always found him to be a very nice and generous guy."

Because of his regard for Nucky and his desire to avoid a clash with him, one morning George told Hilda that it would be better if they stopped seeing each other. Hilda regretfully accepted George's decision to part company.

"She might have resented my putting her down. A few weeks later I was in the Hotsy-Totsy Club with two good friends, Walter Winchell and Mark Hellinger, when she danced by with Nucky. It was around four a.m. and I was sitting there minding my own business, just talking to my pals. Hilda and Nucky danced up close to the table near me and without any words

46

she reached out her hand. I thought she was going to affectionately stroke my face. She sure did," George said caustically. "She raked my face with her long nails and then just danced away, as if nothing had happened."

George's love affairs during those turbulent years on Broadway almost invariably carried an element of danger that heightened their romantic excitement. Another beautiful lady who became George's paramour was Winnie Lightner, one of the stars of the long-running musical, *Gay Paree*, then playing at the famous Winter Garden Theatre on Broadway.

Among the stars in the show were Sophie Tucker, Ben Bernie and his band, and Oscar Levant. Toward the end of the evening the young, but highly talented Levant would play Gershwin's famous "Rhapsody in Blue," and then George would provide the show's climax by dancing his fast Charleston to "Sweet Georgia Brown," a song written by Ben Bernie. For an encore, George would dance another standard of the time, "I'll Say She Does."

One night a perceptive member of the audience might have noted some changes in Raft's dancing style. His dancing was performed at his usual breakneck speed, but the patent leather sex symbol almost ran in a circle on the stage. Also, at times that night he seemed to be gazing toward the heavens as he danced. In reality he was staring at the hundred-pound sandbags that pulled up the curtains. Winnie Lightner's husband was an assistant stage manager at the theater, and George suspected by the man's sudden cold demeanor that night that he knew about Raft's affair with his wife. George feared that the irate stage manager might accidentally bomb him with a sandbag while he was hunched forward doing his popular windmill Charleston.

Years later in Hollywood George and Winnie recalled the episode with amusement when they both danced in the film *Gold Diggers of 1933*. Winnie was now happily married to the famous director Roy Del Ruth, and George, who had just finished working in *Scarface* (1932), was on his way to stardom.

There were other elements of danger in George's life during this period. The El Fey Club, George's home base, always had a quality of intrigue and danger despite its glamorous exterior. Larry Fay had parlayed his profits into the ownership of a legitimate taxi business; but he still retained his contacts and did business with the underworld. In spite of the club's success, there was friction between the partners. Texas drew the Park Avenue crowd and she objected to Fay's gun-carrying hoods who sat the bar and tables sometimes with their guns in view.

George remembers Texas going into the downstairs bar and finding Fay with a bunch of hoods. "They were cutting up dough and planning some capers. She bawled them out because she feared a shootout that would close the place down."

Sure enough, after a series of federal raids the El Fey Club was closed down, but Texas planned to open a new club in Miami and invited Raft to join them. But George—with *The City Chap* and nightclub jobs, including the Parody and the Playground—had steady employment. With so much going for him, he told Fay, he saw no reason to leave. Fay wasn't happy with George's decision, and showed it by his expression. "Fay had a nervous little habit of fingering one ear and licking his lips when he was in a homicidal mood." These gestures Raft used in a movie characterization.

He agreed to see Fay and Texas off at the train station, and the next morning, tired, in his tuxedo and dancing shoes, Raft went off to Penn Station. Before the train pulled out, he kissed Texas good-bye in her compartment. Just as he reached out for Fay's hand, Fay, without warning, uppercut George and put him out like a light. When he came to, he found himself in a compartment on the moving train, shoes and coat missing. He heard Texas laughing in the adjoining compartment but made no move to get to her. The train was rolling into North Philadelphia and his compartment was on the side opposite from the one next to the boarding platform. He smashed the window with a metal water bottle, climbed out, walked the tracks to get out at the station and found a cab driver who was willing to take him to New York.

The next and last time Raft saw Fay was in Hollywood in 1931 when George was achieving success in films. Fay was a pale shadow of his former self and he asked George to help him "muscle into the taxicab business." George quickly let him know he had nothing to do with the rackets on either coast, and shortly after Fay returned to New York.

Two years later, Owney Madden helped Fay out by setting him up with The Napoleon, a little club in the old Woolworth mansion on East 56th Street. Fay made the error of giving the doorman's job to an ex-cop who hated mobsters. On New Year's Eve 1933, a week after the place opened, they got into an argument and the retired cop pulled his gun, chased Fay up a flight of stairs, and shot him. Fay died on the way to the hospital.

Many show business promoters were aware of George's talents, but it was "the old maestro," Ben Bernie, the famous band leader and a good friend of Billy Rose, who gave George a big break by getting him the vaudevillian's dream booking at the Palace.

To see his name on top of the Palace marquee was some external validation for George Raft of a positive identity. He felt a certain vindication from his parents' lack of respect—especially that of his otherwise undemonstrative father—that was important to him. He had seen his father a few times when he visited his mother, but they had little to do with each other. "He never was mad at me. He always told me the same story, 'You're on your own in this world. Whatever you do, you're gonna have to live with it.' From the time I left home at twelve we saw each other maybe five times at the most, and then we had nothing to say to each other. We were like strangers." Raft denied feeling hostility, but real frustration comes when you can't even provoke someone's anger.

But with the 1926 appearance at the Palace Raft's father finally exhibited a certain pride in his son. "I'll never forget it. My father used to bring his friends and guys he worked with uptown. I can see him now, standing out in front of the theater, pointing up to my name on the marquee and telling anyone who would listen, 'That's my son.'"

A year later while he was in Hollywood, Raft received a wire from his mother that his father had died of cancer. He was unable to attend the funeral because of the four- to five-day train trip. "When I got the news, I cried like a baby." But in many ways he had lost his father long ago and had both found other father images and, as exemplified by his intense independence, become his own father.

Raft had gone to Hollywood to appear in the movie *Queen of the Night Clubs* (1929), tenuously based on Texas Guinan's career but including substantial elements of the soap opera drama

Madame X. He recreated his dance act, but the film did nothing to further his career. Perhaps its only significance was that it concluded a phase of his life—Broadway in the roaring twenties.

The Broadway period had provided him with valuable experience, but it also marked him as a gangster—or, at the least, an associate of gangsters. It was his instinct for survival and fierce independence that kept him from any real and destructive involvement in the underworld. If he did not have this, he might have ended up like Madden or Fay or Rothstein or any number of men he knew in those days. Instead, their fates were warning signals which he heeded. What he had learned was self-protection and the ability to capitalize on his own unique talents. But he was not to escape from guilt by association.

Apart from that, George has no regrets. "If you were an entertainer on Broadway during those days you would have to be blind and lame not to associate with gangsters. Look, they owned the clubs. That's where the work was. Besides, all of those people, including Owney, Larry Fay, Frenchy, people like that, were looked up to by everyone. Christ, Owney ran New York in those days. They had a kind of glamour about them. They were more important in those days than a Jimmy Durante, Milton Berle, Ruby Keeler, Ted Lewis, Georgie Jessel, and the others who worked clubs.

"Maybe I got into some things at times a little over my head. But, in those days, the things I did weren't that unusual. Liquor and speakeasies were big business. Everybody drank, even though it was illegal."

In the coming years he would portray a composite of Owney Madden, Larry Fay, Frenchy DeMange, Arnold Rothstein, and Lucky Luciano on the screen. And no one knew better than George how to incorporate authentic gangster qualities into a role. He was extraordinarily convincing in his screen portrayals because he had absorbed every gangster nuance, every quirk of restrained violence and ever-present menace. Maybe he played the roles too well, too true to personality and fact, for he often over-identified with his parts, and this produced an inner confusion. When he walked onto a plyboard movie set to play a powerful racketeer, he thought he was portraying George Raft in the twenties on Broadway.

3

SCARFACE

In 1927, when an enthusiastic Al Jolson accidentally blurted out the line, "You ain't heard nothing yet, folks, listen to this," on the set of the Warner Brothers' musical, *The Jazz Singer*, the "talkies" emerged as a new film art form. The line—a Jolson trademark that captivated thousands of vaudeville fans when he used it regularly at Broadway's Winter Garden Theatre—was not in the script. Sam Warner's original intention was to use only sound during the musical portion of the film; but when he screened the rushes he became fascinated by the dramatic effect of the adlibbed dialogue, and he encouraged Jolson to add other spoken dialogue. At the end of his rendition of "Blue Skies," sung from the stage of the Palace, the errant son, who had run away from home to become a singer, kneels on the stage and emotionally calls to his happy, tearful screen mother: "Did you like that Mama? I'm glad. I'd rather please you than anybody I know." At the film's ending he returns to his father's synagogue and sings *Kol Nidre*.

Sound, limited to orchestral background and sound effects, had been used before, notably in John Barrymore's *Don Juan*, but *The Jazz Singer*, because of its popularity, ushered in the era of the talkies and revolutionized the film industry. It grossed three-and-a-half million dollars and a subsequent film, also with sound sections and starring Jolson, *The Singing Fool* (1928), earned Warner Brothers an astounding five million dollars and put the studio solidly in the black.

The Singing Fool was a sleeper and set a gross record that was not eclipsed until *Gone with the Wind* in 1939. The conversion from silent to sound caught many films in mid-production, and awkward soundtracks were added—for instance, in Murnau's *Sunrise*, Janet Gaynor and Charles Farrell's mouthings were backed by solo instruments.

Although the technical possibility of talking pictures had been available for many years, many film artists—such as D. W. Griffith, Charles Chaplin, and movie moguls with a heavy financial interest in silent films—resisted using the process. Griffith among others felt that the advent of the "talkies" was not necessarily progress. Griffith was quoted in the late forties as saying, "What the modern movie lacks is beauty—the beauty of moving wind in the trees. . . . They have forgotten that no still painting—not the greatest ever—was anything but a still pic-

ture. Today they have forgotten movement in the moving picture—it is all still and stale. . . . Too much today depends on the
voice. I love pictures properly done. Sometimes the talk is good,
often very bad. We have taken beauty and exchanged it for
stilted voices."

Soon after *The Jazz Singer*, Warner Brothers produced an all-
talkie success *Lights of New York* (1928) dealing with gangsters
and speakeasies. MGM produced the first "backstage story"
musical, *The Broadway Melody* (1929). These early films set the
style and subject matter for hundreds of films that have been
made since.

The collapse of the stock market in 1929 and the subsequent
depression slowed Hollywood down, but they did not significantly effect the overall impetus of the movie industry in the early
thirties. In 1930 the talkies brought an average of 110 million
people a week into movie theaters—a staggering figure, never
duplicated, that almost equaled the 130 million population of the
United States. Attendance took a dip from this astonishing figure
in 1931 and 1932; however, attendance rose again in 1933.
Despite the depression years, movie houses averaged seventy
to eighty million persons in attendance every week. Paramount
Pictures told the public in their ads: "There's a Paramount
picture around the corner. See it and you'll be out of yourself,
living someone else's life. . . . You'll find a new viewpoint. And
tomorrow you'll work, not worry."

Unlike the functional, unadorned theaters of today, those
which showed initial run attractions built in the twenties were
Italianate Baroque palaces. In the thirties, they were modernistic
Art Deco in detail—the supreme example, of course, is the Radio
City Music Hall. They were the most luxurious public institutions
in existence, and one entered a big movie theater with reverence
and awe. These were the true American cathedrals, where one
renewed one's faith in existence, found relief and consolation
from distressful reality, gave praise to gods with very familiar
faces, and admired and abhorred the devils.

Not only did films continue to deal with romance and fantasy,
but the Depression and social unrest also came to the fore. In
the "Gold Diggers" musicals money was the true subject—with
Ginger Rogers singing "We're in the Money" in pig Latin and
production numbers about the Forgotten Man. And success—an

almost unimaginable ideal—had either to be gained by luck (chorus girl called at the last minute to sub for star) or by devious or illegal means. The American gangster was morally abrasive; and yet, as a victim of poverty and a rebel against social inequality, he ultimately earned our sympathy.

The first important gangster film was Joseph von Sternberg's *Underworld*, made in 1927, starring George Bancroft and Clive Brook. Its style was influenced by German expressionist movies, a stylistic influence that was to continue through the genre: intense lighting contrasts, a tough, often grotesque sense of character, a vision of a corrupt society. Produced at Warner Brothers in the early thirties were the two still popular classics— *Public Enemy*, with James Cagney directed by William Wellman, and *Little Caesar*, directed by Mervyn LeRoy and starring Edward G. Robinson.

Conceived as films that would expose social evils and debunk gangster heros, they had a different effect. Actually, those films reflected the moral dilemmas and torments of the public and the audience applauded those who rose above the low station where they had been trapped by a complex and heartless society.

Edward G. Robinson, in an interview, commented on his role in *Little Caesar:* "I think the popularity of my role as Little Caesar can be attributed to the public preoccupation with the American dream of success. Rico was a guy who came from poverty and made it big. Remember, almost everyone was poor in those days—right after the market crash of 1929. Rico made it straight up the ladder and everyone could identify with his climb.

"Audiences in those days must have known that Rico died broke in an alley only because of a silly movie code that insisted a villain must pay for his crimes. But even Little Caesar's death provided something people could relate to. After being shot by the police, he cries out, 'Mother of mercy, is this the end of Rico?' I probably expressed a feeling that millions of people had about their own lives."

George Raft seemed to fulfill a similar role. Clearly, this was a man the audience knew well. The public was aware of how Raft had risen above the poverty and slums of New York, and many wanted to believe he was a real gangster who had made it as a movie star. In this sense his associations with the Broadway underworld served his career. Audiences tended to believe that his screen portrayals were based on first-hand experience, an assumption that gave his performances additional authority.

But George was no overnight Hollywood sensation. In 1926 he had toured Europe and enjoyed considerable success, especially in London. When he returned to New York he felt restless and dissatisfied with the four-shows-a-day routine and his old associations. But an opportunity arose in 1927 when Texas Guinan, about to leave for Hollywood to supervise the filming of her life story, offered Raft a part in her movie. He had had a few minor roles in New York films and Texas asked him to play himself, a dancer in her club. Although the film, *Queen of the Night Clubs* (1929), was no great success, at least it brought Raft where he wanted to be—Hollywood.

Raft spent the years 1928 to 1930 in Hollywood trying to establish himself in the films. There were occasional trips back to the East Coast, but they only confirmed that the Broadway he knew was undergoing a change. Vaudeville was on the decline, and in 1933, with the ratification of the Twenty-first Amendment, it was clear that Prohibition and its attendant business (speakeasies, for one) were on the way out. The jobs he could get as a dancer paid little and were also scarce.

He had arrived in California with a sizable bankroll, but, being a big spender and having a passion for the track, his money was soon exhausted. Not since his teenage years had George been so destitute; but, like many street kids he had learned how to survive. With the help of friends from his New York days, and credit extended because of his reputation, he got through. Ben Lieberman, an old friend, owned the Angelus Drugstore in downtown Los Angeles, and at its luncheon–fountain facilities George could run up a tab. Lieberman shared his apartment with another friend from New York, Sydney Weitzman. Weitzman recalls:

"We knew George wasn't going good. He still had clothes and dressed sharp. But, with George, you could never tell by looking at him whether he had a dime or a thousand dollars in his pocket.

"But Ben and I knew because for about a year he slept in our apartment. We were single and we both worked every day. George would arrive around breakfast time, very often with a broad. We'd eat together, then Ben and I would go off to work, and George and his gal would spend the day in bed. He brought home some lookers.

"A few years later, when George began to make it in Hollywood, Ben was in bad financial shape with his store. George loaned him something like $5000 to keep his business going; and George wouldn't have wanted to be paid back."

When he wasn't at the fights at the Hollywood Legion, Raft mingled with Hollywood's upper crust. Few knew George's true financial condition because he kept his wardrobe up at any cost. At a black-tie affair no one's dinner clothes were more fashionable than George's. Although he was often insecure, he looked comfortable wherever he went. Often unsure of what to say, he would remain silent; and this posture, combined with slick handsomeness, gave him an aura of mystery.

At parties most of the talk was devoted to the movie industry and how everyone was making a killing. With bitterness and envy, Raft noted that overnight success was the rule: yesterday's unknowns were today's movie producers, directors, and actors. There were those who the previous week couldn't pay their room rent; now they were buying ranches and building mansions. One day they couldn't even make the delivery entrance, the next they were hosting parties for governors and senators.

Raft's first big party in Hollywood was given by Texas Guinan. "She rented a house at 527 North Camden Drive in what is now Beverly Hills. Texas originally came from Texas and made some cowboy pictures. Before she came to New York, she was a cowgirl.

"The bar was down in the cellar. There were gorgeous dames all over the place. One in particular was Molly O'Day, an actress who had played with Richard Barthelmess in a picture I loved called *The Patent Leather Kid* [1927]. I began to date Molly. She was a gorgeous girl, and one of the sweetest, most gentle women I've ever met.

"She was doing pretty well in films but she loved to overeat and that weight proved to be her downfall. She tried some weird plastic surgery, where she paid quack doctors a fortune for an operation in which they tried to cut the fat off her body. When they sewed her up she had seam scars running up the sides of her formerly beautiful body. The operation ruined her health, her career, and damn near killed her. It was the first time I realized what some people would do to make it and to stay on top in Hollywood."

Raft saw *The Patent Leather Kid* five times. Its story line and theme was of the sort to personally appeal to him. "Barthelmess plays a cocky prizefighter unwilling to go to war. Finally he wants to go but can't since he's been crippled. At the end of the movie Barthelmess is in a wheelchair—paralyzed. When they play the national anthem in the last scene he struggles up from the wheelchair and stands at attention. He stands there in front of an American flag that's waving in the breeze. I always wanted to be that kind of hero in films." Years later, Raft tried to get Paramount and Warner Brothers to star him in a remake of *The Patent Leather Kid*, but the project never materialized.

Raft's reputation had crossed the country with him and, while gaining him entry in certain circles, it quickly proved a mixed blessing. Having won a considerable sum at the track, he was able to take a room at the Mark Twain Hotel on Wilcox Avenue, off Hollywood Boulevard. But soon he was running out of cash again and sold one of his expensive suits for $30 to someone who also roomed there. Two days later, two detectives grabbed him in the lobby. "Your name Raft?" they asked. "They asked me where I had been the night before, and I said I had been sitting right there in the lobby, all evening. It didn't take long to confirm that with the clerks, and soon they were making explanations to me.

"The story was that they'd finally caught up with a stickup artist who'd pulled at least a dozen jobs. It was the guy who was staying at the hotel and he was wearing the suit I'd sold him, with my name sewed in the inside pocket. I was in the clear, but I was off to a bad start with the Hollywood cops because they put my name in their mental file."

After his initial success, work had come easily to George on Broadway; but in Hollywood he soon learned he had to be aggressive to compete for a part. Basically a shy man, unsure of his talent as an actor, George was not attuned to the Hollywood manner.

"I never could ask for a job. If someone told me of some place where they might want me, I'd be there. But I would never put

58

myself in a position where I could be turned down. For example, if I went for a job and there were a lot of people waiting, I'd figure they were all better than me, so what's the use? Without waiting to find out if they were, I'd leave immediately."

Finally, through a director Raft had never met, his lucky break occurred.

In the summer of 1930, after attending the fights, George was sitting with friends in the Brown Derby Restaurant. Rowland Brown, a former Detroit newspaperman, and at the time a rising director, came over and introduced himself to George and told him that he had seen him dance in vaudeville in Detroit and always liked his style. Raft told Brown that he was interested in working in films. "Listen, George, come over to the Fox studio tomorrow. I think I have something for you." Brown was to direct a film, *Quick Millions* (1931), the story of a truckdriver who becomes a ruthless gangster. This was Spencer Tracy's first starring role, and Brown thought George would be perfect as Tracy's bodyguard.

The next day, rather nervous because he badly needed the job, George showed up at the studio. As usual, his calm exterior hid his inner mood. He met with Brown and the casting director, a man named Gardner, for the film. Gardner thought Raft was okay, but he could not understand why they just didn't use one of the studio's contract players. An argument ensued between Gardner and Brown and they talked about Raft as if he wasn't there. For the first time Raft realized that "an actor is like a piece of meat for sale," and he almost walked out. Keeping himself in check, he said nothing.

"I was never much of a talker, so I could never sell myself for a role. These two guys kept arguing back and forth. Finally I said, 'Look, gentlemen, may I say something?' I told them, 'I'll tell you what I'll do. Mr. Gardner seems to think I'm not right. You've got people under contract that should get the job. Still and all, Mr. Brown feels I'm right for it. Suppose I come in tomorrow and read for the part. If my work is satisfactory, you hire me. If it isn't, you don't.'

"I had about two dollars in my pocket at the time and really needed the job; but I never took a job where I wasn't really wanted.

"Next day I took a screen test. In one scene I came into this room with these tough guys and said: 'This town isn't big enough for the both of us and I'm not gonna leave, so you better get out.' Then I touched my handkerchief, touched my hat, and walked out.

"Then they had me do another bit with a cute gal named Dixie, who later became Bing Crosby's wife. She played a secretary and I sat on her desk. 'Say, honey, whattaya do with your nights off?' And she wisecracks, 'I go to wrestling shows.' They liked my test and that's how I got my first real break in the movies."

During the filming of *Quick Millions*, George received a lesson about Hollywood and fame from Spencer Tracy. "Brown knew I wouldn't need any coaching for my small part with Spencer. Finally, we were doing one scene in which Tracy and I are at a banquet table. And among the extras in the crowd was King Baggot, one of the early stars of the silent movie business.

"'Look at that man,' Tracy whispered to me. 'Once a great star and now an extra for a few bucks a day when he can get the work. That could happen to me,' Tracy went on. 'That's what really scares me.'"

Tracy's remark affected Raft so that when the camera closed in for his brief dialogue he was so nervous he couldn't speak. Fortunately, Rowland Brown, a sympathetic and understanding man, waited patiently for George to settle down.

Tracy was very anxious because this was his first big role. Raft, sometimes quick to take offense, was especially nervous, for this was his big chance as well. A clash of temperaments seemed inevitable. "I almost had a fight with Tracy on this picture because he yelled at me. We were filming one scene at the Lakeside Country Club. In those days it was Lee Tracy, not Spencer, who was a big star. Spence and I were waiting on the golf course for the sound truck to arrive. Carved on a bench near where you teed off were the letters A-C-Y. Just for the hell of it, without thinking, I added T and R to the A-C-Y. Spence saw the carving and blew up. Jesus Christ, he got mad. He turned to me and said, 'George, you shouldn't have carved my name on that bench.' I answered, 'Well, who the hell do you think you are? For Chrissake, who the hell knows you, Spencer Tracy? I didn't carve your name, I was carving Lee Tracy's on that bench.'

"He didn't say anything more. Just quieted down. Maybe I scared him.

60

"Well, we did our work that day, and then we went back to the studio on Western Avenue. Tracy was waiting for me and he looked very upset. He said, 'George, are you really going to do what Rowland Brown says?' I looked at him, not knowing what the hell he was talking about. I said, 'What do you mean?'

"'Brown tells me you told him how you're going to get even with me for yelling at you by carving my name and phone number in every shithouse in town.'

"I started to laugh. Spence immediately understood that Brown'd been ribbing him. From that day on Tracy and I became good friends."

After *Quick Millions*, Raft was set for a part in *Hush Money* with Joan Bennett (1931) and was receiving other offers. But once again his past made him suspect.

While at Wrigley Field, enjoying a ballgame, a husky, red-faced stranger sat next to him. "He had 'cop' written all over him, and I was sure I had seen him hanging around the studio. He flashed a gold badge that read: 'Los Angeles Police Department,' and said, 'I'm Lieutenant Lefty James, of the racket squad. We want to talk with you at the station.'

"He drove me downtown and took me to the office of Police Chief Taylor. The chief kicked it right off with a question that floored me. He asked if I had seen Molly O'Day lately. I hadn't seen her for around six months, and I explained that Molly and I had 'agreed to disagree.' Then I asked, 'What are you guys driving at?'

"They told me that Molly was robbed in her apartment at the Garden of Allah of all of her cash and most of her jewels. I was the number one suspect. I really got pissed off. 'What kind of a guy do you think I am?'

"'We know what kind of a guy you are,' Chief Taylor said. 'We've been watching you for a couple of weeks, and you don't look so good. You're a New York hood, which is reason enough for not liking you in our town. Since there're plenty of trains going East, I hope you've got enough for a ticket.'"

Raft told the chief he was an actor and as evidence produced a letter from the studio. After checking out Raft's story with the studio, they released him and later Raft found out that the Los Angeles police had been told by a New York source that he was there not as an actor but as an agent for Owney Madden. Winfield Sheehan, head of Fox studios, who had been impressed with Raft's performance in *Quick Millions*, contacted District Attorney Burton Fitts and told him to leave Raft alone.

The local police seldom gave George any more trouble after that, but old friends from New York called on him occasionally for help with unusual business. One request involved a major star, and possibly saved his life.

"I got a phone call from a mob man in New York who wanted me to handle an emergency job. One of the big men in the rackets back east who'd been looking for his missing girl finally traced her to Hollywood.

"'She's crazy about a young actor,' the guy told me. 'If you want to save this guy's life, Georgie, you'll find the girl and hustle her out of town. Otherwise this actor winds up on a slab.'

"'Okay,' I said. 'Who is he?'

"'Gary Cooper.'

"I got on the phone to Wilson Mizner, now a good friend of mine in Hollywood. He knew everyone in town. The next day he called me back and gave me the girl's address. I went to her apartment, got her packed in a hurry, took her to the station, and got her on the first train east. Six years later I co-starred with Gary Cooper in *Souls at Sea* (1937), but I never told him what I had done, even after we became good friends."

Without his New York past Raft would have been and probably remained just another bit player, for his first parts were playing either a dancer or a gangster.

James Cagney remembered George from New York and got him a role as a competing dancer in *Taxi* (1932). In Samuel Goldwyn's *Palmy Days* (1931), an Eddie Cantor vehicle, Raft played a gangster who was on Eddie Cantor's trail.

It was soon after that his most important role to date came along. Howard Hawks was already one of the most important directors in Hollywood by virtue of the success of films like *A Girl in Every Port*, *The Dawn Patrol*, and *The Crowd Roars*. In 1931, in partnership with Howard Hughes, Hawks was preparing to produce and direct a gangster film about the rise to power of Al Capone—who had a deep scar running down one side of his face. The film was *Scarface: Shame of a Nation*.

Hawks had an idea for a different kind of gangster movie. Hughes was prepared to fund a film based on a book he had bought about two brothers, one of whom became a gangster and the other a cop. Hawks threw out the story line and contacted Ben Hecht, the playwright, who had won the first Oscar given a screenwriter for von Sternberg's *Underworld*. At first, Hecht adamantly refused doing yet another gangster story. But Hawks said, "Well, I've got a little idea. The story will be based on the Borgia family but set in the Chicago of today—Cesare Borgia is Al Capone." Hecht shot back, "We'll start tomorrow morning."

Hawks had heard an anecdote about Al Capone which had given him the idea for the film. "Capone was supposed to have staged a big party for a gangland enemy. First Capone made a long, polite speech about the man. Toward the end of his speech he became angry and zeroed in on how the man had deceived him. At that point, filled with rage, Capone was supposed to have beaten the man to death with a baseball bat.

"That was to me an act so lunatic and duplicitous that it seemed a modern version of Cesare Borgia and the Borgia family. Hecht and I researched the whole Borgia family. Cesare Borgia and his sister Lucretia were supposed to have been lovers. We copied that."

Through a number of Chicago gangsters. Hawks had unusual sources of information and was able to provide Hecht with real material. Together they completed a shooting script in eleven days.

"I remember offering Ben twenty thousand to do that script. He said, 'No, I want a thousand a day, each day in cash.' I said, 'Fine.' On the eleventh day when he finished he looked at me, a little amazed and puzzled. 'We're through, aren't we?' I said, 'You made eleven thousand—and you could have had twenty. You're the lousiest business man I ever met in my life.'

"But I cheered him up: 'Don't look so glum. You can ride back to New York with me next week and I'll pay you a thousand a day.' It took three days and somehow he won another six thousand from me in backgammon. All in all, he managed to earn the twenty grand I had originally offered him."

Before he went to New York to cast the film, Hawks read the script to Hughes. When he finished, Hughes asked, "Where's the brother, the cop?" Hawks said, "There isn't any." Hughes laughed, "You threw the whole book away, but you have one hell of a story here."

The Hughes–Hawks combination had one serious problem: casting. At that time most actors had studio contracts and the studios were not in favor of their players freelancing with independent producers. Fortunately, because of Hughes, Hawks had plenty of money to work with. He selected a few good cameramen, an art director, and rented a little cobwebbed studio. While he was in New York, his staff prepared the studio for action.

Paul Muni had just had a great success in the Broadway production of Elmer Rice's *Counsellor-at-Law*, and Hawks persuaded him to make a screen test for Tony Camonte, the Capone role. Muni resisted: "I'm just not that kind of man." But the test was successful and Muni was signed for the part. The Borgia embroidery on the Capone legend spurred Muni's imagination. The incestuous relationship between Scarface and his sister was broadly suggested by the gangster's overprotective attitude and his fixation about keeping her chaste.

At one point Camonte finds his sister kissing a man in a hallway. He throws the man down the stairs. She bristles, "Sometimes you don't act like a brother, you're more of a——" Before she can get the word "lover" out, he slaps her into silence.

It was a daring subject which certainly would have been forbidden if it had been explicit. But the incest theme seemed to elude most of the censors and audience, who saw only an exciting gangster movie.

In the concluding part of the film the sister initiates an affair with Camonte's number one partner and bodyguard, Gino Rinaldi, a part modeled on Capone's bodyguard Frank Rio, the role played by Raft. "Scarface" Camonte kills Rinaldi in full view of his sister in the bodyguard's apartment; and, in the emotion-packed final scenes, Scarface and his sister embrace, pledge their undying love, and fight to their death in a shootout with the police.

Hawks and Raft first met at a prizefight in Hollywood, but Hawks had seen *Quick Millions* and been struck already by his style and appearance. Several days later Hawks asked Raft to come to his office. Raft, however, was planning to go to Miami, where Owney Madden, in the center of his Primo Carnera enterprise, offered George a job with the Carnera boxing carnival that was touring the country. Raft leveled with Hawks. "There's a chance for me to go to Florida with friends on a business deal. So if this doesn't come off, I wouldn't want to stick around here. I'm doing okay, but right now I'm not in a financial position to lay around and look for another job."

Hawks's answer was immediate. "Starting today, you're on salary." George left Hawks's office and celebrated the good news in a restaurant across from the Fox Studio.

"A lot of actors were there. Now I didn't know Paul Muni, although I had heard of his reputation on Broadway—he was considered one of the great young actors. Somebody points to this man at another table and says, 'There's Paul Muni.' A little later Muni looked up and signaled for me to come over. I did a doubletake like, 'You mean me?' He nodded, so I went over. 'You know,' he said, 'you'd be ideal for this new picture I'm in. It's called *Scarface*.' 'You mean the Howard Hawks movie?' 'Yeah.' I laughed. 'That's really funny of you to say that. I just saw Mr. Hawks and got the job.' He smiled. 'Wonderful,' he said as we shook hands."

The role of the sister was cast when Hawks saw Ann Dvorak with Raft at a party at Hawks' home. "Ann was attracted to George, who looked magnificent in his evening clothes. George was just sitting there, minding his own business. He doesn't drink, and he didn't look as if he was having too good a time.

"Ann asked him to dance with her but he said he'd rather not. She was a little high and right in front of him starts to do this sexy undulating dance, sort of trying to lure him on to dance with her. She was a knockout. She wore a black silk gown almost cut down to her hips. I'm sure that's all she had on. After a while George couldn't resist her suggestive dance and in no time they were doing a sensational number which stopped the party.

"I asked Ann, who'd done a few minor parts in films, to be at my office next day. I gave her the Lucretia Borgia role."

In the film, Hawks used what he had seen at his party. After flirting with George in every scene they meet, Ann finally gets to George in a night club. When they did the scene Hawks told them to do exactly what they did at the party. She comes up to his table and dares him to dance. At first, he turned her down, then he gives in when she does a sensuous dance that initiates their fatal relationship. Hawks believed "the scene played like a million dollars because it was something that really happened between George and Ann."

During the making of *Scarface*, in which Raft played the bodyguard, Gino Rinaldi, a close relationship developed between the two principal actors; and Muni's preparation, acting, and advice were of inestimable value to Raft. Muni had begun his career as Muni Weisenfreund in New York's Yiddish theater, a breeding ground for many of the great actors of the early part of this century. The transition to the Broadway stage gave his reputation wider reknown, and his versatility was remarkable. Although the character was completely foreign to Muni's own, his craftsmanship, intelligence, and ability to transform himself—in manner, voice, appearance—allowed him to play a ganglord convincingly. As, of course, it enabled him to portray Louis Pasteur, Juarez, Emile Zola, and Clarence Darrow with conviction later in his career. While Gable, Harlow, Cooper, Tracy, William Powell were greater "stars," it was Muni who was considered the greatest screen "actor," a sort of successor, but with greater range, to George Arliss who had played Wellington, Richelieu, and Rothschild in films. Later opinions were to alter this judgment somewhat by upgrading the true actorly ability of the "natural" stars and finding the craftsmanship and meticulous impersonations of Muni a bit studied.

It was the "Method" actors, utilizing the theories of the great Russian director Stanislavsky, who first appreciated the sense of reality and immediacy that popular stars, previously employed as mere personalities, could achieve. Raft, like so many film actors, undervalued his own talents. Serious acting was a tradition inherited from England and Europe; the tradition of American acting was in an unsure infancy. It was the film's intense eye that emphasized realism—a realism that Raft's acting possessed—that really altered the approach of American actors. In a film like *The Petrified Forest*, we can see clearly the juxtaposition of styles: Leslie Howard, romantic, studied, graceful; Bogart, idiosyncratic, natural, energetic; and Bette Davis, falling somewhere between.

Muni would be on the set at five-thirty A.M., perfecting scenes and getting made up to be ready to go to work at seven A.M.

Filming would go on to the late hours of the night, for seven days a week.

"Without a doubt Muni was the greatest actor I've ever worked with. He was a perfectionist. He had a full-length mirror in his dressing room and would recite his lines into a dictaphone. Then he would play back the lines and add gestures to fit the dialogue.

"I told him one day, 'If I had to do that to be an actor, I'd quit.' You see, I found it tough work. What I would do would be to think over the scene in my mind and try to become whoever I was playing. I would try to feel like the person in that particular scene. Sometimes my words would be different from the script. But Hawks didn't seem to mind if it came out in the right mood."

Such a procedure had a name, unknown to Raft: improvisation. Untutored and uninstructed, he was working in the method already. Without feature-altering makeup and voice tricks, he developed the character from within, using his own being as the firm base. This was not necessarily a better procedure, just a different one. It is the distinction between Laurence Olivier and Spencer Tracy that Katharine Hepburn once made: great actors both but by different means.

Hawks did not ask George for emotion; he only asked that he play the role out of his own personality. In his movies, Raft worked out certain characteristic mannerisms that he had observed, like scowling a certain way or touching his hat; but on the set of *Scarface* a "bit of business" was developed that became his particular trademark, a gesture totally Raft.

Hawks used Raft in certain scenes when he had no lines or action, because his sinister appearance added atmosphere and a stylistic point. Rather than have Raft just stand there, Hawks had him flip a coin. "Tossing a nickel was Howard Hawks's idea. Of course, I had to learn how to toss the nickel, and practiced for weeks. Finally, I got it so I could almost do it in my sleep."

Also, Hawks was clever enough to know that the coin-flipping would cover a lot of Raft's lack of acting experience. "When he didn't have anything else to do, he would flip a coin. It worked. From beginning to end he looked as if he'd been acting for years."

Another reason Hawks used the gesture is that he heard a story about a gangland killing in which a nickel was found in the hand of a victim. In effect the killers were saying that the crook was only worth a nickel. "Having George flip the coin made him a character. The coin represented a hidden attitude—a kind of defiance, a held-back hostility, a coolness—which hadn't been found in pictures up to that time; and it made George stand out. It probably helped make him a star."

In addition, Raft recalls that, "In those days the cameras were usually stationary, and so were the microphones. Background music wasn't added to the soundtrack—that came later. It was played off camera and recorded at the same time. You couldn't even move your head when you were talking. Also, a speech wasn't broken up into short takes. You had to go through with it to the end. If you muffed a line in the middle, or missed an action, you had to start all over again. So I had to flip the nickel so that my hand was steady and firm, and I even managed to do it while staring at someone."

Maximum use was made of spontaneity and improvisation in *Scarface*, and critics later agreed that Raft's death scene was among the highlights of this classic movie. "We would often sit around, Howard Hawks, Ann Dvorak, Paul Muni, and myself, and discuss a scene for hours. For one scene, Howard explained to Paul Muni, 'This is where you kill George. You find out that he's been foolin' around with your sister.' We all got set up. The cameras are rolling, the music is playing and Hawks said, 'George, remember you've got to toss the coin as he shoots you.' This gave me an idea of how I'm going to end the scene.

"Hawks tried to get me to feel sad, but I didn't really feel that way. Hawks played music to change my mood. Nothing worked. Finally they played a song called *Memories*. 'Mem-or-ies, memor-ies.' And I sorta got a little sniffle. Then Hawks said, 'Okay, let's do it.'

"Now I'm feeling pretty low, hearing that song. It brought back sad memories—things I had gone through when I was a kid.

"We start the scene. I'm wearing a silk robe. Muni knocks on the door, and when I open it he sees his sister, Ann Dvorak, in a negligee. He turns to me. 'You shouldn't have done this to me, Gino. I thought you were my friend!' Then Muni shoots me. I fell back and my head hit hard on the door—and not intentionally. I had really thrown myself into the scene and banged my head. When I slid down the door, I was slightly unconscious and landed in a small pool of my own blood. My eyes sort of rolled up in my head, like people's do when they are dying. The coin I had been tossing fell out of my hand. I heard Hawks say, 'Print.' Everyone there said this was the greatest movie death scene they ever saw.

"Hawks filmed the coin rolling along the floor until it lost its motion, and fell flat. Hawks told me later, 'The roll of the coin and then its falling still told the story of Gino's death.'"

Another memorable scene in *Scarface* was an encounter between Muni and Osgood Perkins (Anthony Perkins's father), who played Johnny Vittorio, one of the gang's enemies. Raft sits to one side, taking apart and cleaning his machinegun almost affectionately. Vittorio, boss of Chicago's West Side, is furious because he doesn't like Scarface appropriating his territory, and he says so in a long, angry, excited speech. "I brought you out here from New York to help me and now you're taking over." Raft starts to load the gun, eyeing him with disgust while he raves. Vittorio finishes in a sputtering fury, and Raft's only line, the last in the scene, demolishes him: "So what about it?"

From that scene, Raft learned some basic things that he frequently insisted on later. First, the length of an actor's lines is not as important as his attitude or look. The other thing was to always try to get the last line in any scene. It is frequently the one that's most effective dramatically and leaves the final impression on the audience. George passed on this tip to Elia Kazan when he came to Hollywood from Broadway in the thirties. Twenty years after, Kazan told Raft he never forgot his advice.

During the production of *Scarface*, Howard Hughes visited the set several times; and, though Raft respected Hughes, even liked the young producer, he almost lost his part because of an unintentional interference in the former aviator's personal life. In the late twenties Raft had met Billie Dove, who was then Jimmy Walker's companion. The three of them saw each other often at "Legs" Diamond's Hotsy Totsy Club. When Billie Dove, a friend of Marion Davies, came to Hollywood, she renewed her acquaintance with Raft—on a more intimate basis.

"I took her out. One thing led to another and we wound up in a gorgeous suite at the Ambassador Hotel. I was in a wonderful position with the girl when the phone rings. It's a pal calling from the lobby. Nervously, he tips me off that Billie Dove was Hughes's girlfriend and that Hughes was in the lobby at that moment looking for her. Believe me, I didn't even know that she knew Hughes. If I had, I wouldn't have gone near her.

"She was pretty upset when I told her what was happening, since the last guy in the world either of us wanted to cross was Howard Hughes. So, as gracefully as I could, I said my good-byes to Billie, slipped down the service elevator, and beat it home."

Hawks was a stickler for authenticity. He used real bullets on the set—principally for sound effects. In a restaurant shootup, bullets were used to break the window glass and to smash things in the background. They then shot the scene with actors and superimposed the shots.

Harold Lloyd's brother was injured on the set. He was warned not to come in because the explosive devices that were being used were dangerous. He went around the back to get a better look and he lost an eye from a ricocheting bullet.

Hawks felt that Hughes was a great help to him when he filmed what they later called their "reign of terror," another important authentic touch that was a first in films. Hawks recaptured the excitement of the filming: "In the big gang fight scenes, the rival gangs in cars rode along shooting at each other. We had a bunch of old cars crashing, some of them running into stores, uprooting fire hydrants, and turning over. We had about sixteen different kinds of wrecks, one right after the other—boom, boom, boom—in that movie.

"We hadn't planned to do it that way. We were only going to do one of these gangster car crackup scenes in the movie. But Howard Hughes saw the rushes and said, 'Hey, that was a great car wreck, let's do some more.'

"I became interested in the technical aspects of the wrecks and showed the rushes to a director friend of mine, Lewis Milestone, who had great battle scenes of another kind in his *All Quiet on the Western Front*. He liked it too. Hughes saw a couple more, and said, 'Keep on, if you can get them all this good.'" These scenes were visually exciting and set the precedent for the hundreds of automobile chase scenes that have been filmed since.

There were a number of versions of *Scarface* made, because in those days, according to Hawks, the picture was "too hot to handle." Due to censorship they had to tone down some of the violence and sexual implications. *Scarface* was even banned in Chicago for a time. They were finally allowed to release the original version only after adding a clip of a city official saying something about gangs being bad.

During the final editing, another censor—an unofficial one—turned up. "When we finished shooting the picture and I was cutting it, three or four real gangsters, tough-looking guys, came into the studio one day and said, 'The boss wants us to look at the picture.' I said, 'You can pay a dollar when it shows in a movie house and then you can look at the picture.' One guy said, with a little smile, 'Oh hell, you didn't scare, did you?' And I said, 'No.' I said, 'Why didn't you just come up and ask me if you could see it? I'll screen it for you if you tell me what you think of it.'

"Then I showed it to them. They said, 'Where the hell did you find all of these things out!' They were amazed at the authenticity of our scenes.

"During the making of the picture, gangsters used to come around all the time. They would say, 'I'm George White or John White.' And I'd say, 'Look I'm so goddam busy today, come in tomorrow morning, okay?' They would agree. Then I'd shoot a wire to Chicago, to my source of information, and I'd get back a telegram, 'Puggy White is a pimp at such-and-such a place and a bouncer at such-and-such a place and carries a gun for such-and-such a person. He was mixed up in this or that killing.'

"When White would come in the next day, I'd say, 'Sit down, Puggy.' 'How'd you know my name?' 'Well,' I'd say, 'I know a lot more about you. You were a pimp and you carried a gun for this guy, you shot So-and-So.' He'd say, 'I wasn't any pimp.'

"Then he would usually tell me exactly how something was done by his gang and we would do that very thing in the movie. That's how we got the realism. We did scenes of killings that had actually happened. For example, in one scene we put guns in a hearse, then drove it by the windows of a café and shot the devil out of the place. That was something that actually happened in Chicago.

"The same thing was true of the hospital scene. Raft and Muni were bringing flowers to this rival gangster who had been shot up badly but hadn't died as he was supposed to. In the hospital corridor they pull these gats out of the flowers and killed the victim. That also actually happened in Chicago."

Hawks invited Capone, who was in Los Angeles, to the studio to look at some of the rushes. "Capone looked at me with a little smile and said, 'Now, tell me, where did you get some of that stuff?' I said, 'Look, Al, don't *you* have some things that you don't tell people?' He said 'Yeah,' and then we both laughed."

Capone reciprocated Hawks's hospitality by inviting him for a visit when he was in Chicago. Hawks called his office, but he wasn't in. Capone's male secretary said he would "let the boss know he was in town." Later that night some hoods visited Hawks at his hotel and asked him out to dinner. "I was about to get into this big black limousine, when one of the men said, 'Mr. Capone sends his regards and asked us to take you to dinner and then show you around since he can't.'

"I paused, 'Where's Mr. Capone?'

"'Well, there was a killing last night. And he had to go out of town on business.'

"I said, 'I'll meet you at the restaurant because I'm taking a cab.' They laughed and said okay." Later on Hawks met them at the restaurant, where they "had some beautiful hard blondes with them, and they all sat with their backs to the wall."

Hawks left for New York the next day and returned to Chicago a week later. He received a call from Capone himself inviting him to a cocktail party in his honor. When Hawks arrived at the party at Capone's headquarters he was surprised to see the arch-gangster in a morning coat and striped trousers. Women were all over the place, and, according to Hawks, "All of Capone's friends and associates, the cream of Chicago's gangster society, were there, all very cordial and polite. The high point of the evening came after dinner when Capone presented me with a small machinegun as a special gift."

Howard Hawks's forte as a film-maker was his involvement with the pure action of his films and his preoccupation with realism. George, throughout his career as an actor, had this same consuming point of view. He always believed, although he was not as adept as Hawks or others in articulating it, that movies were not fantasy, but an extension of his personal life. George was not actually Owney Madden's bodyguard; but he knew on an intimate basis enough people who played that role in life to create an authentic screen image of a bodyguard.

The main attribute George brought to the screen in his first important film was his special look and style. He was fortunate to have this quality recognized by a director of Howard Hawks's ability. According to Hawks, actors like Robinson, Cagney, or Muni worked hard to produce their characterizations on the screen; whereas a personality relied on an innate special quality. According to Hawks, if you had "it," it automatically worked for you on film.

"George had a certain unique look—and he kept it in most of his movies. He was smart enough to keep what he had. It worked for him. When you are a personality like George, the camera does something for you. The camera likes some people, and it liked George. I saw many of Raft's films. Even without lines, he wouldn't do a goddam thing sometimes except think something on camera, and his motivation would show up on film. The audience would learn from that look what he was thinking and what he was going to do about it.

"George had a marvelous impassive quality about him. He underplayed beautifully. I always try to use that tone in a film with an actor. Muni also underplayed a great scene in *Scarface*, the one where he gets his first machinegun, and it worked beautifully. At first, he played it like a tough guy—talking about his newly acquired power with the gun. I felt it was just too tough, too strong. I therefore had Ben Hecht rewrite the whole scene.

"The next day I told Paul, 'I think we got it.' Now he came in with the machinegun and he's all smiles. He carried the tommy gun as if it was a new baby. When he showed the gun to Raft, he said, 'Get out of my way, Gino. It's gonna spit.'

"He shot the tommy gun and knocked every poolball off a rack. In another scene a gang rival said, 'You don't give me orders.' And Muni just patted the tommy gun and replied, 'This is the only thing that gives orders.' George also underplayed it that way in *Scarface*.

"George was smart enough to stick to roles that were successful for him. Actors who become too self-involved or are different every time don't usually get too far. If they stay with roles that vary a certain basic quality, they build an image the public remembers."

Hawks also said, "Raft is one of the few actors who is grateful for the start I gave him. For ten years after we made *Scarface*, Raft would write me every year saying he'd do any story, anytime, anywhere—for half his normal price."

Beginning with *Scarface*, Raft always based his acting on roles that were familiar, stressing different attributes to get a variety of characters. The axiom that each of us has many ways of being is used by the actor. For Raft, he could be a tough gangster, a romantic lover, an elegant dancer, a truckdriver, a loving son—basically all of them Raft or people he knew well—but he could also give each of his performances a distinctiveness. In all of these different characters, the audience recognizes the underlying "real guy."

Hawks was without a doubt a vital force in launching George Raft's career. His perceptiveness about George's potential was actualized on the screen in *Scarface;* and his assessment of George was confirmed by the public and the critics.

Scarface was clearly a landmark film, and it remains Howard Hawks's favorite of the more than fifty feature films he has made. Hawks went on to direct many important films, including Ben Hecht and Charles MacArthur's *Twentieth Century* (1934) with John Barrymore and Carole Lombard; *Only Angeles Have Wings* (1939); *Viva Villa* (1934) with Wallace Beery; *Bringing Up Baby* (1938); *Sergeant York* (1941); *Rio Bravo* (1959), *Red River* (1948), with John Wayne; *To Have and Have Not* (1945) and *The Big Sleep* (1946) with Bogart and Bacall; and *Gentlemen Prefer Blondes* (1953) with Marilyn Monroe.

Now under contract to Paramount, Raft was working in a film called *Madame Racketeer* (1932) with Richard Bennett and Alison Skipworth, when *Scarface* was released. He was asked to leave immediately for New York to make a personal appearance with *Scarface*. The film was breaking box-office records all over the country, especially in New York.

While *Scarface* was playing at the Rialto, another Raft film, *Dancers in the Dark* (1932) with Miriam Hopkins, was playing across the street at the Paramount.

"Ken Murray was master of ceremonies. He introduced me and the crowd went nuts. The way they yelled and screamed made me realize they just wanted to look at me. Still, I had to say something. So I said, 'I don't know what to say, but I can say this. We're on 42nd Street. Just a few blocks away from here is the building I was born in.' Then I broke into a little dance.

"*Scarface* ran all day and all night for about a week, and I appeared every midnight. But I never got used to the way people from all over the theater yelled and screamed. Maybe I was such a big hit because I was a New Yorker. I never got an ovation like that in my life."

Not a man to forget a pal because of his new fame, Raft agreed to appear as a favor at a classy speakeasy, the Biarritz, just off Park Avenue, run by an old friend, Jimmy Collins. Nightclub business was bad in 1932—it was the depth of the Depression, and in one short year Prohibition would be repealed. George offered to fit in two nights on the following weekend, on one condition: that he not be paid any salary.

Word quickly got around Broadway that Raft was to perform, and on the first night, according to Collins, "The place was so packed they were standing in the halls just to get a peek at Georgie." Many of George's friends were there to see his fast Charleston, and this brief revival of the old vaudeville days meant more to him than his new Hollywood stardom.

At the studio's insistence George often toured the country with his movies, for his appearances appreciably helped the box office. All of his old vaudeville fans, plus his new film admirers, jammed the theaters.

The Chicago opening of *Scarface* was delayed, but with the added prologue it was allowed to be released, and when Raft was appearing with the movie in Chicago, he was quietly kidnaped for a few hours by the "big guy"—Capone himself.

"One night after my late show a tough young hood, with a gun bulging under his coat, showed up at my hotel room and said, 'Raft, the big guy wants to see you.'

"All I could manage to say was 'Okay,' and I followed him into a big black limousine filled with other hoods. We went directly to Capone's headquarters in the Lexington Hotel on South Michigan Avenue.

"After passing through checkpoints with the armed guards giving me deadpan looks, I was finally led into Capone's private office, and there he was, seated behind a huge mahogany desk.

I remember a fancy gold inkstand, a small carved Chinese chest, and an odd clock in which little quails and cuckoos sounded the quarter and half hours. There were oil portraits of George Washington and Mayor 'Big Bill' Thompson on the walls.

"I had met Capone once or twice at gambling joints in New York. Then his name was Al Brown. He remembered me as a dancer and seemed interested in my film career—especially my *Scarface* role.

"'Georgie, so you been playin' my bodyguard, Frank Rio, in this *Scarface* pitcher.'

"'Yes, I did, Al,' I said. 'But it's nothing personal. Actors do what they're told.'

"Capone rubbed the long scar on his face. Then, kidding on the square, said, 'Well, you tell them guys in Hollywood that they don't know Al Capone. They bumped me off in the end and nobody's bumpin' Al off while he's running Chicago. Yeah, you tell 'em that.'

"We talked a while longer about people we had known in New York and this and that. I was anxious to leave and finally figured the interview was over. When I said good-bye, and started to walk out, Capone stopped me. 'Wait a minute, Georgie, I see you tossin' a coin all through the pitcher.'

"'Just a little theatrical touch.'

"'A four-bit piece, yeah?'

"'No, it was a nickel.'

"'That's worse. You tell 'em that if any of my boys are tossin' coins, they'll be twenty-dollar gold pieces.'

"I wasn't sure if he was kidding or meant it, but I promised to convey the message to Hollywood. 'You like the picture, Al?' I asked. By now, he was flattered with the attention the movie had brought him, with the name *Scarface* on marquees across the country. 'Yeah, I liked it,' he said."

Scarface received rave reviews not only from the man on whose life it was based, but from most of the critics.

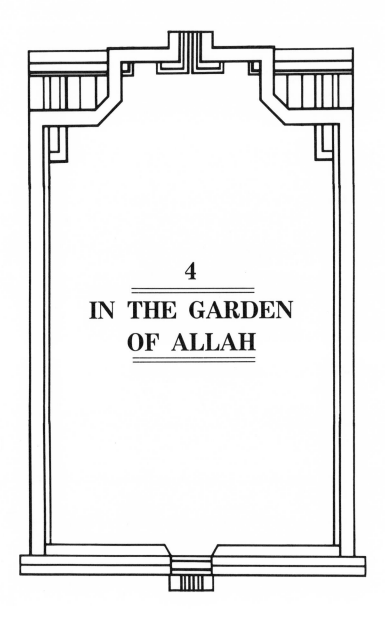

4

IN THE GARDEN
OF ALLAH

In the Depression years of the early thirties twelve million unemployed men rode the rails, sold apples on streetcorners, stood in soup lines, marched on Washington, or sat stoically at home wondering how to pay the rent. To these men and their hungry families, President Herbert Hoover's now-infamous slogan, "Prosperity is just around the corner," was a bitter irony. For all his piety and good intentions, Hoover became a symbol of the Depression. In 1933, the new president, Franklin Delano Roosevelt, rapidly began to move toward positive social change; however, the results of his efforts would not be felt by the average man for several years.

In the midst of all of this gloom there was one bright and glamorous spot, Hollywood, where the hallmarks of the free enterprise system, competition, status-seeking, and conspicuous consumption continued in the traditional American way. A few studios had financial problems in 1932—but these were essentially accounting matters and did not significantly affect the lifestyle of most Hollywood moguls and screen stars.

Hollywood was more than a state of mind. It existed in fact, and its films kept the extravagant hope and faith of pre-Depression America alive. The ultimate activists of the free enterprise system—the gangsters—were glamorized. The sweet life of the super-rich was portrayed as the ideal state of being, potentially available to anyone who wanted to work hard for success; faith in the integrity and ultimate triumph of the common man was expressed in Frank Capra's films, *Mr. Deeds Goes to Town* (1936) and *Mr. Smith Goes to Washington* (1939), but social realities were gingerly dealt with. One exception, King Vidor's *Our Daily Bread* (1934), concludes with an odd mixture of communal living and self-reliance as a solution to the social ills of the time. The stage dealt more directly and more immediately with life in the Depression: Elmer Rice's *Street Scene* (1929), *One-Third of a Nation* (1938), the early plays of Clifford Odets, *Awake and Sing* (1935), *Golden Boy* (1937); Sidney Kingsley's *Dead End* (1935). All these films dealt with urban inequalities. Robert Sherwood's *The Petrified Forest* (1935) and Maxwell Anderson's *Winterset* were concerned with the period's spiritual malaise. The impact of these works was slightly deadened when they were filmed. But incorporated into musicals and comedies were fellas and gals without a dime. In *My Man Godfrey* (1936), the hero seems a bum but is finally revealed to be a millionaire ruined by the crash. Chaplin's *Modern Times* (1936) is given little credit for the rigor of its social commentary. By and large the film industry was successful by virtue of the economic and social problems that were plaguing the country.

The look of John Ford's 1940 film version of John Steinbeck's novel *The Grapes of Wrath*, when contrasted with the photographs of Okies by Dorothea Lange and Walker Evans, gives startling insight into how Hollywood sidestepped a direct portrayal of impoverishment. Usually, social realities were dealt with obliquely and romantically. A safe distance had to be created, such as setting gangster stories in the twenties. Today we must "read through" the films of the thirties, and perhaps they are more interesting now than when they were produced because of the revealing assumptions that shaped them. The social victim and outcast as tragic hero is a recurring theme. This concept was the basis of such films as *I Am a Fugitive From a Chain Gang* (the best of the semidocumentaries, and among America's greatest films) and Fritz Lang's *You Only Live Once* (1937) with Henry Fonda and Sylvia Sidney (the quintessential working-class heroine), *Street Scene* (1931), *Dead End* (1937), and *You and Me* (1938) (the last with George Raft).

George Raft was just such a social hero. He was an ordinary guy, of humble origin, who dressed with class, had pluck, nerve, and guts, and was basically antisocial. He lived by strict moral code, but an extremely personal one. It allowed one to kill, but not to slap women; to rob banks, but not to speak ill of your mother; to be at once ruthless in achieving success and patriotic toward one's country. Such an odd social code is still familiar. To be simultaneously innocent and corrupt is part of America's mythology.

The task of any man confronted with social inequality and rank injustice in a land imbued with democratic ideals and free enterprise is staggering. No wonder audiences went to the movies to find out how to behave and dress. A manner which could incorporate such conflicting notions was hard to arrive at by oneself. Raft, flipping a coin—expressionless, unflappable, with distinctive and self-affirming clothes (and "taste" had nothing to do with it)—was an enlightening presence.

Films not only confirmed and bolstered the audience's hopes;

they also educated them. The films told you not only how life was lived, but more essentially how to live life. Adults in their thirties today have mothers who once behaved like Bette Davis and fathers who dressed and acted like George Raft. And for many it is a curiosity about our parents and their generation that is reflected in the present nostalgia for films by those who weren't even born when they were made.

The geographic center of the film capital was between Hollywood and Sunset Boulevards, bounded by Vine Street on the east and La Brea on the west. On these pleasant palm-lined boulevards out-of-towners could see movie people—from extras to stars—any time of the day or night. The weather was balmy and the clear evening air scented by jasmine. A movie fan would have no problem spotting a Hollywood celebrity's sunglasses and expensive clothing in the rear seat of a passing chauffeured limousine. Sometimes, these luminaries would disembark and mingle with the other shoppers and pedestrians.

A gracious place to lunch might be at the leather-upholstered Brown Derby on Vine near Sunset or at the beautiful, white-framed Hollywood Hotel. A more casual meal could be had at one of the small restaurants up and down the Boulevard. During their lunch break stars and bit players might be seen in their various exotic costumes. On the bulletin boards of these eateries were ads for a room to rent, a call for a special acting type, a tuxedo for sale, or a demand for a performing dog.

In 1932, the red line trolley from downtown Los Angeles ended at Schwab's Drugstore on Sunset. A long block west of Schwab's was the Garden of Allah Hotel. At various times, the Allah and the nearby Chateau Marmont housed such movie greats as Errol Flynn, John Barrymore, Humphrey Bogart, Charles Laughton, Tallulah Bankhead, Marlene Dietrich, Greta Garbo, Ginger Rogers, Laurence Olivier, and Katharine Hepburn, and such writers as Somerset Maugham, John O'Hara, Ernest Hemingway, and F. Scott Fitzgerald.

The literary elite which hung out in Stanley Rose's bookstore on Hollywood Boulevard rivaled the sophisticated clan that gathered daily for lunch at New York's Algonquin. Among them, according to Budd Schulberg in his 1972 reminiscence of that era, *The Four Seasons of Success*, were John O'Hara, Guy Endore, Scott Fitzgerald, Erskine Caldwell, Gene Fowler, Dalton

Trumbo, Dashiell Hammett, Dorothy Parker, and Nathanael West. It was West who wrote the classic Hollywood novel of the era, *Day of the Locusts*, depicting the lives not of the stars but of the "others," those desperate Hollywood hangers-on in the crowds, crazed by envy and frustration. Later he provided the screenplay for a George Raft–Claire Trevor movie, *I Stole a Million* (1939).

Near the Garden of Allah was the Trocadero and Ciro's, favorite celebrity hangouts where Darryl F. Zanuck, Clark Gable, Carole Lombard, Gary Cooper, Jean Harlow, and Louis B. Mayer dined and danced. La Rue and the Mocambo were also famous haunts. Photographers crowded the parking lots and entrances of these exclusive clubs and restaurants, and fans would consider a reasonable evening's entertainment simply waiting across the street to watch these magic people leave their cars. The comparison of these stars with royalty has been made once too often; a more accurate description might see them as fantasy images in human form. It was not merely that they were honored, but they were conceived of in the most intimate terms. The drama of their personal lives was the basis for the most extreme form of the audiences' adulation and identification.

Hollywood figures could gauge their importance by the attitude of the photographers who often opened the door when a car arrived to flashbulb a star. If they found an unfamiliar face they would morosely shout, "Nobody here." A photographer's shrug would indicate you were "out." Sheilah Graham recalled the night F. Scott Fitzgerald was pushed aside as a nobody because Lupe Velez had just arrived with Gary Cooper.

It was this status-conscious, carnivorous, deadly social system that George Raft entered when he achieved stardom in 1932. Now in a position to indulge his sartorial extravagance, Raft joined the Hollywood extravaganza. On a single day he would order four dozen silk shirts, a dozen pair of shoes, and ten suits. Beautiful women—starlets, aspiring actresses, simple "groupies," callgirls—were readily available, and he maintained an awesome sexual diet as his Broadway man-about-town image found new life in Hollywood.

His success and fame did not mean that all was going well. As a relatively uneducated man from Hell's Kitchen, he found himself in a society where he was expected to interact on equal terms with people who were sophisticated, knowledgeable members of an established, if fluctuating, social set. Even politics was a subject Raft had not enough assurance to deal with. He knew whatever was worth knowing about sports: Babe Ruth's lifetime batting average, which horse had won the Kentucky Derby. He knew the hierarchy of the New York underworld bigshots. He knew how to handle women, how to survive, how to overcome poverty. He knew the urgent matters of existence, but they were not subjects for polite conversation.

Discussions of art, music, politics, social gossip flowed around him and, while he had his own valid thoughts on films and a fund of show business lore, he felt inhibited because he lacked a polished vocabulary or broad base of knowledge. He was especially sensitive to any teasing about his New York accent. He kept silent, and that silence also seemed to imply some understandable hostility. This demeanor gave George the reputation of being, if not sinister, then at least mysteriously intriguing. Combined with the roles he played, it tended to confirm the rumors and innuendos that George was in fact a gangster. His fame would not allow his simply blending into a crowd, and, because he was insecure about his manner and shy, he began to avoid parties, dinners, and openings where he might be drawn into conversation. People thought him an enigma. In reality he was lonely and fearful of being mocked; in terror that he might overhear someone call him a lowbrow, "an illiterate" slob in a $300 suit. Instead, he went where he could face life on equal terms: the fights, ballgames, races. Raft's "roaring twenties" act worked beautifully for him on Broadway and on the screen but fell short in the Hollywood social milieu. The change in rules was swift and unprepared for. The same gag or response that went over big on Broadway fell flat in the new setting.

At the fights held every Friday at the Hollywood Legion Stadium, he met his old Broadway friend Maxie Greenberg, now called Mack Grey. Mack was managing a fighter who seldom was left standing after the third round. When George offered him a job as his assistant and also promised to get his fighter work, Mack was delighted.

Raft's main reasons for employing Mack Grey were not only that Mack spoke Raft's language and knew the Broadway crew, but also that Raft trusted Mack's opinions and advice.

They shared a common background and a common sense of life. When George argued with Mack (which was often), it was as if he were arguing with himself. Mack appreciated the problems of Raft's transition from Broadway tough guy–hoofer to Hollywood star. The tension and personal uncertainty of this transformation would cause Raft to explode into violent fits of temper, ending in fights, and Grey was there to provide perspective, protection, and sympathy. Raft's inner anguish precipitated a violence that was always ready to surface.

Despite this personal turmoil, he desperately wanted and gladly received all the accouterments of success. Yet he found, as many others did, that fame and money did not immediately salve inner feelings of unworthiness. At best, the acclaim helped to dull the pain.

On Broadway, Raft had learned the trick of reading someone's lips in a restaurant or nightclub. In those days it provided valuable information about a gangland rival's plans. Mack Grey recalled how, at Ciro's or the Mocambo, out of the blue Raft would say to him, "I'm going to get that son-of-a-bitch." George was responding to a presumed insult he read on a man's lips at a distant table. Mack would frequently restrain George, but he wasn't always successful. One instance occurred after a visit to a plastic surgeon where Raft was having the scar on his ear that was a souvenir of his boxing days removed.

When George did something he loved company. And, on this occasion, since George was getting his ear fixed, he generously booked Mack in for a nose job. A few days after their operations, they went to the Brown Derby for lunch. "No doubt," George smiled as he related the incident, "we must've looked funny all bandaged up. I guess we looked like we'd been in a big fight. Still, we were kidding around about it with different people we knew in the Derby. Finally, when we left and were waiting for my car, some guy standing out front passes a smart remark to a friend, something like—'There's George Raft, the tough guy. I bet he ain't so tough.' I tried at first to ignore him. But he kept at it. Finally I blew up and threw a few punches. The guy went down.

"The waiting photographers caught the action and the next day in the papers—there were headlines, 'GEORGE RAFT, SCREEN

TOUGH GUY, SLUGS CITIZEN.' And there's an awful picture of Mack and me with our bandages. We both looked like ten-ton safes had been dropped on us."

Such incidents stemming from George's repressed hostility tended to foster his tough-guy image with the public. While this hardly promoted the idea that he was an upright citizen, it probably bolstered his career. Audiences believed Raft was actually the guy they saw up on the screen—and, in part, this was true. And his tendency to lose his temper, which added to the publicity, continued. When Raft was doing personal appearances with the film *Bolero* at the Chicago Theater, another incident he later regretted, occurred.

"I was sitting in the Chez Paris with this girl, and there was a big party going on. I was doing nothing special, just sitting there, minding my own business, enjoying the music. The band was playing a tango. Now all eyes were on me because that was the dance I was associated with."

A man at the party came over and asked Raft to dance the tango with his wife. George responded politely, "Well, nobody is on the floor now and I really don't want to show off." The man assured him that his wife was a good dancer. George said he didn't doubt it and excused himself again. The man walked away.

Around midnight, George said good-night to everybody and started to leave. By this time the man was drunk and said, "Raft, you're a shitheel." George was angry. "Wait a minute. You can't say that to me. I don't have to take that from you." The man kept at George and, as often happened in his movies, a mob fight developed. Chairs, windows, and bottles were broken and the police were called in to quell the riot. The next day's headlines read, "RAFT IN BRAWL IN CHICAGO NIGHTCLUB."

His quick temper frequently erupted in the course of his love affairs. In 1934, George was romancing a pretty actress, Marjorie King, who accompanied him to New York, where they stayed at the Waldorf. At dinner one night they quarreled and she bluntly told him that he had bad manners and was crude. At three in the morning he awakened Mack Grey. "C'mon," he ordered, "I'm going to fix this snooty bitch."

They went to Marjorie's room, woke her, and in silence the shocked girl watched Raft with scissors destroy every bit of clothing he had bought her that day. The next morning a bell-hop appeared at her door with an apologetic note from George, a typical gesture after one of his outbursts, and $1500 in cash for a new wardrobe.

Wasting no time, her feelings still hurt, she stormed into George's suite with the money he had sent her to replenish her damaged wardrobe, threw the money in his face, and burst into tears. Mack Grey hated to see money treated badly and carefully picked it up, one bill at a time. He returned the money to Marjorie, who had had a change of heart; and while she dried her tears, still sobbing, she began to count: "Five hundred, one thousand . . . two hundred, three hundred . . . four hundred." Suddenly she screamed at Mack, "You louse, I'm a hundred dollars short!"

Few actors in Hollywood made more trouble for themselves. "Some movie people were afraid of me. And the cops questioned me whenever someone lost an umbrella. Why? Because a bad rumor got around that I could fix things, handle hot merchandise, or get people roughed up."

George never forgot the day a certain underworld character he knew pulled him into a corner at a prizefight and said he had a serious problem with a big boxing promoter. "You got connections, George," he said. "What would it take to get him knocked off?" This amazing and cold-blooded proposition disgusted George. He asked himself, "What had I done that would lead someone to think I'd be part of something like that? If I hadn't noticed how drunk he was, I would have beaten his head into the wall."

Some of Raft's anger was carried onto the set. In 1933, Raft was appearing in *The Bowery*, a film set in the nineties about a milieu Raft knew well—a tough New York neighborhood swarming with gangs. This was the first film Darryl F. Zanuck produced for 20th Century-Fox, and it was directed by Raoul Walsh. Based on an actual feud between two notorious Bowery gang leaders, Steve Brodie (played by Raft) and Chuck Conners (played by Wallace Beery).

Walsh, a stickler for authenticity and a sense of immediacy, would have an extra tell the "hoods" on Beery's side, "All the guys in Brodie's gang think you're a bunch of creeps." And then the shill would say the same things to the extras in Raft's gang.

Beery, Raft, and their gang extras developed real hostility and in one big gang-war scene the movie gangs actually fought, wrecking the sets by throwing real rocks, flowerpots, and anything else they got their hands on. It made for a realistic movie—but a lot of extras wound up in the hospital.

George developed the impression—real or imagined—that Wallace Beery didn't like him; and, at the least, Beery, a big star, was rather aloof. At five o'clock sharp Beery left the set, sometimes leaving George to complete scenes with a stand-in. Finally came the breaking point to George's pride when Raft felt Beery tricked him.

"We were doing a scene on a barge, where we have a big fight. Beery said, 'George, let me throw the first punch just to get things rolling.' I said, 'All right.' I had learned how to frame a fight in a movie. You decide in advance to throw, say, two punches; then the other guy throws two.

"The son-of-a-bitch Beery threw the first punch and hit me with all his might, knocking me cold! When I came to I got up and called him everything I could think of. I told him, 'I'm not afraid of you, you big tub of lard.' Then we squared off for real and I threw a few hard, fast punches into his fat belly. The crew jumped in and stopped the fight. But from then on, of course, we were at odds.

"He was a character, but I learned some things from him. For example, an assistant director got on him one day and said, 'You've got the wrong shirt on, Mr. Beery. It has no style.' His quick response was, 'If they look at my shirt, they won't look at my face.' I remembered that."

Although there was this pronounced wariness between Raft and the Hollywood establishment, he balanced it with loyalty to trusted friends. Always looking for the opportunity to give someone a break, his generosity sometimes backfired and caused him trouble.

Two New York hoodlums he had known casually came to see him because they were broke and Raft got them jobs as extras in *The Bowery*. He lunched with them sometimes, but one afternoon the casting director told him that his two friends had vanished. The next day he found out that they had left the lot to get a bite in a nearby restaurant where they had been gunned down.

Again, Raft got a job for a handsome young man, Jack Gordon, who neglected to tell Raft that he was a fugitive. Gordon received good notices for his performance, and his picture was published in a New York paper where the police recognized him as a suspect in a mob murder. He was extradited, tried, and beat the charge.

In the early thirties Owney Madden came west, and Raft took him on a tour of nightclubs—which didn't help George's image with the police, gossip columnists, and the studios. At one club a private cop, who doubled as a city policeman during the day, had Madden arrested and jailed because he suspected that Madden was violating his parole. When Owney became hungry that night, Raft paid two detectives $150 for a couple of sandwiches. The policeman's suspicions proved correct, and Madden was returned to New York. Madden's waning political connections in New York were not strong enough to keep him out of prison for parole violation. He went back to Sing Sing to complete his original sentence. After his release he retired to Hot Springs.

In spite of the fiercely announced independence and flashes of temper, Raft attempted to alter his image and avoid when he could those who would further tarnish his reputation.

Paramount Studios, to whom Raft was now under contract, felt George was ready for his first starring role. The film was *Night After Night*, based on Louis Bromfield's story "Single Night." Raft shocked the producer when he told him that he would rather not star in the film. He was flattered by the offers, but, as he explained it: "When you fall from the tenth floor you're hurt more than when you fall from the first floor." After some further persuasion, George accepted the part.

Paradoxically, the role characterized some of George's real-life conflicts. The central character of the film, Joe Anton, was an ambitious Prohibition gangster who ran a speakeasy and gambling operation in a palatial New York City mansion that was open "night after night." In the first scene his bodyguard brings him his breakfast in bed. The camera follows him as he discards his silk pajamas and robe, showers, and goes through his elaborate wardrobe in preparation for the evening's activities. As he dresses, he discusses business with his bodyguards and business associates.

Dressed for action, the hero enters his casino, crowded with New York's fashionably dressed elite. He immediately spots Constance Cummings, playing a stunning society lady whose family originally owned the mansion. Beautiful but sad, she appears nightly at the club to dine at her private table. The romance between them is the standard one of the man from the wrong side of the tracks in love with a wealthy woman. She is fond of him but unable to take his attentions seriously. Nevertheless, he attempts to win her by having himself instructed in the social graces by an Emily Post blueblood, played by Alison Skipworth.

The role of Joe Anton's former girlfriend, Maudie, was the one which introduced Mae West to the screen. It was a part originally intended for Texas Guinan. However, George told the director, "Guinan's a friend of mine and she'd be great. But I know a woman who would be sensational." Although Mae West was a famous and somewhat notorious stage star, the director was hesitant, but Raft persisted until she was given the part.

When Maudie, representing the past the gangster is trying to shake, barges into the club, she demands to know what has happened to her former lover. Not only was this Mae West's first time before the cameras, but it became the high point in the whole film. She wrote the scripts for most of her later films, and certainly in all her movies *her* lines were her own. "Mae West adlibbed one line that knocked us all out of the box. Imagine this. Here's a palatial chandeliered lobby with a marble floor. The door opens and in comes Mae West, dripping in furs over a white evening gown. She greets the hatcheck girl and she removes her fur wrap. She's wearing diamond bracelets up to her elbow. Overwhelmed, the hatcheck girl says, 'Goodness, what beautiful jewelry.' Mae West walks toward the casino with her sexy movement, turns back, and hits her with the line, 'Goodness had nothing to do with it, dearie.'"

With only two big scenes in the film, Mae West, as Raft admits, stole the picture. "I always said, 'She stole everything but the camera.' She was gorgeous, stunning, with beautiful skin, perfect teeth, and she sparkled with sex." In Miss West's recollection of the film, however, George held all the cards: "George got me my first big break in the movies. But I had mixed feelings. He played the lead in *Night After Night* (1932) and I was in a supporting role. It was very hard on me since I had been a big star in *Diamond Lil*, *Sex* and other plays. I found it tough playing under him. George dominated all of the scenes. I watched that movie many times. In any scene where George appears, you're not aware of anyone else."

Although Raft had fun working with Mae West, even during this production he lost his professional cool. In one scene he was supposed to pick a shirt out of a drawer. The director thought he was too slow. In front of the crew, he committed the unpardonable crime of yelling at the star. "For Christsake, pick up the goddamn shirt!"

George controlled himself. They did another take and the next time the director still felt he was too slow. "You son-of-a-bitch, just pick up the shirt!" Still, Raft didn't react, but the next morning he arrived at eight-thirty, a half-hour before he was due. When the director came in, George called him over to a corner.

He grabbed him by the throat and said, "Look, you son-of-a-bitch, I want to tell you something. I'm not a tough guy, but if you yell at me again while there're people around I'm gonna punch you out. I'm not that intelligent and don't always know what to say when I get mad. Next time I'm going to have to let you have it right in the jaw. Do you understand?" The director nervously apologized and from then on treated Raft with polite caution.

Unlike most actors, Raft seldom studied his lines the night before shooting. After breakfast, Mack Grey and Raft would drive to the studio and rehearse the day's shooting script in the back seat of Raft's limousine. According to Grey, "By the time we arrived on the set, George would have it all down pat. And if he was nervous, as he sometimes told me in private, no one there ever knew it."

Of course, if a line didn't ring true to Raft's concept of the action or was personally offensive, he stubbornly refused to use it. Instinctively he knew what was right and what was wrong for him. And no one in Hollywood had more direct experience and first-hand knowledge of the tough-guy roles he was playing. Important directors like Howard Hawks, Raoul Walsh, Fritz

Lang, and Billy Wilder welcomed Raft's advice on lines or action, for they knew it would add to the film's authenticity. He realized what it was that made him unique. The attention to movement he had gained as a dancer, the snappy attire and the gestural habits of tough guys, together with his natural gift for impersonation lent the roles he played a vibrant authenticity.

"I was always calm, always spoke slowly, and I never yelled on the screen. I told the coaches and directors, 'Don't ask me to shout or talk too fast. Let me be myself.' And I believed I could write better lines for myself than those given me by many writers.

"The minute they asked me to do anything I wasn't totally comfortable with, I refused. And of course, the minute you try to *force* me to do anything, I'll resist. In one movie I was supposed to climb out on a five-story-high ledge. It was a dangerous shot, but I walked on that ledge, without any resistance, because the director had said, 'That's nothin', George, you can do it.' But if he'd have tried something like, 'You gotta do it,' he would've had to get himself another boy."

He was never at his best in rehearsal, for he needed the pressure and urgency of actual filming. Not a trained actor, he worked best spontaneously when immediate intuition would lead him to the best approach. Therefore, the first two or three takes were the best for Raft. Since movies were made rapidly, this proved a blessing for most directors.

Some critics saw Raft as a limited and unvaried performer, but close attention to his screen portraits reveals a high degree of truthfulness, spontaneity, and subtle flexibility. Despite his monotone voice and tight gestures, audiences sensed some essential reality radiating from within. Raft always "thought the part," and, as Howard Hawks observed, "When George thought something on the screen the audience knew what he meant."

George tended to identify closely with the characters he was asked to play and maintained a stern moral posture toward them. More than once he refused an "evil" part unless the character, by the end of the film, received his just punishment. If he was portraying a particularly ruthless, wholly unredeemable character, he insisted that he be killed at the end. There were some roles that were simply too unsavory and repellent for him under any circumstances. One such rejection led to the first of many suspensions at Paramount—all for similar reasons.

The Story of Temple Drake, a film version of William Faulkner's sensational novel, *Sanctuary*, was being produced by Benjamin Glazer. Miriam Hopkins, opposite whom Raft had formerly played in *Dancers in the Dark*, was starred. Raft was assigned to play Popeye, a psychotic who rapes a girl with a corncob and then kills her feebleminded son. In the novel Faulkner describes Popeye as

> A man of under size, a cigarette slanted from his chin. His face had a queer bloodless color as though seen by electric light; in his slanted straw hat and slightly akimbo arms he had the vicious depthless quality of stamped tin. . . . He twisted and pinched cigarettes in his little doll-like hands. His skin had a dead dark pallor. He had no chin at all. His face just went away like the face of a wax doll set too near a hot fire. . . . Popeye's eyes looked like rubber knobs. . . . Popeye looked about with a sort of vicious cringing.

As if Popeye's appearance wasn't horrendous enough, he had a shrunken, nonfunctional penis (an unthinkable condition for George Raft), a result of having been castrated for a previous crime.

This image was so offensive to George that he bypassed Glazer, who wouldn't comply with Raft's wishes to not play the role, and appealed to Paramount executive producers, Emmanuel Cohen and Adolph Zukor. After several heated meetings, he finally told Zukor: "I'll do the movie on one condition. You put two million dollars in my account. Because when this movie comes out—I'll be through as an actor. Everyone will hate me. The two million would be my insurance policy."

Raft's "moral" stance became national news and produced a controversy. It became a *cause célèbre*, and church leaders and citizen groups who had thought the novel obscene when originally published sided with George Raft.

George explained his position to the press: "I always ate before I went into pictures. And the movie business got along pretty good without Raft. Maybe this Paramount break, if it comes to a real split, is all to the good.

"I've been lucky enough to get a break on the screen. People have been good to me—they've liked me. If I had done what Paramount ordered me to do and played the part of Popeye they wouldn't have liked me any more. That's the way I got it figured out. That part was plain suicide for me. Any other actor might play it and maybe get away with it, but if I played it there'd be just one thing for the public to think and they'd think it—'George Raft, himself, is like Popeye.'

"I was promised, before I made my last personal appearance tour, 'No more gangster and racketeer roles.' Then they spring this on me. Listen, I know my luck won't always hold. But I'd like to leave the screen exactly when people could point up at me and say, 'That's George Raft. He was hitting on high when he quit.'

"I'll never be one that takes a bum part, loses the respect of the public, and by-and-by has to panhandle bits while he hears people say, 'That's Raft—remember him?'

"I'm not panning Paramount for making the picture. That's their business. I'm only thinking of me—George Raft. I wouldn't play a heel like Popeye because I don't choose to commit suicide. And for me playing that part would be plain suicide."

The battle was finally resolved and Jack La Rue took the part. George may have been right, for La Rue's career was definitely on the rise—but after *The Story of Temple Drake* it plateaued, and, although he played in many subsequent films, he seldom got past second billing and was restricted to a series of villain roles.

George bounced back from his clash with Paramount's top brass and co-starred with Sylvia Sidney in a melodrama, *Pick-Up* (1933), in which he played an honest cab driver who befriends a recently released jailbird, Sylvia Sidney. But this role was only a temporary change, because Paramount had him slated for more tough-guy roles.

By 1934 George felt that he had exhausted his repertoire of gangster variations, and Paramount might have kept him on the "heavy" track indefinitely if he had not taken the initiative himself. Outside of a brief role in *Taxi* with Jimmy Cagney, a fast shuffle on stage with a chorus in *The Bowery,* and the early self-portrayal in Texas Guinan's *Queen of the Night Clubs,* George had not been cast as a dancer.

Musicals were becoming extremely popular again, and Warner Brothers led the field. Their productions of *Forty-Second Street,* and *Gold Diggers of 1933,* both of which bubbled with elaborate Busby Berkeley musical numbers, were instant hits. Other studios were trying to latch onto the trend, and at RKO they discovered they had a dynamite pair when two featured players, Fred Astaire and Ginger Rogers, were the sensation of the film *Flying Down to Rio.* It was Astaire who brought real dancing to the films—making dance sequences the focal point of his movies. Raft thought this a good time to capitalize on his own dancing ability.

Sam Katz, a Paramount executive, had worked for the Public Theatres Circuit and had hired Raft as a dancer in the twenties. Raft approached him with the idea of putting him in a musical and allowing him to utilize his romantic manner in the way Valentino's had been in *The Four Hoursemen.*

Katz commissioned a screenplay. But George was not completely happy with it. *"Bolero* was good, but I didn't particularly like it because they made me unsympathetic, someone too conceited, only interested in dancing and success. Carole Lombard played my dancing partner. We're in love with each other but I only talk to her about rehearsals, making our act better, or about how important my career is to me.

"I wanted the story to be different, where I could love the girl more than my career. I was tired of being a rat. But they wrote the movie their way, and I went along with it."

George's nemesis in the *Temple Drake* battle, Ben Glazer, was assigned to produce *Bolero,* and once again they clashed, this time about the dialogue. The dancer was to tell his press agent that it would be good publicity to have pictures taken of him as he knelt at his mother's grave.

According to Mack Grey: "George fumed for days over this. He took it so personally that it seemed as if he was being asked to say it about his own mother. The morning he was supposed to do this scene, he was rehearsing a dance with Carole Lombard and, just as they were doing a dip, he spotted Glazer coming on to the set. He was so anxious to get at him that he dropped Carole on her behind. By the time Carole said, 'Thanks a lot, George,' he was halfway over to Glazer. George laid it on him how he felt about it and that he wasn't going to do it. So what does Glazer do but tell him flat out—'You'll do it, because I say so.' George let him have it right on the jaw, and Glazer went down! After more arguments, and a few apologies, the speech was finally deleted."

Although George might have hated Benny Glazer, he adored his leading lady, Carole Lombard. *Bolero* was a great hit, and they repeated its success with *Rumba* (1935).

"I truly loved Carole Lombard. She was the greatest girl that ever lived and we were the best of pals. Completely honest and outspoken, she was liked by everyone.

"Carole was wholly generous, always seeing to it that people she knew or felt sorry for worked as extras. If they didn't work, she wouldn't go on the set.

"She was always playing jokes. One day she put little tin stars all over my dressing room, even in my toilet. Another time she sent me a big package from Bullock's, tied with a big floral ribbon bow. I opened it. There's another box, then another. Finally I get to the last box and there's a ham!"

One of Lombard's legendary practical jokes that delighted all Hollywood was a trick she played on her agent, Myron Selznick. As a matter of routine, Carole was asked to renew her contract with Selznick. He gave her three copies to study and sign. Reversing the standard actor-agent split, Carole changed all copies so that she was to receive ten percent of all of Selznick's earnings.

Selznick was delighted at the pleasant signing ceremony the following day, and never took the time to reread the contract he approved. Several weeks later Carole wrote Selznick asking why she had not yet received her ten percent. He checked the contract and with horror saw what it was he had signed. Fortunately for him Lombard relented and agreed to sign a more routine contract.

At the time Lombard and Raft became friends she was separated from William Powell and was in the process of divorce. It was rumored, because they were seen so often together, that they were lovers. George never told the complete story, but apparently these rumors had some basis in fact. Lombard was unlike any woman Raft had ever known. Her candor and casual approach to life totally disarmed Goerge. With most women, he felt called upon to perform and was even a little nervous, but with Lombard he was always relaxed—except once.

"We talked about anything and I could express exactly how I felt because she liked the sort of words you were used to only using with guys.

"One day I found out Carole wasn't a natural blonde. We're sitting and chatting in her dressing room, and as we're talking she starts undressing. She had one of the sexiest, most sensational figures I've ever seen in my life." The dressing room door was unlocked and any minute they might be called on the set.

"I didn't know what the hell to do after she undressed. She's talking away and mixing peroxide and some other liquid in a bowl. Still talking casually, with a piece of cotton she begins to apply the liquid to dye the hair around her honeypot.

"She glanced up, saw my amazed look, and smiled, 'Relax, Georgie, I'm just making my collar and cuffs match.'"

Mack Grey also remembered Carole Lombard with great affection. He was in the hospital with a double hernia and Carole came to visit him almost every day during his recovery.

"One day I told Carole that *killa* is the Yiddish word for hernia. She thought that was a riot. After Carole heard this, she called me Killer. Carole would walk up to the hospital receptionist and say seriously, 'Can I see the Killer?' She had everyone scared of me. They all knew I worked for George Raft and he had this gangster image, and everyone thought I actually was a killer.

"Another day, while she was visiting, the doctor came in looking scared. He said, 'Are those guards in the hall really necessary?' I didn't know what the hell he's talking about, and I got up and looked in the hall. There were two tough-looking guys holding toy pistols that look real, marching back and forth as if they're protecting my room.

"Finally the hospital supervisor showed up. He said to Carole, 'We can't have this here in the hospital. What's going on?' The guy almost had a heart attack when she told him, 'Look, the mob put out a contract on the Killer's life. He's got to be protected.' The supervisor was terrified. 'We can't have a shooting in the hospital.' But then, by the look on Carole's face, he surmised it's a gag—and we all began to crack up laughing."

George was very much in love with Carole, but he felt, "What was the sense in it? I had nothing to offer her. By then I had signed over ten percent of my earnings to Grayce, and she refused to divorce me. I was trapped.

"Regardless of my personal feelings, I was happy for her when she married Clark Gable."

Gable and Lombard were the king and queen of Hollywood for many years. Their idyllic marriage came to a tragic end in 1942 when Carole died in an airplane accident while on a War Bond tour for the government.

Now that Raft's career was well established, he could vary tough-guy roles with other character parts. In *Midnight Club* (1933) he was a detective out to get Clive Brook; he was an ex-convict trying to go straight and finally driven to suicide in *All of Me* (1934), which also featured Fredric March, Miriam Hopkins, and Helen Mack; in the first film version of Dashiell Hammett's *The Glass Key* (1935; remade in the forties with Alan Ladd), George played a friend of Edward Arnold, who played a politician who was accused of murder; with Alice Faye and Frances Langford, he appeared in a thriller musical about radio broadcasting, *Every Night at Eight* (1935), directed by Raoul Walsh; he did a comedy, *It Had to Happen* (1936), with Rosalind Russell; a love story, *She Couldn't Take It* (1935), directed by Tay Garnett, with Joan Bennett; with Sylvia Sidney as co-star and Fritz Lang as director, he appeared in *You and Me;* in William Wellman's *Spawn of the North* (1938), George headed an all-star cast that included Henry Fonda, John Barrymore, and Dorothy Lamour.

George's acting was primarily self-expression, and he gave little thought to the notion that his performances would be considered serious actorly work. This modesty aided the veracity of those portrayals he did commit himself to, but the caution also served to keep him from roles that others took on with tremendous success. And it was Humphrey Bogart who inherited some of these roles and with them made move history.

Samuel Goldwyn was preparing the screen version of Sidney Kingsley's hit play *Dead End.* It was adapted for the screen by Lillian Hellman, to be directed by William Wyler. The stars were to be Joel McCrea, Sylvia Sidney, and George Raft. Raft was to play Baby Face Martin, a psychopathic killer sought by the police who hides out in the New York slum where he was raised.

97

The film also introduced the Dead End Kids, who later became known as the Bowery Boys. Raft, however, balked at certain aspects of Martin's character and particular actions he would be called upon to perform.

"Here I was, on the lam, hiding out around this neighborhood in cellars and places like that and I met this gang of kids. One gang member recognized me as a killer. The gang begins to idolize me — and I'm supposed to teach them how to be tough and how to be a criminal. I couldn't bring myself to do that.

"I told Mr. Goldwyn how I would like to play the part. I want a scene where I tell the kids how bad my life is, 'Just look at me crawling around like a rat, hiding. You don't want to hide all your life. Make something of yourself. Don't grow up like me.'

"In another scene I'm supposed to be with my mother and she slaps my face and calls me 'a no-good bum.' The way they had it I was just supposed to walk away mad. I wanted to play it with a tear in my eye, so the audience would know that my mother is right, and that I felt bad about my life as a criminal."

Goldwyn and Wyler were anxious to get Raft and Goldwyn pleaded with him, "George, I think you're wrong. Do it our way." Despite this powerful pressure, Raft turned down the part.

Bogart played Baby Face Martin brilliantly; it was his best role since that of Duke Mantee in *The Petrified Forest*. Eventually there were to be more roles that Raft would refuse and Bogart would turn into triumphs.

Raft suffered from his inability to clearly distinguish between the character of a film part and his own character. Despite this continuing confusion and his perpetual edginess and social discomfort, he was becoming more accepting of Hollywood's ways. But the old angry Kid Raft would still surface at the most unexpected times.

Now that he could easily afford tickets, seeing every important baseball game fulfilled a childhood dream. His movie star status provided an additional benefit: entree to meeting ballplayers. He came to count among his friends top players and managers.

The last game of the 1935 Detroit-Chicago World Series was a close contest. It was decided in the ninth inning when Goose Goslin broke it up with a sharp single that won the series for Detroit. After the game the crowd swarmed onto the field and carried Goslin on their shoulders back to the dugout. "Goose," a friend and fan of George's, came over to his box and respectfully presented him with a prize gift—the bat that won the game. "Here's a present for you, Georgie. Take it home with you."

That bat to George was as valuable as any Oscar. Still clutching it, Mack and George jumped into a cab to head for the train station. They had to rush in order to catch a westbound train to California to fill an important movie commitment. George told the driver, "Step on it. Get us there in time and I'll give you an extra ten-spot." The driver went as fast as he could through the jammed traffic near the stadium. A truck pulled out in front of them, almost forcing the cab off the road, and made them miss a green light. When George's cab caught up with the truck at a stop light, George leaned out the window and let the truckdriver know what he thought of him. The truckdriver, as he pulled away, yelled at George and Mack, "Drop dead, you Jew bastards."

This was all George had to hear. George was mad enough to pull the driver out of the truck and beat him up properly, but he didn't have the time. He instructed the cab driver to pull right alongside the truck at the next stop light. The cab driver did as he was told. Just as the light was turning green, George leaned out the window, took careful aim, and threw the bat like a spear at the truckdriver's head. George never found out how hard he hit the man, because the cab driver took off on cue, peeling rubber, for the station. They made their train.

On the way to California, George was filled with remorse, not only because he lost a treasured memento, but also because, once again, he had lost control of his temper.

Soon after this outburst, George had dinner with a respected and close friend, the famed Hollywood director Gregory La Cava, and he told La Cava about the bat incident and his other uncontrollable outbursts. He wanted desperately to do something about these emotional problems that were making his life a constant torment, keeping him from enjoying his own success, and ultimately damaging his career. He was aware that his distrust verged on paranoia. La Cava sympathized with George and suggested that he should consider consulting a psychiatrist.

Reluctantly—his self-reliance and pride causing him to hesitate—he took his friend's advice. The next day he made an appointment with a reputable Los Angeles analyst. "But I never went. What was I gonna do? Tell this guy about how I felt about my mother? Also the guy would probably find out how dumb I was—and I couldn't stand that." For Raft, the transformation from Broadway hoofer to Hollywood star was filled with emotional tumult. Each successive incarnation required alterations in moral codes and increasingly complex social abilities. From indulged favorite child to street kid, to nightclub entertainer, to underworld hanger-on, to Hollywood idol—it was a journey of incredible difficulty and baffling confusion. His hostile impulses distressed him, but the prospect of intensive self-examination was frightening for it threatened the very defense mechanism he had so carefully constructed in order to survive.

When he was a child, he earned his mother's approval as a "good boy." But the minute he entered the world of neighborhood gangs, he was forced to assume an attitude of rough and ready aggressiveness. Being tough was a matter of survival, as anyone who has grown up in this milieu will attest. Hell's Kitchen did not encourage or reward tenderness or compassion. But despite Kid Raft's exterior, his mother had implanted in her son a natural warmth and generosity that in his earlier years had little opportunity for expression. Success, for Raft, brought the power and the means to indulge his generous impulses without fear of ridicule or restraint.

George resented being connected in his private life with Gino Rinaldi—the character of the coin-flipping hood that had originally brought him fame. He wanted to be accepted for his own personal sensitivity, kindness, and generosity—but most people preferred Raft as a tough guy. This public preference, coupled with his own insecurity, forced him to play a role both on- and off-screen for which he had unwittingly typecast himself: George Raft, tough guy. The frustrating limits of this role fostered an aggressive behavior that only served to strengthen his image.

Few actors will deny that the roles they play effect their personal lives. And character actors who are strenuously typed, so that their very personalities become typecast, run the risk of suffering from an identity crisis. The average person may have identity problems, but he generally has a relatively solid sense of himself. John Smith plays John Smith, and he does not ordinarily attempt to play Hamlet or any other role foreign to his nature. But an actor with the studied ability to become someone else may smother and confuse his personal identity. Marilyn Monroe and Jean Harlow as sex goddesses presumably suffered from this confusion, which left them with a sense of emptiness and frustration.

At first, George Raft enjoyed playing Gino Rinaldi and similar roles. It gave him a chance to "play" the gangster heroes he had admired in his youth. Moreover, it was a legitimate profession that involved no danger and earned him the envy and adulation of the crowds. Problems emerged, however, when he attempted to break away from his tough-guy role and explore other acting possibilities.

His friendship with people like La Cava, James Cagney, and Gary Cooper and a relationship with a woman like Carole Lombard had changed his demeanor and point of view — but Kid Raft, George's own dependable and successful characterization, was not so easily dismissed.

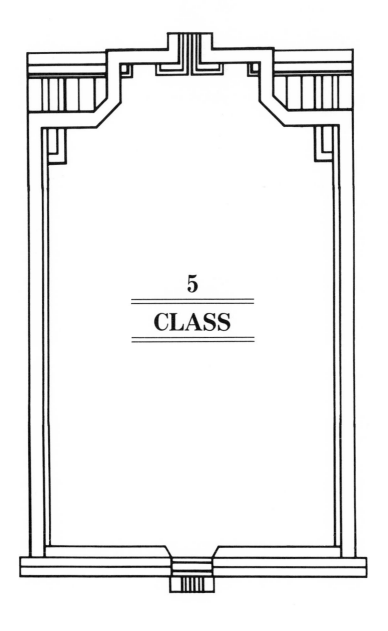

5
CLASS

The story of this play is not so much the story of a prizefighter as the picture of a great fight—a fight in which
we are all involved, whatever our profession or craft.
What the golden boy of this allegory is fighting for is a
place in the world as an individual; what he wants is
to free his ego from the scorn that attaches to "no-
bodies" in a society in which every activity is viewed
in the light of a competition. He wants success not simply for the soft line—automobiles, etc.—which he talks
about, but because the acclaim that goes with it prom-
ises him acceptance by the world, peace with it, safety
from becoming the victim that it makes of the poor,
the alien, the unnoticed minorities. To achieve this
success, he must exploit an accidental attribute of his
make-up, a mere skill, and abandon the development of
his real self.

> —Harold Clurman on
> Clifford Odets's play,
> *Golden Boy*

Social mobility—the dream of shifting freely from one social
class to another, of stretching oneself to the limits of one's imagination, of climbing the ladder of success from the lowest to the
highest rung—is supposedly one of the great benefits of American society. The move involves changes in values and expected
behavior, and the achievement of higher status is accompanied
by anxiety about fulfilling new requirements and expectations.
It also involves negating a previous identity and assuming a new
one. But for those on the bottom moving up is a tantalizing goal
to be achieved at any cost.

For Raft "class" had a precise meaning. It meant a single
family living in one palatial residence in a fashionable neighborhood rather than twenty families crowded into a Hell's Kitchen
tenement. "Class" was wealth and the security and luxury that
money afforded. He was very aware of his social origins and was
anxious to overcome them. He felt driven toward the top, for it
was there that he imagined his problems would be solved. For
most people, though, "moving up" produces more problems than
it solves. Outward trappings of success sometimes become a dis-
guise, an inappropriate and undeserved costume that masks the
real man. To compound the confusion, when these very trappings

and insignias are altered in the course of a short time, one can find oneself having achieved the wrong kind of success. Because of rapid social change, the goal—because it doesn't remain steady or because it was, from the beginning, incorrectly viewed—remains impossible to achieve. Ironically, great success causes greater confusion: on one hand, the loss of the original self; on the other, the need for even more and a different kind of success. The theme in various forms floods American literature; it is exemplified by virtually all the Americans in James's novels, Frank Cowperwood in Dreiser's *The Financier, The Titan,* and *The Bulwark,* Sinclair Lewis's *Dodsworth,* and the most often cited, F. Scott Fitzgerald's *The Great Gatsby.* Jay Gatsby's vision was shared by millions of young men. They wanted class and style—and they were assured that these things could be purchased for the right price. Everyone has felt that strange guilt and discomfort after buying something expensive—a suspicion that you are unworthy of your purchase, that it wasn't meant for you.

Class to George was the opposite of the tough world he was born to. Classy people not only lived in mansions, they ate in the best restaurants, like Delmonico's, they rode in the biggest carriages, their clothes were always impeccable and uniquely styled. You were what you owned, lived in, wore—and the best could be had. And luck was no mean element.

Now that his screen image blanketed the country, Raft was often mobbed by his fans—a constant concrete affirmation of his new status. He was amazed by the manifestations of stardom. As a man who had experienced alienation and pain in his youth, he enjoyed every precious evidence of the fact that he was no longer "nobody." Scenes like the one described by Thomas M. Pryor in *The New York Times* on July 23, 1939, were occurrences Raft took pride in:

> Like a swarm of locusts in a cornfield, a pack of famished autograph hounds pounced on George Raft the other luncheon time as he emerged from No. 21 West Fifty-second Street after a hearty repast consisting of honeydew melon and a glass of water. They popped out of doorways, from behind parked automo-

biles, and before the astonished Mr. Raft could beat a hasty retreat behind the sturdy iron-grilled fence of the establishment he was surrounded by fifty-odd youthful demons equipped with fountain pens, pencils, autograph pads and candid cameras. Their excited babble of voices attracted another crowd of curious passers-by and soon three of Mr. Valentine's finest came on the double-quick to see what caused all the commotion. They looked, saw that the Hollywood Killer-Diller was holding his own and retreated to the sidelines. . . .

This response by the "average guy on the street" was a source of special personal satisfaction. "It made me feel good to know that I got across to the five-and-ten-cent-store girl, to the guy on the street. Maybe intellectuals and bigshots didn't like me, but the average guy and gal did and they still are the majority of people in this country. And they were my main audience."

Raft always considered himself as "just another guy." Always identifying with the "little guy" who he felt wasn't as bright or as talented as those on top, he believed that he was nevertheless someone of value who deserved respect. And in many ways he thought that his own "making it" was a feat of arch-chicanery. He had fooled the bigshots, but the "big joke" was not played on the people, but by and for the people. A man flips a coin, looks tough, and earns three hundred grand a year doing it. For many of his average-guy fans, this was part of the reason for his great appeal.

"I love it when people recognize me. They come up and talk to me as if I lived next door, on their block, around the corner, or hung out with them in the corner beer parlor or poolroom the night before. I was at New York City's World's Fair in 1939 with Charles Boyer. There were the two of us in the middle of this big crowd. And Boyer was a bigger star than I was, a great actor; but no one spoke to him. I had just made *Each Dawn I Die*, a prison picture with Cagney and the crowd was yelling, 'Hi, George' or 'Hi, Stacy'—as if I was in the prison yard with Cagney—'How are you?' Letting me know they saw and liked my pictures.

"The average guy identified with me. It would have sounded funny for them to yell 'Hi, Charlie' to Boyer. It was all right for them to think they knew me personally."

George Raft

Despite the pleasures of recognition and adulation, George resolutely refused to watch himself on film. Mack Grey attempted to describe George's odd phobia: "George always felt he looked terrible. In the early days he worried, 'What will the guys on Broadway think of me? I'm awful. My face will scare babies.'" When Raft finished *Bolero* with Carole Lombard, Mack recalled his co-star had a showing at her Malibu beachhouse. George couldn't turn Carole's invitation down; he was just too fond of her. But as soon as the lights went out and the screen titles came on George went outside. He walked along the beach with Mack until he was sure the film was over.

George reflected a number of times, "I always had the feeling if I had looked like Tyrone Power or Bob Taylor, I wouldn't mind looking at myself. I just do not feel I look good. I'm kind of the greaseball type and I guess some people like me—so I must be passable. But I'm sure not good looking."

His achieved position and its derivatives temporarily salved his deep feelings of personal inadequacy. That it wasn't a total solution has already been mentioned. Excessive approval from large numbers of people can be a valuable therapeutic defense— while it lasts. George Raft was lucky. There were many in Hollywood during that era who did not make it; and for those who fail in Hollywood the consequences can be devastating. One aspiring starlet, Frances Farmer, who ran a losing race in Hollywood, cogently described the Hollywood battlefield and its characteristics in her autobiography, *Will There Really Be a Morning?*, the account of her painful destruction in movieland:

> The Hollywood of the thirties cast a wide beam of magic that peered into every corner of the world, and the stars of that era were unique creatures known only to one generation.
>
> Time and economics have wiped out the star system and rendered its species extinct. But for a while I was one of those gossamer ladies who played a small role in the legend known as the Golden Era of the Silver Screen.
>
> There were kings and queens in those days, idols to be adored. All perfect. All untouchable. And there were the idol makers. Men who created the image but destroyed the reality. . . .

> I was also a very small pebble. The giant studios
> bulged with potential stars, all straining to run the race.
> All beautiful. All ambitious. All eagerly anticipating the
> magical transformation from an unknown to a star. . . .
> There was an abundant array of beauty-contest
> winners and muscle-flexing beachboys, none of them
> trained to act. None sensitized to a performance, and
> few whose minds extended farther than Ciro's or the
> Brown Derby. It was an untutored assortment, but
> from this raw meat the talent coaches waded through
> and selected, as one would a prize bull or promising filly,
> a prospect with potential. . . .
> No camaraderie existed among this select few, only
> open competition and unabashed ambition. A do-or-die
> life-or-death atmosphere left a desperate aura in the air.

George's wish to become somebody, somebody important,
seemed to be fulfilled. Stardom, celebrity, and money gave him
status — and a sense of security that he had always yearned for.

Though he was now on top, he never forgot the deprivations of
those early years. He was one of Paramount's biggest contract
stars and was sought after by other studios. His weekly salary
averaged over $5000 — an enormous income for the Depression
thirties. But his expensive habits and expansive generosity made
it impossible for him to hold on to money for long. That generosity was, in part, the uncomplicated gesture of a man who knew
the pain of being down and broke. In another sense, his giving
money away was like the act of a guilty gambler who would rid
himself of an undeserved (and therefore dirty) bankroll. Perhaps
he unconsciously questioned his right to his own success.

But being a big spender was an attribute of those who were at
the top in George's Broadway world. He had fought for his place,
and he would perform with the best of them. Giving a handout,
or just throwing money around, confirmed one's status.

Bellhops, parking attendants, waiters, doormen, and cigarette
girls could always count on big tips from George Raft — and when
Raft bought seats for sporting events, it was never for himself
and Mack Grey alone, but also for fifteen or twenty others who
were financially short.

Panhandlers or old pals who approached him with the right
story walked away with a ten or twenty for their trouble. A

Hollywood reporter once asked him if he wasn't aware that he
was an easy target for professional moochers. "Sure," he replied,
"sure, I know a lot of people are taking me. But can I let that
stop me from helping someone who really needs a buck? I couldn't
sleep at night if I thought I turned someone down who really was
hungry or had rent to pay. I remember how it used to be for me.
And I never want to forget it."

During the filming of *The Bowery*, he packed as many extras
as possible in the crowd scenes of his movies—movie-set streets
would be filled with old pals of George Raft. He personally saw to
it that certain people in need of work were hired for weeks on
end. While this added to the film's budget, producers considered
it insurance against Raft becoming difficult on the set. They
knew he believed for a favor received, a favor returned. It has
been rumored that there were times toward the end of the day
when George might deliberately flub a line so that the extras
and grips could collect overtime.

Once when Raft boarded the elevator of the El Royale apart-
ments, he tipped the operator five dollars. Grateful, yet with
sincere admiration, the operator rhapsodized about the suit
Raft was wearing. Before the elevator operator could stop him,
George gave him the coat and vest, and when they arrived
at Raft's floor he told the man, now in a state of shock, "Stop in
later for the pants."

While an easy touch, George was sensitive to certain subjects,
and the wrong approach could evoke a brutal reaction. He was
especially touchy about aspects of his earlier years. One cold
morning while staying at New York's Waldorf-Astoria there was
a loud unexpected knock on his suite's door.

"I put on my robe and yanked the door open. Standing there
was a creepy little guy with a peculiar face. After looking at his
face closely for a few seconds I recognized him as a second-rate
New York racketeer.

"'Remember me, Georgie? I knew you when you worked at the
El Fey Club.' I didn't like his attitude. 'Yeah, I remember, so
what can I do for you?'

"'I just thought—well, you know, the old days and the time
they confiscated your car because it was full of cases of booze.
I guess people don't know too much about those days and I'm

sure you wouldn't want me to tell the press. I could use about five bills.'

"I had an uncomfortable feeling in my gut. 'So you want five C's to keep your mouth shut?' He squirmed a little and then he said, 'Yeah, Georgie, that's one way to put it.'

"We were still standing in the doorway. I grabbed him by his coat and heaved him into the hall and told him in a way that he could understand to 'get lost.' I was a generous guy with most people, including guys looking for a soft touch, but I had no patience with shakedowns and petty chiselers who knew me when, and who thought I didn't dare have my background during the twenties exposed."

It was fellow actors who could evoke his deepest sympathy, with his knowledge of how tenuous movie success was, and how difficult it was to achieve.

In the early thirties when Raft was working with Eddie Cantor in *Palmy Days* he came to know a beautiful girl with flame-red hair who was in the chorus. One day, on the set, he noticed that she seemed downcast. He asked her if something was wrong, and if he could help. "I'm flat broke, need rent money, and on top of that my mother is coming out from the East. I don't know what to do." George peeled a hundred dollars from his wallet and insisted she take it. She agreed to accept the money only as a loan; and, according to the lady, "He insisted that I borrow his grand limousine that was a mile long. The deal also included George's chauffeur.

"I met my mother at the Pasadena train station. When she saw my car, she was overwhelmed. That night was one of the most marvelous evenings of our lives. The chauffeur drove my Mom and me to a fancy restaurant and we had a terrific time."

Several years later, to Raft's surprise, Lucille Ball approached him in the Brown Derby and insisted on repaying the loan he had long forgotten. In later years, Lucy made many efforts to pay some interest on the debt she felt she still owed George for his generosity.

During his Broadway days as a dancer at the El Fey Club, Raft's relation to "society women" was always inhibited by his awareness that in their eyes he was at best a one-night stand.

He could have little realistic expectation that a romance or any sort of intimate association could emerge. Now he was a movie star, and anything was possible.

In New York Raft had become friendly with the well-known millionaire playboy, Jock Whitney. They met again in the mid-thirties at a Hollywood racetrack and reminisced about the good old Broadway days, the El Fey Club, and old friends. With Whitney was a woman who listened attentively to these curious exploits. Virginia Pine was, among other things, an aspiring actress who had played several bit parts, and though she concealed her pleasure she was thrilled at meeting Raft.

She was a slender woman whose fair skin, light hair, and blue eyes gave her a gossamer beauty. Her appearance and well-bred manner made Raft feel like an overdressed peasant. Confronted with her aloofness, Raft was entranced by the challenge of aspiring to such an obviously unattainable ideal.

While Virginia's family was not among the Top 400, her society credentials were more than adequate to Raft. Virginia had grown up among the comfortable, solidly upper-middle-class worlds of Chicago, New York, and Greenwich, Connecticut. A divorcée, she had been married to a wealthy department store owner in Chicago and had a two-year-old daughter.

Through friends, George acquired Virginia's phone number; but he was afraid to call. Rejection was too likely and an abhorrent prospect. At a party given by Darryl and Virginia Zanuck, he met her again and asked her if she would dine with him the following evening. She coyly hesitated, but before the evening was over she told him to call the next day. Finally, with an edge of reluctance she agreed to the date. They went to Ciro's that evening and on the dance floor Raft was unmatchable. Raft was finding the evening a surprising success. Later, he drove her to the small, attractive Hollywood Hills house she was renting.

Totally disarmed by her gracious ease, Raft told her as much about his life as a taciturn tough guy could reveal. His trusting candor, a novel manner for him, both impressed and moved her.

The remainder of the evening, as Raft recalls, did not go off so well. "Virginia excused herself and went into her bedroom. She came out in a stunning emerald green negligee. I was nervous as hell. Maybe for the first time in my life with a woman, I wasn't sure of what to do because she had me off balance. I had never felt this way with any other woman.

"Finally we sat together and I kissed her. It was very exciting." George started to make love to Virginia, an instinctive movement for him, and he was confused and surprised when she resisted.

"She had dressed up in this sheer gown and I figured that was the go-ahead. But it wasn't. I felt really hurt. Sure, I'd been rejected before, but it wasn't the fact that we didn't make it that bothered me. It was my feeling that I had made a fool of myself with this beautiful woman—and I had ruined my chances. She might not want to go out with me again. That was what depressed me. We talked some more and then I left. I figured I had struck out for good, but I couldn't help thinking of her constantly."

Later, when they were lovers, Virginia confessed she was being a disgraceful tease. She thought it would be "great fun saying no to this big Hollywood ladies' man. I just wanted to see the great George Raft squirm a little."

Despite the apparent rejection, George called her again a few weeks later, and from then on, for several years, George Raft and Virginia Pine became one of Hollywood's most devoted and loving couples. George's inability to marry and their "prizefighter and the lady" image provided good copy.

Her initial aloofness attracted George because, as he explained, "I figure, who am I? If a woman goes for me right away, I would think she had poor taste." For Virginia, a man like Raft was a new experience. His speech and concept of the world were less cultivated, but there was a tenderness about him that appealed to her. He was especially thoughtful in his care and affection for both her and her daughter, Joanie.

All three of them would fly to Catalina for weekends, attend sporting events and shop together in Beverly Hills. In time they established a relationship that was probably the closest Raft ever enjoyed as an adult. Later on, as their relationship deepened, he built a quarter-of-a-million-dollar house for Virginia and her daughter in Beverly Hills. But George did not live there.

"I would never disgrace anybody. A woman like Virginia was to be treated with respect. If I'd lived with her, Louella Parsons would've headlined it in her column. That would've degraded Virginia. No—it wasn't then like it is today, when living together means nothing. When I built the home for her in Coldwater Canyon, I lived with Mack at the El Royale on Rossmore."

A Hollywood fan magazine of the day describes the relationship in its own inimitable jargon:

> . . . George Raft, a one-woman man if there ever was one, is as true to Virginia Pine as a model husband would be. He has been, for three years. He has just bought her an expensive home in Beverly Hills. Recently, when they had a slight tiff, George took out some other girls, but was plainly so torch-burdened he could hardly stand it. He has never seriously looked at anyone else. Nor has Virginia.
>
> Consider the results—strictly out of wedlock.
>
> Before they met and fell in love, George was the easiest "touch" in Hollywood. He made big and easy money and just so easily did it slip through his fingers and into the outstretched palms of his myriad down-and-out friends. George, who came up the hard way, still has a heart as big as a casaba melon and as soft inside. But he is more careful with his money now. He invests it—and well. . . .

Before George met Virginia, his flashy clothing with its extreme cuts was fashionably theatrical. His trousers had the highest waistlines in town, and the jackets were tight across the shoulders and sharply tapered at the waist. From his hat to his narrow, pointed, and Cuban-heeled shoes he personified Mister Broadway.

Virginia suggested that he shop at conservative establishments favored by bankers and executives—Oviatt's and Pesterre's. With her advice they selected a wardrobe that befitted a gentleman who enjoyed owning fifty suits, a hundred silk shirts, and an astonishing number of ties and pairs of shoes.

Modern Screen (February 1936) reported the revolutionary sartorial conversion:

> Farewell-to-Elegance item: George Raft announces, possibly with a nostalgic tear in his eye, that he has

given up the high-waisted trousers which have so long been identified with the Raft wardrobe. "Natty," which used to be a one-word description of all the Raft finery, has been deleted from George's dictionary and his tailors have been instructed to mold his future garments along more conservative lines. We, who always wondered how George got his hands in his pockets without breaking an arm, congratulate him on his momentous decision. Goodbye, fond memories of former splendor; so long, classy cuts and dreams of checkered magnificence; and a polite hello to a brave new — and awfully Bond Street — world!

Since Raft was a trend-setter, men over the country revised their wardrobe. It was a fashion event equal to Gable's revelation in *It Happened One Night* (1934) that he didn't wear an undershirt. George, formerly a restaurant habitué, also changed his dining habits. Evenings he supped with Virginia and Joan as a family at their Canyon home. No real father could have been more attentive to Joan than Raft, for he had the innate qualities to become a model parent: concerned but indulgent. Conservative in his projections of the future, he provided for Joan's college education through a generous annuity. There are many who, having suffered the deprivations of unconcerned parents, are instinctively well schooled in what a child needs. It is a negative way of learning, but a painfully effective one. At night Raft lay awake to plan unusual surprises for Virginia and his "adopted" daughter.

Virginia Pine strengthened Raft's position in Hollywood society. In subtle ways, their relationship furthered his career, for her social ease made him a more comfortable party guest and served to ameliorate any underworld aura. His new respectability was capped when in 1937 he was nominated for an Academy Award as best supporting actor for his role in *Souls at Sea*. The film, directed by Henry Hathaway, who made *Lives of a Bengal Lancer* (1935), also starred Gary Cooper and Francis Dee. Miss Dee was a genuine lady whose genteel, proper manner was an important aspect of the character she was playing in the film. Her manner and style bore a striking resemblance to that of Virginia Pine. Whatever the requirements of the script, throwing a rock at Francis Dee was equivalent to throwing one at Virginia Pine. One simply didn't treat real ladies like that.

"We were supposed to go to Catalina for the scene where I was to throw a rock at Frances Dee, but I told them to forget it—I wouldn't do it, so they'd better go without me. It would've been different if Frances was playing a whore, or a no-good sort of a dame. But she's a real lady in this picture. I reasoned with Hathaway, 'How can I throw a rock at her, for what reason?' I asked him. 'I'd look like a real rat.'

"When I didn't show up in Catalina, they called me at the studio, and I went in and told them to tear up my contract. Mr. Zukor said, 'How can you do that? You have a lifetime contract with us. This is ridiculous.' Maybe it was, I told him, but I wouldn't do the scene.

"Finally they arranged a meeting with Gary Cooper and his manager, Jack Morse. At that time there were dirt roads in Beverly Hills, and Coop and I walked and talked along one of them for a few hours. I told Coop what I thought and why and he finally agreed with my position and told Hathaway he wouldn't do the picture without me in it. With Coop on my side, Hathaway cut the scene.

"*Souls* was a helluva good adventure movie about the slavery days. My hair was marceled and I wore a ring in my ear—like some sailors did in those days. In one scene Coop and I are drinking rum together. Both of us were quiet actors. You know, we didn't like a lot of dialogue. Mainly, we looked at each other. Finally he said to me, 'You know I love you.' The script had 'look at him, pause, and then say, "I know I love you too."' The director yells, 'Print!'

"After we both stopped laughing, Coop jokingly told Hathaway, 'You can't put that in the movie. People are going to think Cooper and Raft are a couple of fags.' I guess he figured we were right because he cut it."

With the Academy Award nomination, 1937 was an enormously successful year for Raft. His triumph was marred, however, by a severe personal tragedy: the loss of his mother, whom he had visited often in New York and supported in a generous fashion, was a severe blow.

On his last visit to her other apartment on 173rd Street and Audubon Avenue in Washington Heights, she looked very ill.

"I knew she was dying from a lung condition. My mother had had hard times with me when I was a kid and worried especially about me during the twenties, when I was on Broadway. She suspected the worst about my way of life then, but it had all turned out okay."

After her death, a neighbor told him that his mother had seen all of his films. She made no distinction between her son and the characters he played, and while watching a film in which the police were chasing him his mother got so excited she jumped up and yelled at the screen, "Run, Georgie, run! They're catching up!"

"I knew she was proud of me. Every wall of her apartment was hung with stills from my movies and fan magazine cutouts. Neighbors told me how she would go around the neighborhood and trade autographed pictures of me with the druggist or grocer to complete her collection. If she went into a store that didn't have a picture of me, she would scold the owner, give him an autographed picture, and make sure he hung it.

"When she passed away, God rest her soul in peace, she was proud of me."

None of George's Hollywood friends except for Mack Grey came to the funeral. Owney Madden, with his sidekick Frenchy DeMange, also attended. Madden was now a figure from the past, but his consideration was evidence of the best part of that past. Raft well understood the meaning and actions of true friendship. No matter what the consequences, he could never deny his friends. That humanity would cause no end of confusion in the public eye.

George was so emotionally distraught that Mack Grey had to handle all of the funeral arrangements. "George was very broken up about his mother's death. He always loved her dearly, sent her money regularly, and gave her everything he could. At the church I held his arm. He kept sagging, and I thought, I can't let him faint like this. I kept pulling him up.

"The third time I whispered to him, 'George, I know how you feel but control yourself. You'll look foolish if you faint or fall down. People are looking. They think you're a strong guy. Don't do it.'

"At that moment George pushed away from me and knelt on the ground. Suddenly I realized what he'd been trying to do all along. He simply wanted to kneel down in the church, cross himself, and say a prayer."

After his mother's death, as far as he knew, he no longer had any family. There may have been a few brothers still living—but George never cared enough to find out. As far as he was concerned, he was now alone.

After the funeral, George returned to California and Joan and Virginia. For Virginia there was no future in the relationship unless he obtained a divorce. Virginia wanted a marriage and George wasn't free. No matter how Raft pleaded with Grayce, she remained adamant. The tension increased, and Raft had bitter quarrels with both Grayce and Virginia. Lucille Ball, who occasionally dated Mack Grey, filled the role of a close and devoted friend.

"I was Virginia Pine's best friend during the four years of her romance with George. When it was clear George couldn't get the divorce they both desperately wanted, the relationship began to fall apart. I remember some of their fights. We would all go out together, everything would be great fun, but then an emotional tornado would hit.

"One night in particular, we went dancing at the Trocadero on the Strip and were having a great time. Virginia seemed happy— even though she was a little angry about something George had said. After our great night on the town, we went to the fabulous home George had built for Virginia. We were sitting around, talking happily—then suddenly, I can't say how, they got into this terrible fight. Finally Virginia stormed into her bedroom.

"George was a perfume nut and he'd bought Virginia several thousand dollars' worth of imported perfumes. She had this wall full of fantastic perfumes. George and I were in the living room, but we could hear her smashing bottle after bottle. George was burning up inside, but he just sat there quietly, seemingly calm, saying nothing. When I got up enough nerve to go to Virginia, her bedroom looked like it had been hit by a hurricane. And the room reeked of perfume for months."

Desperate for a solution, Raft made many attempts to redirect Virginia's concerns and interests. "Virginia always wanted to be an actress, so I tried to get her into a picture I was in, *The Lady's from Kentucky* (1939). I felt Virginia was perfect, but the studio was dead set against anybody getting into their features through

118

a boyfriend. Even though I tried hard, desperately hard, I never could do anything significant for her career."

Finally, Virginia Pine began to see other men. Not only were these dates an attack on Raft's ego, they inflamed his jealousy. Mack Grey remembered many a night during this period when George, restless and depressed, would ask over and over, "Where's Virginia? Where the hell did she go?" On certain nights George would follow her.

The heaviest blow came when he learned that Virginia was lunching with Joseph Schenck, a 20th Century-Fox executive. George parked across from the restaurant and when they came out he followed them to Schenck's house. George rang the bell, and when no one answered he broke down the door.

"What could I do when I found them together? I just looked, turned around, and walked out without a word. I couldn't offer her marriage, which was what she really wanted. Later I said to her, 'Go ahead, go with Schenck. He's the kind of man you should have. You know, if you drive into the studio in his limousine—everyone would turn around. That's what you really want. Someone who's a bigger shot than I am!'"

He made a last attempt to reason with his estranged wife when he was in New York on a personal appearance tour.

"Virginia and I were battling, and it was awful, so in desperation I decided I'd make another try. I called Grayce, asked if I could come over and talk to her. She hesitated, then said okay after I told her it was important.

"I had just got a large chunk of dough, in cash, as an advance on an independent movie I was going to do.

"Full of hostility toward Grayce, I drove out in a studio-rented limousine. After all, I didn't deserve what she was doing to me. I didn't feel I owed her anything—but I had signed an agreement where she got ten percent of all my earnings. I felt enough was enough.

"Grayce had a pretty nice house—nothing elaborate but neat and clean. What shocked me was the way she looked, because I remembered her as attractive, good-looking. All of my talks with her after we separated were by phone. Now she was very fat and frowzy, and looked like an old lady. Sitting with her reminded me of how far I had come—and how much I wanted to unload this burden from my past.

"We sat in her living room and exchanged a few words before I pulled out this envelope of money and put it on the table and said, 'Grayce, I don't have to tell you our marriage was a big mistake. You know we really didn't even have a marriage.'

"She says, 'That's your side of it.'

"I went on, 'Look, I don't want to argue or to fight with you. All I want is a divorce. There's a hundred and fifty thousand dollars in cash in that envelope. It's yours if you'll divorce me.'

"I couldn't believe what she answered.

"'George,' she shakes her head, 'are you trying to bribe me?'

"Then I start to see red, but to get anywhere I had to contain myself. 'Look,' I pleaded, 'I want to get married and have a life for myself. What the hell did I ever do to you?'

"I knew then I was arguing with a stone and there was no way out. With her, I had the feeling it wasn't just because of religious reasons. She wanted more money. And she thought it would be worth more over the years to stay married to me.

"When I got back to California I told Virginia what I'd tried, and instead of understanding she blew up, began to smash things, and went to pieces.

"From then on our relationship, what was left of it, turned to dust. Virginia would be out when I called from the studio. My career was still going great, but my personal life was worse than a dog's. Finally, I had to accept calling it off. I gave Virginia fifteen thousand in cash and she moved back to New York. Mack and I moved into the house I'd built for her in Coldwater Canyon. I'd hoped to move in as Virginia's husband. I moved into it as a bachelor, probably the most miserable one in the world."

Some years later, Virginia Pine married the noted journalist, Quentin Reynolds.

The liaison with Virginia Pine, coupled with his greater maturity, forced him to recognize that he preferred a long-term relationship to the stream of one-night stands that he used to assuage his loneliness. A major star, acclaimed by the public and respected by his colleagues, he was now a member of the Hollywood establishment. No longer was he the brash, slightly disreputable sharp young man of the early years.

There was no incongruity when after a party at Jack Warner's house he escorted Norma Shearer, by any standards one of Hollywood's great ladies, to her home. They had known each other slightly for a number of years.

Norma Shearer had been married for eight years to Irving Thalberg, the man F. Scott Fitzgerald used as the model for his unfinished novel, *The Last Tycoon.* Thalberg was considered a young genius. He was Louis B. Mayer's most trusted and influential protégé at Metro-Goldwyn-Mayer when he met the young Norma Shearer. Although Mayer loved Thalberg like a son, he warned his own daughters against any interest in him, for since childhood Thalberg had suffered from a rheumatic heart condition and was destined for a short life. Thalberg was dedicated to upgrading the cultural level of films. He starred Shearer in Eugene O'Neill's *Strange Interlude* (1932), as Juliet to Leslie Howard's Romeo, in Noel Coward's *Private Lives* (1931), and as Elizabeth Barrett in *The Barretts of Wimple Street* (1934). He treated her as the screen's answer to Katherine Cornell, Lynn Fontanne, and Jane Cowl. These films were Hollywood's most prestigious, and if they sometimes lack vitality they undeniably possess tone.

Their marriage was considered an ideal one, and they were at the center of Hollywood's intellectual circle. Thalberg was an ambitious man who drove himself incessantly. Under the extraordinary pressure of this existence his health gave way and on September 14, 1936, at the age of thirty-seven, he died of lobar pneumonia, leaving Shearer a widow with two children.

After the completion of *The Women* (1939), in which she starred with Rosalind Russell and Joan Crawford, Norma Shearer traveled to New York for a stopover at the 1939 World's Fair before continuing on to Europe. Raft was in New York at that time and supposed to return to California, but on the spur of the moment he joined Norma on the *Normandie.* Raft's popularity again demonstrated itself, for a news report from the *New York World Telegram* of August 2, 1939, the day after the sailing, reported:

GEORGE RAFT IS NO. 1 ATTRACTION AT SAILING OF
NORMANDIE
Old Neighbors Ignore Other Celebrities Including
Mrs. Roosevelt and Norma Shearer
George Raft, the movie actor, who was born on W. 41st St., went back resplendently today to the old neigh-

borhood and for a time was No. 1 attraction among a large group of celebrities, gathered about W. 48th St. pier for the sailing of the liner *Normandie*, including the wife of the President of the United States, a Cabinet officer and so many top-flight film favorites they could hardly be counted.

Oldsters of the district that bred Raft scarcely stirred when Mrs. Eleanor Roosevelt passed toward the gangplank to bid goodby to traveling friends; longshoremen didn't even look up when beauty in the form of Norma Shearer floated by; but there was a prodigious stir among them, a stoppage of work, and a crowding around when Raft appeared.

Workmen and idlers grabbed for Raft's hand for hearty shakes, and they asked for autographs and spoke to him with easy familiarity, awed only by the garments he wore.

"My God," said a longshoreman, "that coat talks to you."

The coat was a brown affair with enormous checks, setting off a checked sports shirt and sundry other articles of various shades of brilliant browns.

Raft was among the largest group of passengers — 1,397 — to sail.

Mrs. Roosevelt bade goodby to her uncle, David Gray, and to Henry Morgenthau, Secretary of the Treasury, Mrs. Morgenthau and their three children.

Rafael L. Trujillo, dictator of the Dominican Republic, sailed for the Riviera.

Other passengers who got some attention, after the Raft brilliance faded into a cabin were, besides Miss Shearer, Charles Boyer and his wife, Pat Patterson; Edward G. Robinson, his wife and their son; Bob Hope; Frederick Lonsdale, playwright; Gilbert Miller, producer; Roland Young.

Louella Parsons wryly reported at the top of her column of August 13, 1939: "The laugh of the week was George Raft's cable to his Hollywood pals that the reason he sailed on the *Normandie* at the last minute was to make a fourth at bridge. The truth, of course, is that George and Norma have fallen in love."

As a group the celebrities visited London, Paris, and the south of France, to be mobbed everywhere by movie fans. In this gathering of notables, Raft, according to several headlines, received the lion's share of the attention.

As the Shearer-Raft romance deepened, headlines followed them around Europe. The August 8, 1939, *London Daily Mail* headline read: NORMA SHEARER AND GEORGE RAFT DENY ROMANCE. MOBBED BY CROWD ON PARIS ARRIVAL.

After several weeks, Raft left the touring party to return to Hollywood and begin filming a new movie. Shearer followed shortly after, and the affair continued. It was precisely the differences in their cultural background, interests, and friends that encouraged their delight in one another. With Thalberg, Shearer had attended formal dinner parties and concerts and led a rather domestic, determinedly private life. Now she was thrilled at the new world of clubs, the track, fights, and ballgames which George introduced her to. As Mack Grey said, "She was like a kid, playing hookey from school."

For his part, Raft, as Norma Shearer's escort, was frequently with Hollywood's upper social set. He had previously feared the formal manners of dinner parties. Yet now he found himself liking Norma's friends more than he had expected; and they in turn liked him, because he was a man with neither pretension or guile. Now more sure of himself than ever, Raft insisted on being accepted as himself. When he had something to say, he said it. When he had nothing to contribute, he remained silent.

This new social awareness called for significant alterations in the life style of Raft's Coldwater Canyon house. Formerly, George and Mack made use only of the den and their bedrooms. The other rooms were furnished but ignored. Now, with some zest and a sense of the unexplored, Raft gave dinner parties, with Shearer as hostess.

He had always had special rapport with children, and Norma's were no exception. He took Irving Junior to ballgames, and occasionally drove to Norma's Malibu beach house when she was not at home to build sand castles with baby Katherine, a posture completely incongruous with the George Raft image.

Neither of them thought of marriage—for one of them it was impossible, for the other undesirable, although they behaved toward each other with that tenderness and consideration that is the mark of new-found lovers. Raft seldom passed a shop window without searching for something that might please Norma. Whatever her dinner menu, she always saw that there was steak for George, the only meat he has ever cared to eat. There was even talk at MGM about co-starring them in a remake of 1931's *A Free Soul,* one of her early successes with Clark Gable and Lionel Barrymore; but nothing came of it. (Raft did appear in a radio version with Frances Farmer in 1941.)

"Yes," George reminisced, "Norma and I had a wonderful romance. It lasted about a year and a half. She was one of the most marvelous women I'd ever known. I never saw such maternal feeling for children. Sometimes we'd be dressed for some formal function, but Norma wouldn't leave without a long good-night talk with her kids. I'd wait, patiently, enjoying their laughter and giggling. Then I'd open the door to the kids' room and see a wonderful sight. They'd all be on the floor, rolling around and laughing. Norma would have to change clothes completely. But she wouldn't have it any other way. Neither would I."

For almost a year they were inseparable. Mervyn LeRoy once accompanied them to Saratoga Springs for the racing season. "They were a beautiful couple. You could tell that they adored each other. She loved to go everywhere with George. And she was very kind to him. He had never been with a lady like her.

"I remember in Saratoga they were staying in a charming house next to mine. Norma knew George loved perfume. Well, she sprayed perfume all over the room and on the bottom of the curtains.

"It was strange to see them act like a couple of young kids in love for the first time. Here was Norma, who had been protected and sheltered most of her life, madly in love with the screen's number one tough guy, up from the depths of Hell's Kitchen. Even for Hollywood it was an odd scenario."

Yet not everyone in Hollywood approved. Many of Shearer's friends were deeply concerned by their romance, and Louis B. Mayer was heard to observe, "A nice Jewish girl like Norma shouldn't go with a roughneck like that."

Pressure was applied steadily to Norma, who was urged to find someone closer to her own world. It seemed to some her attachment to Raft was an act of defiance, a hesitant sampling of a life style that was foreign to her. Perhaps, they thought, it was a way of dealing with sorrow. This pressure, however, was not the problem. Norma's love and affection for her children, coupled

124

with George's inability to marry, finally drew an inevitable conclusion to their romance. "We loved each other, but knew the relationship wouldn't get anywhere, and we just drifted apart."

Raft belonged to a set of male pals who met for dinner every Tuesday night. "There was Cagney, Ralph Bellamy, Spencer Tracy, Pat O'Brien, Lynn Overman, and Frank McHugh. We'd go to different restaurants each time. Like Chasen's one night, Romanoff's the next week, or La Rue on the Strip. We rotated picking up the tab. For most of these guys it was the boys' night out, because they were married.

"After dinner we might go to the fights or a ballgame, but sometimes we would just sit around and talk about work, sports, or dames. I remember I'd say, 'You guys can talk about dames, but you'll go home to your wife and I'll have one waiting for me.'"

Although he enjoyed and took full advantage of his freedom, Raft had mixed feelings about being past forty without a family. The father role he enjoyed playing with Joanie Pine and the Thalberg children expressed itself through visits to hospitals and orphanages and appearances at children's benefits, where he gave freely of time and money. He once offered to adopt a boy who was in trouble with the law and had other behavioral problems. Almost at the last moment, the boy's natural parents intervened and the adoption fell through.

As all behavior of the film stars was newsworthy, so was Raft's consideration for children. A fan wrote to *Photoplay*'s March 1938 *I Saw It Happen* column:

> My husband and I are baseball fans, and as our home is in Los Angeles, we've seen a number of movie celebrities at the different games. Most autograph hunters confine their activities to before and after the game, but this afternoon a particularly impatient little boy couldn't wait to ask his idol, George Raft, to sign his book. It was the last half of the ninth inning and the score was tied. Everyone was tense with excitement, including Mr. Raft, who rose from his seat with the others to see if there was going to be a home run.
>
> Just then the little boy tugged at George Raft's coat and said, "Could I have your autograph, please?" Mr. Raft didn't hesitate a moment, though I am sure he was as anxious as the rest of us to learn the outcome of

the game. He gave the kid a big smile, said "Sure, Sonny," and sat down amidst all the excitement to write in the boy's book. A great guy, I think!

It was Mack Grey who served as George's family. Raft relied on his advice, and they were companions at the fights and other athletic events. He had little time to dwell on loneliness because the studio kept him busy with film after film, and when he wasn't making a movie, the studio required that he do country-wide promotion tours. The spark of seeing George Raft in person sometimes generated small riots. *The Jersey City Journal* (March 1939) reported a typical occurrence:

> George Raft, leading man in many knock-down, drag-out scenes in the films, was the center of a real-life rough-and-tumble in Jersey City last night as he struggled and fought for forty minutes to escape from a mob of a thousand or more autograph seekers and hero worshippers in front of the Stanley Theatre. . . .
>
> He lost a pretty light fedora hat, and his coat was ripped but he took it all with a smile and was probably pleased with his first personal appearance in Jersey City.

With ten years of experience in over thirty movies, Raft had become a distinguished movie star to millions of fans around the world. In this short period he had built a recognizable, powerful image that clearly established a position for him in the upper strata of one of the most competitive social systems in the world. Hell's Kitchen now seemed but a small echo from the distant past.

GEORGE RAFT

George's mother, Mrs. Eva Ranft, whose dark, attractive looks her son inherited. (GEORGE RAFT)

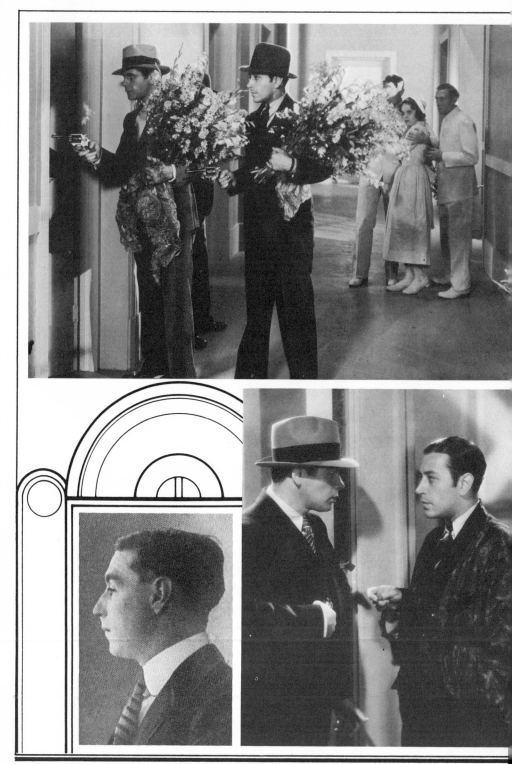

Above: In *Scarface: Shame of a Nation* (1932). Paul Muni and George Raft are unwelcome tors. (UNITED ARTISTS) *Inset:* Owney Madden, loyal friend and notorious underworld figure. *Below: Scarface.* Raft's familiarity with underword life served him well in his first major rol Guido Rinaldo. Raft holds the coin he flipped throughout the movie; at left is Paul Muni. (UNITED ARTISTS)

ther publicity photo which recalls the attraction of Rudolph Valentino. (GEORGE RAFT)
*: Paramount vacillated before deciding on Raft's most promotable image. In this publicity still,
played on his short baseball career. (PARAMOUNT)

Above: Night after Night (1932) was Mae West's sensational film debut.
Below: With Al Hill and Constance Cummings in *Night after Night*. (PARAMOUNT)

ve: Raft appeared in a segment of Paramount's all-star multiepisode *If I Had a Million* 2). (PARAMOUNT)

w: Raft as Steve Brodie in *The Bowery* (1933), surrounded by his "gang." (UNITED ARTISTS)

Raft made two films with Carole Lombard, *Bolero* (1934) and *Rumba* (1935). Their on-scr[e]
rapport carried over into real life. (PARAMOUNT)

Inset: Decked out in Latin ruffles, Raft dances with Margo in *Rumba*. (PARAMOUNT)

set: Edward Ellis (center) and Mischa Auer teach Raft bullfighting in *The Trumpet Blows* 934). (PARAMOUNT)

low: From the first screen version of Dashiell Hammett's *The Glass Key* (1935), with Edward nold. (PARAMOUNT)

Above: With Rosalind Russell in *It Had to Happen* (1936). (TWENTIETH CENTURY-FOX)
Below: As a bandleader in *Every Night at Eight* (1935), with singers, left to right, Alice Faye,
Patsy Kelly, and Frances Langford. (PARAMOUNT)

ith Virginia Pine's daughter, Joanie. (GEORGE RAFT)
set: Being interviewed by Hedda Hopper. (GEORGE RAFT)

Above: On the beach with Dolores Costello Barrymore and a pampered pooch in *Yours for the Asking* (1936). (PARAMOUNT)

Below: The all-star, action thriller, *Spawn of the North* (1938), featured, left to right, Dorothy Lamour, Lynne Overman, Henry Fonda, Louise Platt, Raft, and John Barrymore. (PARAMOUNT)

ove: On the set of *Souls at Sea* with Countess Dorothy di Frasso, who had figured prominently
Cooper's early Hollywood years, and was also Bugsy Siegel's friend. (GEORGE RAFT)
low: With Gary Cooper in *Souls at Sea* (1937) in the role for which he was nominated for an
ademy Award. (PARAMOUNT)

Above: Costarring with Sylvia Sidney in Fritz Lang's *You and Me* (1938). (PARAMOUNT)
Inset: Raft's first film for Warner Brothers was *Each Dawn I Die* (1939). (WARNER BROTHERS)
Below: From the violent conclusion of *Each Dawn I Die.* (WARNER BROTHERS)

ove: One of Raft's best films was Raoul Walsh's *They Drive by Night* (1940), with Humphrey
gart and Ann Sheridan. (WARNER BROTHERS)
ow: Bogart, Raft, and George Tobias in *They Drive by Night*. (WARNER BROTHERS)

With Marlene Dietrich in *Manpower*. (WARNER BROTHERS)
Inset: An extraordinary cast became the main ingredient for the success of *Manpower* (1941). (WARNER BROTHERS)

h Sydney Greenstreet in *Background to Danger*. (WARNER BROTHERS)

et: Director Raoul Walsh positions Osa Massen, with Raft in doorway, for *Background to*

ger (1942). (WARNER BROTHERS)

Above: As a director of London's Colony Club Raft played a familiar role and became the center of controversy. (UNITED PRESS INTERNATIONAL)

Inset: Raft and Betty Grable were one of Hollywood's most highly publicized romances. (GEORGE RAFT)

Below: George Raft with Jack Warner, and long-time friend Danny Goodman. (GEORGE RAFT)

Above: With Vera Zorina in *Follow the Boys* (1944), an all-star production. (UNIVERSAL)

Inset: In *Johnny Angel* (1945), Raft played a sailor searching for his father's killers. (RKO)

Below: Outpost in Morocco (1949) starred Raft as a Foreign Legion officer attempting to quell an Arab rebellion. (UNITED ARTISTS)

Above: Raft made two films with Jerry Lewis. *The Ladies Man* (1961), shown here, and *The Pats* (1964). (BUD FRAKER)

Below: A Friar's Club Roast in Raft's honor brought out Hollywood's top celebrities. Front row, left to right, Dean Martin, Frank Sinatra, Robert Goulet. Peering over Sinatra's shoulder is George Jessel, and in back row, among others, are Glenn Ford and Robert Wagner. (GEORGE RAFT)

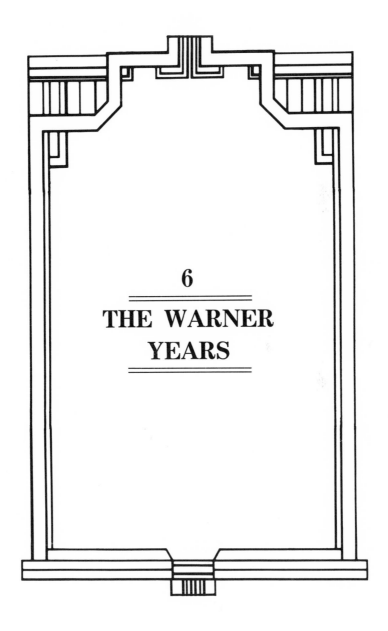

6

THE WARNER
YEARS

At Ciro's: "Who's that? He looks familiar."
The Brown Derby: "Isn't that George Raft?"
At the Beverly Wilshire: "Look, there's George Raft!"
On Sunset Boulevard: "My God! I'm going to faint!
It's George Raft!"

The year was 1938; George Raft was a star. His unquestioned cinematic importance freed him from his former reputation. He no longer had to behave or be known as a tough customer who had fought his way onto a set or into Hollywood society. What he had done financially for Paramount Studios could be seen in the grosses of his pictures; a George Raft film was invariably a box-office success. The taxi dancer, the vaudeville circuit hoofer, and Prohibition tough guy were no longer relevant to the new Raft, now one of the ranking ladies' men about town. His romances with Carole Lombard, Virginia Pine, and Norma Shearer helped to fill hundreds of inches of Hollywood copy. Beyond that, Raft's bedroom prowess with second-string Hollywood starlets and regular hookers was a day-and-night wonder. Many of them referred to George with awe as the "black snake."

He was also a fashionplate style-setter for a significant number of American men. Black pinstripe suits, long roll collars, highly polished and pointed black shoes, high rise pants—to which he had returned—were Raft-popularized trends.

Although he did not drink, George still loved to dance, and he was seen regularly with such distinguished Hollywood citizens as Darryl Zanuck, Harry Cohn, Gary Cooper, Norma Shearer, and William Powell at Ciro's, the Coconut Grove and the Mocambo in Hollywood; the Chez Paree in Chicago; the Hurricane and Copacabana in New York. And his position in Hollywood was concretely confirmed when in 1940 the forms of his handprints and signature were immortalized in cement at the entrance to Grauman's Chinese Theatre.

Wisely he continued to use his past experience as a resource for his acting. On loan to Universal for *I Stole a Million* (1939) with Claire Trevor, Raft worked with director Frank Tuttle. During rehearsal Tuttle explained the action of a particular scene. "You're on this main street, George. And you walk into the post office with a gun and say, 'This is a stick-up.'"

George thought it over for a moment, then he said, "Sorry, Frank, the post office won't work."

Astonished, Tuttle asked, "Why not?"

"I'm not sticking up a post office," George said. "That's a federal rap. As a kid I learned that no gunman in his right mind fools around with Uncle Sam."

At first, Tuttle thought George was kidding, but Raft refused to do the scene until the post office set was converted into a tourist bureau.

It was these small, realistic touches, combined with the contributions of directors like Frank Tuttle and writers of the stature of Nathanael West, that gave George's films of this period an unmistakable authenticity.

Variety, July 14, 1939, gave the film an enthusiastic review:

> In a vehicle well tailored to his specific talents George Raft turns in one of his best and most persuasive performances. . . . Complementing with an equally sound and convincing portrayal is Claire Trevor, just coming into her own as a highly talented actress capable of meeting the most exacting demands.
>
> Screen play by Nathanael West is a concise and conclusive story detailing the logical evolution of a circumstantially created criminal who retaliates for initial injustice against himself in a succession of lawless ventures which ends in his own death—a sacrifice to make life easier for his wife and child. Plotting is legitimate and emotions are genuinely built up with suspense and valid character development.

George Raft's complicated typecasting battles continued at Paramount, and after more than twenty disagreements with Paramount about roles, and almost the same number of suspensions, Raft concluded that he should move on. Paramount was reluctant to release him from his lifetime contract, which guaranteed him more than a quarter of a million dollars a year. Nevertheless, Raft demanded termination of his contract and in 1939 he signed with Warner Brothers.

Although he no longer had the security the contract with Paramount guaranteed, he felt more comfortable at Warner Brothers, where he was obligated to do no more than two pictures a year.

He was also assured by Jack Warner that, although the roles might include the familiar "criminal" ones, he would have greater control over how these would be depicted—with the inclusion of redeeming personality traits.

Jack Warner was the dictator of his studio, and, like Harry Cohn at Columbia and Louis B. Mayer at MGM, he ruled with a firm hand that inspired terror, respect, anger, and extraordinary loyalty. He treated his actors like a kindly circus ringmaster. With his brothers, Sam and Harry, he created a studio as powerful as the others, with just as distinctive a style. Jack Warner gave his unequivocal praise to only one star who had been on his roster and that was during the twenties. He fondly reminisced about him in one of his famous rambling after-dinner speeches:

"He was the only leading man who always gave a good performance; he faced one hazard after another in filming and never once complained. He seldom argued with the director or pushed for more closeups. He didn't ask for one raise and any dressing room on the lot was satisfactory. At lunch he was grateful for an extra hamburger." He was, of course, talking about Rin Tin Tin, the dog.

Rinty, as the handsome German shepherd was affectionately called, along with John Barrymore, kept Warner Brothers solvent during the twenties, until their first talkie with Al Jolson moved the studio into a top position in the industry. The studio, under Jack Warner's tough leadership, produced in the thirties the great romantic adventures with Errol Flynn: *The Charge of the Light Brigade* (1936), *The Adventures of Robin Hood* (1938), *The Sea Hawk* (1940), and *Captain Blood* (1935); the Bette Davis dramas, such as *Jezebel* (1938), *The Private Lives of Elizabeth and Essex* (1939), *Marked Woman* (1937), and *Dark Victory* (1939); the Paul Muni films *The Story of Louis Pasteur* (1936), *The Life of Emile Zola* (1937), and *Juarez* (1939); the musicals reknowned for the Busby Berkeley extravaganzas and the gangster films that made cinematic history in the early thirties and continued to grow increasingly popular with age.

The studio became so involved in making gangster films during this period that they hired their own gun and explosion experts. Warner relates the story of a group of United States Army officers who watched the shooting of one gangster film, and later expressed amazement at the fact that not one machinegun jammed during a lengthy scene. They told Warner the trouble they had with the same guns. Warner explained that the cost of filming was so great that they could not afford delays. Later, according to Warner, his studio experts advised the army and they adopted the firearm devices used at the studio.

When George Raft became a Warner Brothers contract player in 1939, Jack Warner was the boss of the toughest mob in film history. No other studio could match the formidable gang of Jimmy Cagney, Humphrey Bogart, Edward G. Robinson, and George Raft. Raft's first big film at Warner Brothers was *Each Dawn I Die* with James Cagney. Almost ten years before, Raft had played a bit part in Cagney's *Taxi*, and this had proved to be an exciting pairing. In a *Detroit Free Press* article titled "Cagney's Pal: George Raft's Friendship with Jimmy Dates Back to New York's West Side," aspects of George's relationship to Cagney were recalled in conjunction with a preview of the film:

> Two youngish fellows made their way from a small neighborhood movie theater in one of the innumerable and undistinguished suburbs of Hollywood. It was night, but they wore dark glasses. Also, they had soft straw hats pulled down over their eyes. Had it not been for these accessories you would have seen that one was a slightly freckled, blue-eyed redhead, the other a brown-eyed, olive-skinned, patent leather haired brunet.
>
> The pair had been to a sneak preview. . . .
>
> A block up the street from the little theater, where their car was parked, the two young men took off their glasses, pushed back their hats and were themselves again. The disguises were worn simply so that the audience in the house might not know that the two stars of the film were present, and might not feel inclined, therefore, to be over-enthusiastic.
>
> The redhead extended his hand and shook the other's warmly. "George," he said, "you're great in that show! You've never done anything better and I can't recall any of your pictures in which you gave quite so good a performance!"
>
> "Thanks, Jim, I appreciate that," said the dark chap. "But I'd have been an awful dope if I hadn't shot the works trying to keep step with you throughout the picture. You pepped me up and encouraged me, and I hope

that some day I may be as good an actor as you. It's your show, Jim, and I'm proud to have had the share in it that I did."

This wasn't merely actors' talk. It was on the up and up, a couple of frank statements by a couple of good friends. . . .

Like so much overblown reporting on films and movie stars, the meeting had occurred—but not exactly in that manner. George went to the sneak preview with Cagney, but as usual he didn't watch the movie. He paced up and down the block outside until Cagney came out. One part of the article was true. Cagney was enthusiastic about the movie, and so were their fans.

The film has always been one of George's favorite movies because "I had an opportunity to work with Jimmy Cagney, a guy I admired. Also I liked the role. Stacey, the tough criminal I played, showed great courage and helped a pal, Cagney, out of a tough spot."

Ads for *Each Dawn I Die* read, "Cagney meets a Raft of trouble in prison." Typical of the prison melodrama, Cagney played a crusading reporter, Frank Ross, who had acquired enough information to expose the tie-in between the district attorney and the mobs that ran the .city's rackets. Warned to lay off, Cagney ignores the threats and finally falls victim to the mobsters. They hit him over the head, shove him into the driver's seat of his car, pour liquor over him and throughout the car's interior. Sending the car into a busy intersection, it careens and kills three people and Cagney goes to prison on a "bum beef."

In the penitentiary he learns to be tough, yet makes every effort to stay clean and do his time so that he can return to fight corruption. Although he avoids prison politics, he comes into frequent contact with Stacey (George Raft), the tough king of the big yard.

At first Stacey, a respected stand-up con who is feared by the prison's stoolpigeons, thinks Ross (Cagney) is an outsider and a punk. While the two of them are working in the prison jute mill, a stereotypical crippled prison stoolpigeon, Limpy, is about to stab Stacey from behind. Ross saves Stacey's life by tripping Limpy. Stacey's thank-you line is, "You're okay, kid. I owe you one."

Ross comes upon Stacey as he practices the throwing of a knife for the express purpose of killing Limpy. During the showing of a prison movie in the prison auditorium, Limpy is stabbed by someone else, but Ross thinks Stacey is responsible for the murder.

Shortly thereafter, Stacey asks Ross to turn him in as the murderer, because he has been sentenced to a term of 199 years, without possibility of parole, and he had planned to kill Limpy to get into a courtroom on a murder charge. Therefore he insists that Ross rat on him. This may earn Ross a pardon, will certainly put Stacey on trial—and will make possible an ingenious escape.

Ross complies and this leads to one of the most extraordinary and impressive prison movie scenes. Stacey, brought to court for his trial, dives out of a three-story window and through the canvas top of a truck, upon which a cross has been painted. He lands on a bed of mattress padding in the body of the truck and then escapes in a car which pulls up next to the truck.

Ross has not been granted parole and Stacey, on the outside, learns the identity of a man who had framed Ross in the car incident and who is now in the penitentiary. Since Ross was "the only pal who ever did anything for me—without being on the take," Stacey decides to help him. Stacey returns to prison voluntarily; then, during an abortive prison break, gets a confession from the rat who framed Ross. Of course, the confession is made in the presence of the warden. Stacey is shot down—and Ross is on his way to exoneration and freedom.

In addition to its being a major box-office success, *Each Dawn I Die* set a standard for all subsequent prison pictures. Along with a taut story line that has not become dated, the film is almost documentary in its sociological coverage of prison characters and their related penological problems: the prison psychopath, the sadistic guard, and the concerned warden. Moreover, Cagney was superb in portraying how the modern political prisoner can become hardened, calloused, and embittered by incarceration. A screen gem is Raft's portrait of the classic American criminal and his value system. The film was a critical success and gave Raft's new career at Warner Brothers an impressive send-off. *The New York Journal American* of July 20, 1939, singled out Raft's performance for special credit:

If it weren't close to heresy to say so, indeed, one might even go so far as to aver that it is Mr. Raft who comes nearest to stealing the entire picture, even in the face of the usual masterful playing of Brother Cagney in "Each Dawn I Die." Mr. Raft is once again back in his own element, the role of a tough guy with a heart of gold, a convict with a stretch of 199 years before him, and taking his time about playing it out. In such parts as these Mr. Raft literally shines, the sinister shadow of his playing dominating every scene in which he appears, and most of the rest in which he isn't seen at all. If that isn't picture stealing, then I don't know what is.

Variety, July, 18, 1939, in its review, agreed:

Raft shoulders up, inspirationally, to equal level in a role of difficult transitions as a tough repeater convict who makes himself the instrument for the unjustly convicted reporter's vindication through voluntary reprisonment and heroism in the surging battle of the cons with machine-gunning militia. A fiery, wholly persuasive and telling enactment.

During the filming of *Dawn*, a ruthless union racketeer, Willie Bioff, whom Raft knew from his New York years, was extorting huge sums of money from Hollywood producers and other industry leaders, including Harry Cohn and Joseph Schenck. With his partner, George Brown, Bioff controlled the International Alliance of Theatrical Stage Employees union. Their blackmail was paid because they threatened work stoppages and other trouble. If their payments were delayed, "accidents" would happen on the sets of films. Bioff and Brown's threats would be carried out by thugs imported from Chicago.

George saw Willie on the set of *Each Dawn I Die* more than once looking with obvious dislike at Cagney. Bioff stared at the overhead lamps and exchanged meaningful looks with some of his goons. Although nothing happened, Raft suspected something was wrong.

Sometime later, after the picture was finished, Raft met Bioff in New York. "You did pretty good with *Each Dawn I Die*," the gangster turned labor leader said. "You can thank me for that."

"How come?" George asked.

"The studio wasn't going to pay off and we were planning to take care of Cagney," Bioff explained. "We were all set to drop a lamp on him. But I got word to lay off because you were in the picture."

"You son-of-a-bitch," George swore. "It's a good thing nothing happened to Cagney. Jimmy's one of the greatest guys in Hollywood and if you had hurt him—you would've hurt me."

At a later time, Raft, behind the scenes, helped some studio heads and the courts to clean up the Hollywood unions.

Soon after the Cagney episode, Bioff retired as a labor organizer and moved to Arizona where, under an alias, he went into the grocery business. On the morning of November 4, 1955, when he turned on the ignition key in his pickup, the truck exploded, killing him. No one ever found out who put the dynamite under the hood.

The success of *Each Dawn I Die* led to another film about convicts, *Invisible Stripes*. Raft and Humphrey Bogart played ex-convicts. Raft means to go straight, but his prison past, the "invisible stripes," hinder him. Bogart continues his criminal activities. In the exciting climax of the film both are shot down. Raft atones for his misdeeds in this film by protecting his younger brother, played by Willian Holden, from a life of crime. The part had the required redeeming features. As Wanda Hale, in a review in the *New York Daily News*, commented, "George Raft makes his Cliff Taylor so sympathetic and real that you hate to think of what is obviously going to happen to him."

Seated next to Raft on the Johnny Carson Show, Holden recalled his experiences while making *Invisible Stripes*.

"I had only been in one film, *Golden Boy* (1939), before I went to work in *Invisible Stripes*. I wasn't a very experienced actor, and besides I was pretty nervous working with two stars like Raft and Bogart.

"In one scene, I square off with George in a fight because I resent his help. When we did the scene I must have still been bobbing and weaving from my fight scenes in *Golden Boy* because my head hit George's eye. I remember, when I saw the blood, thinking, 'Christ, it's George Raft. Now I'm going to really

136

get it.' Well, he was as nice as could be even though his wound needed several stitches later at the hospital.

"He really was my big brother, in and out of the movie. In fact, if he had not helped me, I might have been thrown out of the picture. However it began, the director, Lloyd Bacon, was always yelling at me. I couldn't seem to get anything right—my lines or my movements. It was hell.

"Then George stepped in with the director and told him to go easy on me. The director finally lightened up on me because of George's insistence."

During these early days at Warner Brothers, Raft recalled that, "I was in prison so much I had a special prison suit made to order for me by an exclusive Beverly Hills tailor. Christ, during those years when pictures put me in every joint in the country, I wanted to look stylish in my cell. I carried the suit in a leather case in the trunk of my Caddy. And got more wear out of it than I ever did from any other suit in my wardrobe."

In the 1940 *They Drive by Night*, directed by Raoul Walsh, George put aside his prison garb and gangster image for the role of Joe Fabrini, a hard-working, tough-talking guy who was trying to make it in the trucking business. Fabrini, the paradigm of the two-fisted hero, meets Ann Sheridan, a hardboiled waitress at a truck stop, and falls for her "like a ton of bricks." Ann complains to Raft about the diner boss's hands, "all ten of them." In one scene a truckdriver seated next to George smirks and says of Ann Sheridan as she turns to draw a cup of coffee, "What a set of headlights." George proves how much he resents this crude compliment by punching the driver in the mouth.

Bogart plays Paul Fabrini, Raft's younger brother who loses an arm when he falls asleep at the wheel and Raft cannot prevent their speeding truck from crashing. Ida Lupino plays the frustrated wife of a jovial but foolish truck-fleet owner, Alan Hale. After George has lost his truck in the accident, he goes to work for Hale. Ida is interested in Raft, but he is stuck on Ann Sheridan. In an attempt to get Raft, Ida Lupino suggests that he can acquire the trucking firm if they get rid of her husband. Turned down by Raft, Ida decides to murder her husband herself. In a chilling scene she leaves her drunken husband in their garage to die of carbon monoxide poisoning from the exhaust fumes of their idling car. The garage has an automatic electronic door, and Ida, to insure her husband's death, deliberately closes the door on Hale. She is charged with Hale's death, and later, in prison, goes mad at the sight of prison doors as they open and close automatically.

This scene is a memorable one and validated Raft's judgment, for he had recommended Ida Lupino for the role, which was her first major part. Previously she had won attention for her playing of the spurned model in William Wellman's *The Light that Failed* (1940). She was almost replaced in *They Drive by Night* because her astrologer forecast that the movie was bad luck and therefore recommended she leave the set. Jack Warner later claimed that Ida's absence added over a quarter of a million dollars to the picture's production costs. Yet, by coincidence, Miss Lupino's faith in astrology was almost confirmed when a near fatal accident that might have taken the lives of Ann Sheridan, Humphrey Bogart, and Raft occurred during the shooting of an exterior scene.

Raft shuddered as he recalled the incident, "I could drive a car blindfolded. I learned how when I was helping to move booze, and the associate producer of the movie and my old pal, Mark Hellinger, must have known that when he assigned me to *They Drive by Night*. Some people say I got nothing from Owney Madden but a bad reputation—but the driving skill I acquired when I worked for him in New York years before undoubtedly saved my life and those of the people in the picture with me.

"In this scene, Humphrey Bogart, Ann Sheridan, and I are highballing down a long hill in an old beat-up truck. Halfway down, the brakes really went out—a situation that wasn't in the script. Bogart saw me press the pedal and when nothing happened, he began to curse. 'We're going to get killed!' he yelled. Ann screamed and turned her eyes away from the road as I fought the wheel. I couldn't have been more scared myself. The speedometer hit eighty when I saw a break on the right where a bulldozer had started a new road. I pulled hard on the wheel and the truck went bouncing up the embankment. Thank God—it finally stopped.

"Ann was too upset to talk, but Bogart said, 'Thanks, pal,' with definite appreciation.

"'Don't thank me,' I thought to myself, because I didn't have the breath to answer, 'Write a letter to Owney Madden or Feets Edson.'"

On location with *They Drive by Night,* George may have saved Humphrey Bogart's life—and in other ways, by default, he continued to help Bogart's monumental career.

In 1941 George again let it be known that he no longer cared to be cast as a hood or gangster. He rejected the lead in Raoul Walsh's film of W. R. Burnett's *High Sierra.* Here he would have played Roy Earle, an aging and weary bankrobber, and been co-starred again with Ida Lupino. The screenplay was by Burnett and John Huston. Raft objected not only to the character he would play, but also to that character's death. As with *Dead End,* Humphrey Bogart was given the role.

Subsequently, with Bogart as beneficiary, Raft turned down more parts in films which are now considered Hollywood classics.

Sam Spade in *The Maltese Falcon* (1941) was neither gangster nor hood, yet George's contract with Warner's called for two pictures a year, with no remakes, and the Dashiell Hammett novel had been filmed twice before in the early thirties, in 1931 with Ricardo Cortez and Bebe Daniels and in 1936 as *Satan Met a Lady* with Warren William and Bette Davis. Another uneasy situation was that the film was to be directed by John Huston. Huston already had a reputation as an exceptional screenwriter, but this was his first directorial assignment. William Wyler, who had proved correct about *Dead End,* again advised Raft to accept the role.

Wyler at the time told Raft he had nothing to fear. "Huston is a brilliant guy and you can't miss with him." Then Raft at tempted to make a package deal. "All right, I'll do the picture," he told Wyler, "if you'll direct my next picture." Wyler told him, "Sure, George, if I have a role that suits you." Raft interpreted this as rejection. Unwilling to take the risk, he telephoned his agent, Myron Selznick, and instructed him to turn down *The Maltese Falcon.* His agent used the contract clause that entitled Raft to turn down remakes.

A place in film history was assured for everyone associated with *The Maltese Falcon,* but the principal beneficiaries were John Huston and Bogart. Bogart, with the supporting cast of Mary Astor, Peter Lorre, Sydney Greenstreet, and Elisha Cook,

Jr., became a sort of repertory company: Bogart, Astor, and Greenstreet again in Huston's *Across the Pacific* (1942); Bogart, Greenstreet, and Lorre in Michael Curtiz's *Passage to Marseille* (1944); and, most memorably, Bogart, Greenstreet, and Lorre joined Ingrid Bergman, Claude Rains, Conrad Veidt, and Paul Henreid in the film version of a forgotten play, *Everybody Comes to Rick's*. Raft thought the role of Rick not right for him; the film of course, was *Casablanca* (1943). *Casablanca* won Academy Awards for Best Picture for 1943; Best Director, Michael Curtiz; and Best Screenplay. In 1973 it was voted Warner Brothers' most popular film.

The roles in the films *Dead End, High Sierra, The Maltese Falcon,* and *Casablanca* were quite a legacy, but such refusals and inheritances were common occurences. What is remarkable is that so frequently it was to be from Raft to Bogart; earlier, it was only on Leslie Howard's insistence that Bogart repeated his stage portrayal of Duke Mantee in the film of *The Petrified Forest*. Warner Brothers had wanted Edward G. Robinson. Although Raft and Bogart never became close friends, Raft liked Bogart. In fact, at Warner's George became friendly with the all time big-three tough guys—Cagney, Bogart and Robinson. He considered them, unlike himself, to be "educated guys." "I think Bogart was a college grad. Cagney was a very bright guy. And Robinson, the very least you could say about him was how intelligent and cultured he was."

Raft, unlike Bogart and the others, knew the hard streets and tenements and had survived the back alleys and docks. At this stage in his life he no longer felt any need to prove that the tough roles he played for the camera were an expression of his real personality.

George recalled being in a New York club when Bogart, who often took his tough, cynical screen image home and on trips with him, did everything possible to start a fight with several patrons. The proprietor, a man known to Raft from boyhood as a rough street fighter, told Bogart he was going to be kicked into the street. At that point Raft intervened. "Don't hold it against him," George explained to his old acquaintance. "He works hard and he's just unwinding in his own way."

One difference between Raft and the others was George's

preoccupation with ridding himself of his criminal image. Encouraged by the great success of *They Drive by Night*, Jack Warner developed a property in the same genre as *Drive*, again to be directed by Raoul Walsh. The film about workingmen called *Manpower* (1941) furthered the harmonious relationship between Warner and Raft. The film strengthened George's desired image as a man of the people, and promised to become another box-office winner for the studio.

Manpower was a story of the men who worked with high voltage lines. Raft was co-starred with Edward G. Robinson and Marlene Dietrich, supported by strong character actors like Alan Hale and Frank McHugh. The advertising campaign used an electric triangle to stimulate the movie goers—"Robinson's mad about Dietrich. Dietrich's mad about Raft. Raft is mad about the whole thing"—as they went on to promise a movie of "crackling tension." Then the studio flacks did everything possible to encourage the public to believe that the romantic conflicts they saw on the screen had been inspired by real-life situations of the picture's three principals. In fact, as is often the case with legends that Hollywood promulgated, there was a measure of truth in the conflict.

As with most Hollywood films (and *They Drive by Night* was no exception) the plot of *Manpower* contains clichéd situations, relationships, and characters. What distinguishes it and others like it are the vitality of the performances, the immediacy of emotion, the colorful setting detail, and the tautness of the film's movement. The manner of varying the formulas is sometimes the gauge of the film's success. Today we honor directors and actors for the personal imprint that makes the real differences in these formula films. *Manpower's* plot delineates the clichés and shows how they could be made viable.

Raft and Robinson played tough, fearless men whose specialty was high-voltage installation and maintenance. The picture opens with Pop Duval, another linesman, asking George to give him a lift to the women's prison where his daughter Fay—played by Marlene Dietrich—is to be released. At the prison gate a tight closeup of Raft's face tells the audience that he sees her as "a dame who can only be trouble."

On their drive to the prison, Pop confesses to Raft that his failures as husband and father were responsible for Fay's life. From now on, he swears, he will make amends and become a father to his daughter. When Raft sees how she meets her father without a flicker of emotion, he doubts if anyone, especially her father, could reach Fay Duval. All she asks for is a cigarette and to stop somewhere for rouge, powder, and lipstick—things a girl didn't get while she did time in the "birdcage." At the drugstore Raft puts a penny in the weighing machine Dietrich stands on. With a bitter twist of her mouth she reads aloud her fortune card: "Your future will be as bright as your past."

In a short time, Marlene is again at work in a dancehall. There she is the cliché tart with a heart of gold that could be stolen, if she ever permitted herself to relax her hostility. Raft and Dietrich are attracted but distrust each other, and they quarrel bitterly because neither of them dares be gentle; nor can they believe in a love that gives all and demands nothing.

Meanwhile, Robinson, a naïve, warmhearted pal of Raft's, falls for Marlene and wants to marry her. Raft advises against this, and when his warnings fail he attempts to buy off Marlene with a "few hundred bucks." His interference infuriates her and she tells Raft, "I wasn't going to marry Hank, but now nothing will stop me." Robinson proposes, Dietrich accepts him, and Raft reluctantly goes along with their marriage—but not before he warns Marlene that if she cheats on his friend Hank he'll "take care of her personally."

In true Hollywood fashion, the prostitute, once married, is metamorphosed into the perfect housewife. Raft, quite pleased, accepts the miracle and begins to believe that she has gone straight. Suddenly there are complications. Raft is hurt in a fall from a high wire, and Robinson, against George's wishes, insists that he convalesce at his house. Alone with Fay, he realizes that he wants her—and she wants him. Yet Raft reacts angrily when Marlene, now the wife of his best friend, confesses that she is in love. "Why, I never gave you a tumble," he lies despairingly.

On a stormy night Raft and Robinson go out with a crew to repair a power line. Coincident with this, Marlene decides she must leave Hank because, while she respects her husband, she doesn't love him. She packs her suitcase, but before she leaves town she stops at the dancehall to say good-bye to the girls just as the place is raided. Robinson and Raft have returned to Robinson's house when the phone rings and Raft answers it to learn that Fay has been arrested. Without telling Robinson, George bails Fay out of jail. When she swears that she has done nothing wrong, Raft slaps her, and she reacts with scorching irony: "I've been hit harder than that."

Now, for the first time, Robinson believes that Raft has tried to take his wife away. He and Raft are at work on the poles during another storm and in a murderous fury he swings at Raft with a large wrench and slips and falls. Before his death, Robinson realizes he has been contending with forces beyond all of them and reconfirms his love for them both.

In the final scene, Raft takes Dietrich to the bus depot. A bus enters and blocks the view of Dietrich; but when it pulls out, to the relief of the audience, Fay is still there. Raft and Fay then leave the depot together. The ending implies a new life but doesn't confirm it—a movie ending as familiar as it is disarming.

The making of *Manpower* was far from tranquil. George had several heated arguments with Jack Warner and Edward G. Robinson. When Warner viewed the early rushes, his happy liaison with Raft was shaken because·he bullishly objected to "the George Raft longpoint shirt collars." They were, he believed, too long, and would "distract the audience's attention." Jack Warner's executive opinion was transmitted by note to Raft and he was ordered to change his shirts for the picture. Raft complied, but felt strongly that he had been unnecessarily censured, and humiliated, by the studio's executive producer. Criticism about the length of a collar would mean little to Robinson or most other men—but with George Raft Warner had dealt a uniquely personal blow that deeply wounded him.

Mirroring their screen roles, wariness developed between Raft and Robinson. Raft was enamored of Dietrich; and he believed, perhaps with reason, that Robinson also was interested in their leading lady. It was this unstated rivalry for Dietrich that might have provided the spark to their animosity, and Little Caesar and Gino Rinaldi threw real punches at each other in several scenes.

This friction on the set received wide press attention. The September 1940 issue of *Movie Life* did not mention any romantic triangle. They put the blame on Robinson's being a "camera hog."

> Much publicity has appeared in public prints about alleged maulings both on and off the *Manpower* set, where E. Robinson and G. Raft are said to be indulging in one of the fieriest feuds Hollywood has enjoyed in many a moon. Story is that one of the boys is a camera hog and the other isn't having any of it; so, being pretty pugnacious, himself, he's said to have taken a poke at his co-star.

George recalled his conflict with Robinson from his own standpoint: "I had top billing for the movie, but I was willing to co-star to get Marlene in the film. I was always nuts about her. Then Jack Warner insisted on Robinson. I never thought Robinson was right for the role, which was written to be played by a big guy. I'm not sure why I got mad at Robinson. I resented his trying to put me down with advice, you know, how to handle lines and business. He made me madder and madder.

"In one scene, I'm supposed to take him out of a bar. And Eddie suggested, 'George, let me struggle a little bit. Let me fight back.' Our director, Walsh, thinks exactly the opposite, and said to me, 'Just pick him up and carry him out—without a struggle.' Now who was I supposed to listen to? So in listening to Walsh, in doing the right thing, I lost out with Eddie.

"From then on, we didn't get along too well. Finally we had this one particular scene where it's raining. Dietrich of course was stuck on me, but out of spite she marries him. I don't know if you ever looked up into rain. It's pretty tough. And the scene calls on us to repair what's wrong with the high tension wire way on top of the pole since the power failure's blacked out the entire city. Yet it's raining cats and dogs. Okay, we're supposed to go up the poles without dialogue, since we're climbing, but Robinson wants to add dialogue before we start up.

"Robinson said, 'I want to say some new lines down here.' And I told him, 'I don't want to say anything down here.' When we get to the top of the pole, and work on it, then we can say a few lines. I explained, 'That would be more authentic.'

"What I think is right Robinson tells me is wrong. So he continues to insist that he wants to say something down here. His attitude burned me, so I said, 'Fine. Talk to yourself, because I'm not gonna answer you.' Now we're all standing on the outside of the set because of the rain that's pouring down. There's Frank McHugh, Ward Bond, and a lot of the other characters in the film.

"Finally the dialogue director comes over and says to me, 'Do you want to go over the scene you're supposed to do down at the base of the pole?' I says, 'I'm not gonna say anything at the base of the pole.' Robinson repeats, 'I think we've gotta say something.' Again, I repeat myself, 'We don't know what is wrong on top of the pole yet with the wire.' He says, 'Well, I want to say something.' I says, 'Why? To me, silence is golden.' We began to argue."

One thing led to another and the "two linesmen" threw a few real punches, before they broke it up. A photographer snapped a picture of the fight and it was a front-page story around the country. Both Robinson and Raft refused to continue with the movie.

The problem was partly a clash between a "personality" and an "actor." George always preferred acting with a look or a body gesture. Robinson, on the other hand, was an accomplished actor who attempted to integrate all aspects of his acting talents including the verbal in any scene. The hassle was finally resolved by Raoul Walsh and representatives from the Screen Actor's Guild in discussions with Raft and Robinson.

There were other mishaps. One concerned the scene where Raft was supposed to slap Marlene. In keeping with his code, he refused to hit a woman, especially Dietrich. Also George knew by now that when he warmed up anything might happen, because he was not a man who could always pull his punches. Marlene convinced him "it was only a movie" and that he should follow the script. When Raft at last agreed to play it, he hit her so hard that she fell down a flight of staris and fractured her ankle.

Another accident occurred when Raft was climbing a pole. Over thirty feet above the ground his safety belt broke. He fell eighteen feet, hit a crossbar, and then fell another twenty feet to the ground. In shock and unconscious, he was rushed to a hospital with three broken ribs and contusions of the abdomen. In the film's hospital bed scene, Raft didn't require any bandages from the costume department.

Despite their differences at the time, Robinson was one of Raft's fans and boosters, and in their later years both men valued their long association and friendship. In an interview with Robinson some months before his death in April 1973, he spoke with insight of Raft.

"George always wore this fantastic, arresting mask when he acted, yet you sensed that underneath his cool façade he was seething—boiling—writhing. I've worked with many great actors both in Hollywood and on the stage. And in my opinion no one matched George for this quality of personal power and manhood. His range was limited—he always played George Raft. But that character—there was no other like it—always evoked a sympathetic response and identification from a mass audience.

"He believed so completely that he was George Raft in the role, not George Raft playing a role, that there were times when he could get carried away with his inner forces. Why, when I worked with him in *Manpower* he reacted so personally to a scene with me that it turned into something I'd never experienced before. And it never happened again. The scene called for George to drag me out of this bar. Raoul Walsh put us through the scene, then called, 'Cut.' George went right on shaking me furiously and he wouldn't let go of me until several people pulled him off. It was as if the role had taken over the man.

"Also, we had that misunderstanding that I still can't figure out. I've never had a physical fight on a set with anyone. First of all, in spite of being Little Caesar, I'm not a physical person. I think George just resented my being in the picture. He once told me later on that he felt my role called for a bigger guy, someone like Victor McLaglen, whom he wanted. I guess tension built up and we clashed.

"I've always been very fond of George. Once we did a shtick at some function that seemed to amuse everyone. George and I stood eye-to-eye, glaring viciously at each other. Then I pointed my finger at his face and said, 'See here, you. No one fools with Little Caesar. See! See!' George responded by staring at me with that glowering deadly Raft look before he retaliated by taking out his famous coin and flipping it a few times. Then he said, 'This town isn't big enough for the two of us. One of us has to leave, and it ain't gonna be me.' We paused, then danced off the stage in each other's arms. The audience loved it.

"Actors like George and me probably lasted as long as we did because we were people before we were stars. You can promote a new face, someone with a few tricks never seen before, and people might go along with this promoted figure—but only for a little while. Then they see through him. You must be real to last. Have the integrity of being human, flawed, understandable. And you have to work. I still work as hard today, at each role I get, as I did at the beginning of my career. I can say the same for George.

"To my mind, the true actor understands the great responsibility of playing another human being. A true actor may not be a great actor. Yet the true actor understands that his craft demands that he take on another person's attributes and life experience and do what he can to interpret them sincerely. Again I'm describing Raft. Although he always played himself, he tried hard to put validity and integrity into his part. If the part had some moral quotient that fit Raft's own personality, he was fine and people on the set knew it immediately."

Manpower was important for Raft because it gave him a chance to fulfill his dream of working with Marlene Dietrich. "Over the years I'd known her casually, and I ran into her now and then. Nothing ever developed because in the early thirties, when she was at Paramount also, Joseph von Sternberg was her director and I guess her man. Still, when I knew she was at the studio I'd be on her set just to look at her. Coop and I were pals from all the way back and in 1930 he'd just made *Morocco* with her. After the last day of shooting, we both watched her walk down the street in a man's suit. 'Oh, Jesus, isn't that wonderful?' I said to Coop. 'Oh, Jesus, just once! I'd give a year's salary for one night!'

"Coop looked after her and nodded. 'I guess she is fabulous.' I said, 'You son-of-a-bitch, you worked with her for fourteen weeks, and you haven't noticed until now!'

"A few years later when Coop and I were making *Souls at Sea,* some days we had to be up at six to make our boat to Catalina.

One day, while we were in the sun on the beach, Dietrich popped into my mind (by now I'd seen her around town in this big old-fashioned Rolls-Royce, with a German driver who looked like Erich von Stroheim) and stayed there all day, all night, and all of the next day. And I don't ever remember fluffing so many lines.

"Then it happened. I was having dinner alone at the Brown Derby and she comes in alone and asks me to join her. I couldn't believe it. So very slowly, to give her a chance to change her mind, I got up and sort of shuffled to her table. We just talked and talked for hours about ourselves and our careers. I was on suspension at Paramount then and I told her jokingly, 'They won't allow me into the studio. Why don't you hire me as your bodyguard, so I can get into the place?' She laughed, which made me think she liked my style. I was excited, thinking I was going to get the chance to take her home. But she said, 'I have my car, and my driver.' I didn't push—with her I didn't dare—so I walked Marlene to her car. At the time she was living at Malibu. As she drove away, I thought, 'There goes my big chance.'

"Now and then I'd see her, casually, at different parties or openings, but always with von Sternberg. I was so afraid she would say no if I asked her to go out that I used the idea of avoiding an insult to von Sternberg as an excuse. I had a helluva crush on her. I thought she was the most elegant woman that ever lived."

On and off the set of *Manpower*, George apparently did fulfill many of his fantasies about Marlene Dietrich, although it is a part of his past he refuses to discuss. She stayed at his Coldwater Canyon home for a time. Because of the complications of their other relationships, the Raft-Dietrich romance never went as far as it might have. They both admired each other immensely, and during the time when *Manpower* was filmed their names were frequently romantically linked in the columns.

Raft's position among Hollywood's galaxy of stars reached its peak in the early forties. In addition to a heavy stream of movie part offers, he was vigorously sought after for participa-. tion in many events, including personal appearances. He found that he had to place rigid priorities on his time. One event, however, that he was proud and happy to attend was an official function at the White House.

President Franklin D. Roosevelt's Birthday Ball in January 1941 helped raise funds for victims of infantile paralysis and was a gala national affair. Top national dignitaries and select Hollywood stars were invited. Raft's invitation was another confirmation of his popularity and stature as an actor and citizen, and he was one of the most celebrated stars at the ball. The Washington *Times-Herald* of January 31, 1941, in a column by Peter Carter, reported:

> George Raft, who came to this party, now knows definitely, if he didn't before, just what price popularity, for he was smack up against the wall with admirers five feet deep around and finally had to be rescued and escorted out of the room by J. Edgar Hoover and a few able assistants who looked so stern that persons promptly cleared a path for them. . . .

Jack Warner's authoritarian rule—evidenced by the shirt-collar directive—was becoming unendurable for Raft. They often clashed about matters of much more importance. Columbia's president Harry Cohn, when asked why he was so hard on his staff, responded: "I am king here. Whoever eats my bread sings my song." This was Warner's attitude as well. His dominance required Raft's subservience, and this was a posture George was unable to assume.

During his tenure in the late thirties and through the forties, Jack Warner managed to wage more battles with his stars than almost any other studio head. Bette Davis, Jimmy Cagney, Olivia de Havilland, Errol Flynn, and Humphrey Bogart, among others, were on suspension so often that people wondered how the studio was able to make so many important and financially successful films.

Bette Davis's battle was representative of those of other actors. Against his direct orders she played Millie in the 1934 screen version of Somerset Maugham's *Of Human Bondage* for R.K.O; and she gave in that film what many consider to be among the best screen performances in movie history. Her instantaneous success calmed Warner's wrath, and she won her first Academy Award the next year for a Warner film, *Dangerous*. But disputes broke out several times over what she considered "dreadful roles," a complaint Raft often made. Unlike Raft, Bette Davis was more concerned with the dramatic quality of a film rather than the personal connotations of a role. Programatically, she alternated playing wicked women and good women. In 1937 she was offered starring roles in two pictures in England, and against Warner's orders she sailed off to begin work. Warner issued an injunction against her working anywhere but at Warner Brothers. Since the freedom of film artists was at stake, all Hollywood was intensely interested in the outcome of the case. The landmark decision forbade Bette Davis to break her contract and established a harsh precedent of studio power and bondage for the actor which later specifically affected George Raft's position at Warner Brothers. Bette Davis resumed work at Warner's, but there was now little doubt whose power was supreme. In fairness, there were concessions made: Davis virtually dictated the choice of director, crew, and property on many movies. While on loan to Samuel Goldwyn, for which Warner exacted over $300,000 from Goldwyn, she played in one of her best, *The Little Foxes* (1941), directed by William Wyler, who had guided her at Warner's in her second Academy Award performance for *Jezebel* and in *The Letter* (1940). Eventually, Jack Warner did real damage to her career by insisting on her playing in the much maligned but intermittently brilliant *Beyond the Forest* (1949).

In later years, in a more philosophical mood, Bette Davis wrote in her autobiography, *A Lonely Life:* "In all fairness to Jack Warner, he was singular as a movie mogul. No lecherous boss was he! His sins lay elsewhere. He was the father. The Power. The Glory. And he was in the business to make money. . . ."

Bogart, also in a mellow mood after he left Jack Warner, reminisced with a tinge of fondness: "I kind of miss the arguments I had with Warner. I used to love those feuds. It's like you've fought with your wife and gotten a divorce. You kind of miss the fighting."

Stars in Warner's paternalistic system were of course not truly suffering—they did have fame and fortune. But they were in a very real sense children to the studio, a status evident by the discipline and punishment that followed for those who did not behave.

As mentioned, Raft's earlier years at Paramount had produced many suspensions, so his initial year at Warner Brothers seemed like a honeymoon. He had socialized with Jack Warner for many years and considered him a friend, and fully believed that "Jack's word was his bond," which made him a singular man in Raft's mind. Without argument, Warner approved the two-picture-a-year arrangement, and there was allowance, with J.W.'s approval, which Raft believed would not be withheld, to accept outside roles. Beyond the contract, Warner assured Raft that his personal preferences about roles would be respected.

And, after the success of *Each Dawn I Die, Invisible Stripes, Manpower,* and *They Drive by Night,* why should there be any trouble? Therefore Raft became outraged when he was handed a role that involved playing a "heel" who refuses to help his family and becomes embroiled in Nazi spy activities. Edwin Schallert, a *Los Angeles Times* columnist, sympathetically summed up Raft's problem at the time in an article on August 1, 1941:

RAFT REFUSES TO PLAY "HEEL" ROLE AT WARNER'S
George Raft and Warner Bros. are embattled again. The actor doesn't like the role he is supposed to play in "All Through the Night," which was to start today, nor the subject matter of the story. I understand from sources close to Raft that he feels the part in the production makes him out to be a heel, because he is willing to throw money away in gambling and refuses to assist members of his own family. . . .

Raft has been often charged with being a kicker-upper in the movies, but, more times than not, he has been just about right in his arguments. He has a clear and logical conception of what is good for his own career, and the stamina to say so. His first big flare-up took place over *The Story of Temple Drake* at Paramount. . . .

Because of his type, Raft is very likely to be cast as a heavy without sufficient redeeming traits. Of course, he did just such a villain in "Scarface," but that was right at the outset. He managed to maneuver his way out of that kind of assignment and doesn't want to go back to it again. He'll portray a type that isn't too good nor too bad, but there must be some rays of sympathy. Otherwise, he judiciously refuses.

The easiest thing a studio can do is to suspend a player when he commences to rebel. Warner Bros., I understand, has already done this in the instance of Raft, or will if he doesn't do the picture. The establishment would be much smarter if they studied the psychology of actors' contentions. Then there wouldn't be so much of a melee about the whole issue.

All Through the Night (1942) starred Humphrey Bogart, and Raft was placed on suspension.

In November 1941, George received an offer from Universal Studios of $150,000 for ten weeks' work in a film with Rosalind Russell. Since he had played previously with Russell in *It Had to Happen* (1936), he looked forward to working with her again in a comedy.

Jack Warner, then in New York, did not return the calls of Raft or his agent. Raft wanted the Universal deal badly, but—as stipulated in his contract—had to secure Warner's approval, so he flew to New York.

"I caught up with Jack in his Waldorf suite. And he was a different person when he wasn't behind his desk. Outside of business he could be very cordial and friendly. He listened sympathetically as I told him there was a new chance I might get a divorce from Grayce, since she'd told my lawyer that $150,000 wasn't enough, but she might consider $300,000. The $150,000 I'd be getting from Universal would certainly help me put together that kind of dough. So I put it to Jack as if I was a soldier, he was the general, and I was requesting a ten-week furlough to go on another assignment. After some discussion, nothing to worry me, Jack gave me his okay and appeared to be embarrassed at my thanking him so much.

"I left the Waldorf elated that I had Jack Warner's okay. I didn't have anything in writing, but who needed that when I had Jack Warner's word? That night, at Reuben's Restaurant on 58th Street, I ran into one of Jack's associates. We had a bite together and talked about this and that. I told him about my Universal deal and how I was anxious to try this new role, plus how good the money was.

"He shook his head. 'Jack Warner isn't going to let you do it.' I got a little angry at this guy, 'What the hell do you mean? The man gave me his word. Are you calling him a liar?'

"'Look, George,' he put up both hands, 'I don't want any trouble with either of you. But I know Jack Warner. And, as yet, you don't.'

"That upset me, so the next day I called Warner back at the Waldorf. And found out he'd left for California. Sure enough, when I returned to L.A., the studio informed me that Jack had changed his mind and I couldn't go on loan. Boiling mad—because to me a promise is a promise—I tried for days to see Jack, but he avoided me. Finally my agent told me they wouldn't let me go to Universal because they wanted me to do a picture at Warner's called *The Dealer's Name Is George*. Now that property was a title, nothing else. There was no script, no nothing, only a name they'd pull as a gimmick on me whenever they didn't want to let me do something on my own."

At Paramount he hadn't been disturbed by the studio's attempts to force him into undesirable roles because they had never said they wouldn't. But the arrangement with Jack Warner was different, and Warner had broken his word. After over six months on suspension, Warner finally permitted George to go on loan to Universal to work in *Broadway* (1942) on the condition that he return to star in a spy film.

In *Broadway*, an updated rehash of a twenties stage hit by George Abbott and Philip Dunning, George played a character whose outlines were similar to those of his own during the early years. The story begins with a film star arriving in New York to raise funds for shows put on by Hollywood stars for the benefit of men in the service. Walking along Broadway, he arrives at the site of a club he used to work at as a dancer. His reminiscences with his bodyguard, played by Mack Grey, is the cue for a flashback to the roaring twenties—and gangsters, speakeasies, and entertainers.

George's last film for Warner's, *Background to Danger* (1943), the spy one he had agreed to, was directed by Raoul Walsh and co-starred Peter Lorre and Sydney Greenstreet. In it, Raft played a G-man, and in one scene, which had to be reshot several times, he is tied up by spies Lorre and Greenstreet. Perhaps out of boredom, Lorre began to blow smoke in George's face. According to Mack Grey, "George told him at least five times to 'knock it off.' Remember, George was actually tied up. Lorre would laugh and he spitefully kept blowing smoke at George. Finally, when George was untied, he was so furious he ran into Lorre's dressing room and clobbered him. But this was one time," Mack added, "when a guy really deserved it."

In December 1942 Raft demanded and had his contract with Warner Brothers annulled. According to Raft, the studio owed him around $75,000, but he was so anxious to be free he told them to forget it—and even paid Warner $10,000. Jack Warner gives his own account in his autobiography, *My First Hundred Years:*

> In one way my association with Raft was unique. When we had serious performance problems with other actors and actresses, I usually wound up paying off their contracts to get them off the lot. Raft says: "I had nothing but trouble with Jack Warner." After five pictures he wanted out.
>
> "Tell you what, Georgie," I said. "Why don't we settle the argument for . . . well, let's say ten thousand."
>
> "Fine," he said.
>
> And what do you know? He gave us a check for $10,000 and I practically ran to the bank with it before he could change his mind.

From then on Raft never entered into any long-term studio contracts. His later films were contracted on a single picture basis. He gave up the benefits of continued studio backing— which was a basis for financial and career security—so as not to compromise his idiosyncratic principles. The independence he selected might have troublesome consequences, but it would not cause any regret. What a studio could do to torment and denigrate an actor is accurately depicted in Clifford Odets' *The Big Knife* (1955). Raft remained his own man.

The Warner Years

Ultimately, with the gradual waning of the star system and the breakdown of the big studios in the late forties, the magic careers—those of Gable, Cagney, Robinson, Davis, Bogart,—suffered a decline. The continued durability of John Wayne or James Stewart are remarkably untypical. One of the great stars, Raft took his career into his own hands, and he learned early by choice what the others would be forced to learn.

7
THE FORTIES

"The lights are going out in Europe! Ring yourself around with steel, America!"

With these impassioned words, Joel McCrea in the final scene of Hitchcock's spy thriller *Foreign Correspondent* radioed warning to the United States from a bomb-devastated London. The year was 1940, and Hollywood was playing a major role in communicating World War II to the American public.

As Hitler, the man with the Charlie Chaplin moustache, devastated Poland and marched on France, the bulldog British spirit was heralded in such films as *A Yank in the RAF* (1941) and *Mrs. Miniver* (1942). When Chaplin's *The Great Dictator* (1940) was released, the first sardonic attack on the villain of the century, the subject was already too grim for comedy.

After Pearl Harbor, FDR assured the nation that "We have nothing to fear but fear itself," and the public rallied to the cause. Those who could not fight bought bonds, planted Victory Gardens, served as air-raid wardens, and participated in the programs of rationing with spirited cooperation. Popular songs included *I'll Walk Alone, The Jersey Bounce,* and *Don't Sit under the Apple Tree with Anyone Else but Me;* and jitterbugging in zootsuits worked off a lot of nervous energy for young people not old enough to fight.

In 1943, zootsuited pachuco gangs clashed with servicemen on the streets of Los Angeles; and hysterical bobbysoxers knocked down policemen to get a glimpse of Frank Sinatra at the Paramount in New York. In sports, the "Doc" Blanchard–Glenn Davis combination launched the 1944 Army football team, Ted Williams hit over 400 for two seasons in 1940 and 1941, Don Budge was an international tennis star, and Whirlaway won all of the major horseraces.

Millions of citizens identified vicariously with the drama of war depicted in such films as *Thirty Seconds over Tokyo* (1945), *Story of G.I. Joe* (1945), and *A Walk in the Sun* (1946). In the early forties, Hollywood felt courageous enough to deal with the German incursions into European countries: *The Moon Is Down* (1943), *This Land Is Mine* (1943), *Hangmen Also Die* (1943), *Mrs. Miniver* (1942), all of which were late reporting but presumably inspirational. To strengthen our ties with the Russians Warners produced, at Roosevelt's suggestion, *Mission to Moscow* (1943); and Samuel Goldwyn made *The North Star* (1943).

159

These films were to be particularly vilified by the infamous House Un-American Activities Committee in 1947. Tribute was extravagantly paid to the homefront, in *The Human Comedy* (1944), and in David Selznick's *Since You Went Away* (1944). And nurses received honor in *Cry Havoc* (1944) and *So Proudly We Hail* (1943). More important there were the "war" movies: *Objective Burma* (1945), *Bataan* (1943), *Destination Tokyo* (1944), *The Purple Heart* (1944), *Wake Island* (1942), *Guadalcanal Diary* (1943), *Thirty Seconds over Tokyo* (1945), *A Walk in the Sun* (1946), *Desert Victory* (1943), *Sahara* (1943), *The Story of G.I. Joe* (1945), and a host of others. Preston Sturges poked malicious fun at the soldier cult in *The Miracle of Morgan's Creek* (1944) and *Hail the Conquering Hero* (1944), and George Stevens's *The More the Merrier* (1943) and Vincent Minnelli's *The Clock* (1945) are good examples of wartime romantic comedy.

Hollywood's participation in the war was not only on the screen. Hollywood stars rallied to entertaining and supporting the troops through Bob Hope's U.S.O. entertainment, George Raft's traveling Cavalcade of Sports fight shows, and War Bond drives. Millions of pinup pictures of stars like Betty Grable and Rita Hayworth decorated the lockers and walls of barracks around the world.

As the grimness of the war became pervasive, light-hearted entertaining movies filled a real need. James Cagney put back on his dancing shoes in *Yankee Doodle Dandy* (1942); *Cover Girl* (1944) was considered a breakthrough musical; a priest sang in *Going My Way* (1944); in *Springtime in the Rockies* (1942), *Sweet Rosie O'Grady* (1943), and *Pin-Up Girl* (1944), Grable was the bouncy, naïve American Girl imbued with sex appeal.

Going to the movies in the early forties was either an escape from the hard realities of involvement in the European conflict or a lesson in how to deal with it. It was less important that the lessons were misleading, inapplicable, and unreal or the entertainment tasteless and witless—the audience needed to be told something, anything, and needed to be distracted. Movie stars became crucial cultural heroes.

For many stars, the studio's role of stage mother–father and patron saint was an imposition to be happily and heartily welcomed. The studio provided guidance, comfort, and security. The ultimate pinup girl, Betty Grable, for example, slid with little hesitation from the protective custody of her mother into the waiting arms of 20th Century-Fox. Under the paternal tutelage of Fox's head of production, Darryl F. Zanuck, Betty Grable became a reigning box-office queen in a series of campus, gay nineties, and Latin American musicals that were a popular diversion of the early forties.

Grable was born in 1916 in St. Louis and moved to Los Angeles with her mother, Lillian, at the age of twelve. One report referred to young Betty as "brash, cherry, friendly, and one of the crowd." For a time she was under contract to RKO, where she appeared in the chorus lines and was given a number, *Let's K-nock K-nees*, in the 1934 Astaire-Rogers *The Gay Divorcee;* but she eventually returned to bit parts. Paramount also signed her, with similar disappointing results.

Grable married Jackie Coogan when she was quite young and both the marriage and her screen career seemed failures, so she gave them both up and went East. There she appeared in the Cole Porter musical *Du Barry Was a Lady* (1939), which starred Ethel Merman and Bert Lahr. This part earned her rave reviews and 20th Century-Fox brought her back to Hollywood in triumph to replace an ailing Alice Faye in *Down Argentine Way.*

Raft fell for Betty Grable when she was a glamorous young actress of twenty-two. Apparently Grable first had a crush on Raft when she was just a wide-eyed, sixteen-year-old chorus girl, possibly on the set of *Palmy Days*. A *Modern Screen* (August 1941) article, written in the peculiar "popular romance" style of that period, presented an historical account of Betty Grable's first reaction to Raft.

> Betty looked with admiring eyes at the important people on the set.
>
> Among them was a dark, Latin youth who was probably the complete personification of all that Glamour could spell. A sultry face under blue-black hair, a touch of cynicism and sorrow in eyes that were hooded and remote. A Latin who could dance like the wind across a plain.
>
> An eyeful for a little girl with too-curly yellow hair and big, excited blue eyes.
>
> So, when somebody told her that George Raft wanted to take her to the six-day bicycle races, she didn't be-

lieve it. She went to her mother. . . . "I couldn't go—
could I?" Well, her mother thought, her heart suddenly
wrung and pitiful at this uncomplaining child, maybe
she could go. But they must take Marjorie, her sister,
and Betty must be home by 11:30 P.M.

She dressed with shaking hands, too excited for
speech. Too excited, alas, to speak at all, all evening.
Her smile was ready, and her eager, responsive look,
but she still didn't believe it.

George Raft was embarrassed, fidgety—people were
laughing at his bundle of girlhood, whispering about
"cradle-robbers." And although something inside him
had clicked like a clock striking an hour of destiny, he
decided destiny was kidding.

He took them home, and somebody told Betty that
he'd said, "I'm giving her back till she grows up."

But, in fact, Raft was smitten with the child star and followed
her mushrooming career from the sidelines. Her next leading
role after *Down Argentine Way* was in *Tin Pan Alley* (1940), a
musical with Alice Faye, John Payne, and Jack Oakie. Faye
was Fox's reigning musical star, but she was to be eased out and
replaced by Grable—as Grable was to be replaced by Monroe in
the early fifties. By 1942 Betty Grable was one of the top ten at
the box office, and her famous legs, Grable's gams, were insured
by Lloyd's of London for more than half a million dollars. Countless men in the Allied Armed Forces drooled over Betty's pinup
pictures, and her photo was a favorite fighter plane insignia.
Grable was a national darling, and the drums and fifes of Fox's
publicity department played overtime to hail the girl in whose
arms, flacks said, every GI wanted to die.

Raft was hesitant to approach Grable directly. Instead, he
asked a mutual friend, Jack Benny's wife, Mary Livingstone,
to sound her out and build him up. Mary's sales talk was un-
necessary, since Betty remembered George and was eager to
date him. Along with Jack and Mary Benny, they planned to see
each other one Sunday night for dinner at Ciro's after Benny's
radio broadcast.

On that Sunday morning, Grable was ill, and by midafternoon
she knew she could not keep the date. She feared Raft might
think she was using illness as an excuse not to see him. There-

fore when she called she asked her mother to get on and confirm her daughter's indisposition and disappointment. Raft assured them both that he understood and hoped she would be well when he returned from Washington, where he was to appear at President Roosevelt's Birthday Ball. When Betty hung up, she was convinced that Raft would never again try to see her.

The Sunday after Raft's return from Washington, George called Betty and escorted her to a Bundles for Britain benefit, then took her dancing at the Mocambo. They had a grand time, and at her door he asked to see her again. "'When?' she asked me. 'Tomorrow night?' I suggested. Betty smiled at me. 'That's a date. And don't *you* get sick.'

"We hit all the Hollywood nightspots. At first we had two things in common. Neither of us drank and we loved to dance. Between dances we'd have fruit-juice drinks or I'd send for ice-cream sodas, which both of us were crazy about. Sundays I'd take her to baseball games. Sometimes we'd drive to Caliente for the races. On Tuesdays and Fridays we went to the fights.

"My dates with Betty—well, they were different. Virginia Pine went to the games and fights to please me. Norma Shearer went for the novelty. But Betty Grable went because she, personally, liked sports as much as I did, and she proved this by helping me organize my contribution to the war effort—'George Raft's Cavalcade of Sports.' I was too old for the service," George continued, "so the Cavalcade was my contribution to the kids who were fighting for me. The Cavalcade consisted mostly of a traveling team of fighters who put on bouts at Army and Navy bases. I'd referee the fights, unless such ring greats as ex-heavyweight champ Jim Jeffries or Henry Armstrong were scheduled to officiate. Then I'd entertain. You know, it only stood me about fifty thousand. Next to what I gave my mother, spending this gave me the most satisfaction."

In the early forties the Raft-Grable romance became important to the financial security of the fan magazines in much the same way the Liz-Dick alliance of the sixties did. It could be wildly speculated that the lurid and larger-than-life fan magazine accounts of the Raft-Grable romance served as an aphrodisiac to the real-life relationship of the two stars—now both at the very peak of their film careers. The powerful publicity offices of 20th Century-Fox and Warner Brothers were seldom unresponsive to the unrelenting requests for the release of new and exotic data about the dynamic duo. The puffed-up visions of romantic love created by the studio and the press gave the relationship a dimension of surrealism that would be difficult to measure against the truth.

Betty shared George's interest in sports and got along well with Mack Grey and the other people around Raft. If they were working, Raft and Grable preferred quiet evenings at his home where they dressed casually for informal meals. After dinner they would play gin rummy or bridge, just as any married couple might. A typical fan magazine article, written in the silly ping-pong prose of the genre, captured a sense of domestic fun and friendly thoughtfulness that characterized their romance:

> He thinks she's more fun than any girl he's ever known—sunny-hearted, full of laughs, easy to please. She insists he can outclown her, only he's not so noisy about it. She calls him her straight man—or, to tease him, Sinister. He calls her "Goodlookin'." She says he's soothing. She's never seen him excited or heard him raise his voice. Her tendency is to rush around. "Take it easy," he says. "Everything's under control."
>
> George loves to give but hates the act of giving and will run a mile to escape a thank you.
>
> "Think your brother-in-law'd like to go to the fights, Betty?"
>
> "Why don't you ask him?"
>
> "You ask him."
>
> Or, "Here's some perfume I got for your mother. You give it to her."
>
> It's come to be a running gag in the family. "Betty Alden," she says, "speaking for Miles Standish Raft—" He can't bring himself to hand even her a gift. "Go look on the table in the other room," he tells her.

Betty characterized George as "one of the kindest and most generous men I have ever known. Once I went to the hospital with an infected wisdom tooth. My jaw was throbbing horribly. Somehow George assured me it wasn't swollen at all, or, if it was, it looked lovely that way. He sent flowers every hour on the hour.

"Then there was the time when I told him I'd taken my mother to dinner on the maid's night out. Once told was enough for George. From then on he never forgot that Thursday was the maid's night out, and never failed to ask my mother to be with us."

Unfortunately for the principals, their romance was tailormade for gossip columns, so that accounts of their love inspired some of the worst prose in the history of syntactical composition ever dredged up for the readers of fan magazines. But it wasn't the journalistic excesses that caused difficulty; it was the unseen presence of Grayce Mulrooney that clouded an otherwise promising affair. Day by day Betty felt more strongly that there could be no lasting future with Raft. When she began to date other men, they quarreled bitterly.

A friend recalled an evening with Betty and George at Ciro's: "Betty was table-hopping, greeting and hugging other guys. George sat at his table with me looking depressed. I said, 'What's wrong, George?' He waved his hand in disgust at Betty. 'Look at her jumping around. I could give that broad half of Sunset Boulevard and still wouldn't know where I stood with her.'

"I could tell he was really hurting with jealousy and anger. I got the sad feeling that it was all over between them. And now he was really going to feel pain."

Betty confided in Louella Parsons, who dutifully used almost every detail of their romance in her column:

"I would have married George Raft a week after I met him, I was so desperately, so deeply in love with him. But, when you wait two-and-a-half years, there doesn't seem to be any future in a romance with a married man.

"I am doing my best to try to forget him. You can't see a person every day and have them do all the little thoughtful things George did and break off without feeling lonely. I don't expect to get over George today, tomorrow, or next week. But I do know there's no turning back."

Studios might allow romances, but long-term affairs were not tolerated. Raft lavished expensive gifts on Grable—diamonds, furs, even racehorses. "My much-publicized romance with her finally ended on a slapstick note. Shortly before our thing went on the rocks, I'd ordered as one of her Christmas gifts a stone marten coat, which was delivered to my home after we'd said good-bye for the last time. Still, I felt Betty should have it. Bought for her—it was hers.

"I handed the big box to Mack Grey and said, 'Drive this over to Betty Grable's house. If she doesn't want it, spread it out in front of her door and she can use it for a doormat. Just don't bring it back here.' Mack took the coat and, as I expected, Betty didn't want to keep it. So he laid this gorgeous hunk of fur on her doorstep and drove back."

Time does heal ruptured and bruised relationships, and in the years that followed Raft and Grable became good friends again and occasionally went out together, with her husband Harry James. Her untimely death in July 1973 was a terrible blow to Raft.

For Raft, Betty Grable was his last important romantic involvement. He at last accepted that he could never again endure the pain that came from breaking up with a woman. Casual relationships required no emotional involvement and therefore could not be heartbreaking. Easy come, easy go became his active social philosophy; and this intensified his sexual activities.

Dean Martin, then Jerry Lewis' partner, was a newcomer to Hollywood in the early forties, and he vividly remembered George's lifestyle during this period. George missed Betty but he carried his torch in grand style.

"Shortly after I first arrived in Hollywood, I had a chance to go to George Raft's house. As a kid, I guess I'd seen every picture he ever made, and to me he was a super-star. I was awed by his place in Coldwater Canyon. It was like the temple of a brothel. The most gorgeous women in town would be there. It wasn't just sex. They would swim nude in the pool or we would sit around and talk. George would lounge all day in his silk robe at poolside. He never swam. In fact, the only exercise he ever had was with broads or shuffling a deck of cards. Dinner was a special event. When the girls would unfold their dinner napkins there would either be a hundred dollar bill or some expensive earrings, or for special broads a brooch or a bracelet. George had class."

Perhaps it was Dean Martin's admiration of Raft's lifestyle that years later prompted him to hire Mack Grey as part of his entourage. As a close associate of George Raft's for many years,

Mack Grey was able to observe the private lives of many Hollywood stars of that era. Even when compared with Hollywood's top romantic heros, Mack never ceased to be amazed at George's exploits.

"There was never anyone like him. You know, a man of affluence and leisure might get up on a day off and play a round of golf, some tennis, or take a swim. Not George. Screwing was his only game. He would get up in the morning and put in a whole day at it. He was a sports-screwer.

"Whatever he did during the day with women, at night, after a regular date, George would take some gal home and by the time he'd get back to the house there'd be another gorgeous number waiting and willing. Let me tell you—I knew all the bedroom athletes, studs like Barrymore and Flynn. But on the mattress George topped them all.

"The truth," Grey swore with a raised right hand. "For year after year after year, George averaged two different women a day. Say that George had a lull, wasn't working, was free one morning, he'd have some hooker or starlet in for a matinee. Then she'd leave. Rested up, George would go to dinner and to bed with another dame. After he got her home—another one might come around midnight. And next morning I'd see another pretty face at the table with us."

In spite of George's Don Juan exploits with women, he continued to have little confidence in himself as an attractive lover.

"I guess women thought I was a sexy guy. I don't know why. I don't think I'm handsome. I guess they like the Latin lover or greaseball type. I never had trouble getting almost any woman I wanted. But yet I was always afraid of rejection. A woman always had to come toward me seventy-five or a hundred percent before I would make an advance.

"After I had all those romances fall through I just figured it was better to be alone than be rejected. That's why for many years I stuck with callgirls. If you got the dough, with them there's no rejection."

Paradoxically, George generally went either with callgirls or women he rated as "stylish high-class ladies" who were "above him." His 1945 film *Nob Hill* reflected a characteristic of George's relationship to women. He was cast as the rough, crude gambler from the Barbary Coast; Joan Bennett was the unattainable "lady" at the top of the hill. As in *Night After Night*, he overcame seemingly insurmountable odds and won the lady.

He always thought of himself as the guy from the other side of the tracks who was disparaged for thinking he could ever marry the lady, whether she be Virginia Pine, Norma Shearer, or Marlene Dietrich. This self-doubt may have motivated George to play such screen roles.

"Let's say a tough guy goes for a bitchy broad like the kind Jean Harlow, Shelley Winters, or Ava Gardner played. Who cares? They're two of a kind. But if he wants to win a Kate Hepburn, a Greer Garson, or a Joan Bennett, the audience watches every move he makes. It's exciting. Will he slip up? At the last minute, will his background keep him from getting this special girl?" This stock situation was just as often played in reverse: the girl from the wrong side of the tracks in love with an upper-class swell.

Although Raft presented many women with gifts of all kinds from perfume to diamonds and fur coats, there were times, he confessed, when he wondered if this generosity was not simply an expensive ego prop. "Say I give a girlfriend a ring. She looks at the ring and says, 'Gee, this is wonderful.' *This* is wonderful — instead of 'Gee, you're wonderful.'"

He freely admits that he was for many years the "hooker's delight." "Wherever I was in those days—at the Friar's Club, at a friend's, or at home—around midnight the phone would start ringing, almost falling off the hook. I was in the little black book of every high-class hooker in Hollywood."

One starlet had, in her opinion, a steady job with George.

"First you must understand," she explained, "I'm really an actress. I never had any big roles—but I've played some pretty good bit parts. Because there was no work, I went into the business. Through a girlfriend of mine I met some customers and after a few months I put together a pretty good book.

"I found out that George Raft was definitely *numero uno* to any girl working Hollywood. So when a friend asked me to come along one night to his house I was superdelighted.

"When he met us at the door, he didn't say much more than hello, but my friend knew the scene. We went into the bedroom, took off our clothes, showered, and used some of his perfume.
168

Before long my movie hero came into the bedroom, took off his silk robe, and the party began. He made love to each of us, and even though it was a business date I must say I was into it.

"A few days later he called me and I went to his place alone. Hundred-dollar tricks are always special—but with George it was really great. He would talk to me like we were on a date and had a romance going. Sometimes we went out to dinner, or he gave me a little extra gift. He was so good to me that I really dug him. He never asked me to do anything weird sexually like some Hollywood tricks I could tell you about. I always hoped he would offer to help me with my acting career, but he didn't and I never had the nerve to ask.

"Anyway, George turned into a three-night-a-week steady date. He always had me show up at exactly midnight, we'd talk and then ball for an hour or so. It became a steady gig and three hundred dollars a week is good money. For about six months I cut out all my other dates, since three bills was enough to cover my living expenses.

"Now that I think about it, he did help me with my career. It was really great for me because now that I had the bread I got new pictures—composites—made, changed my agent, and went on some good interviews for parts.

"But all good things end. First of all, I didn't make a full three hundred a week because once in a while I had to bring along a friend. One night I brought along this far-out looking chick who's new on the scene. She was around five foot ten, had a groovy body—she looked like Verushka. I knew she was exactly the type George went for. I know I dug her myself. She was a little loaded on pills and it didn't matter to me. But when George noticed she was high, he blew. He never minded me having a few drinks when we went out but this was the first time I knew he was absolutely down on dope. He called me a few choice names and then told the two of us to get lost. When I called him the next day, it was no use. He just told me 'No hard feelings,' but he couldn't get involved with anyone on dope and thought I knew better. That was the end of my romance with George Raft. After that I had to go back to work again, and not at the studio."

He would never tolerate any brusqueness or a businesslike attitude. "If a broad came in and acted as if she wanted to get it over with fast and get out, I would tell Mack to pay her and get rid of her. I always wanted it to be like a date. Nice and pleasant.

"Or if a hooker came in and mentioned the name of anyone else she had been with, or even that she had a boyfriend, it was all over between us.

"I wasn't different from a lot of guys in the public eye who spent a lot of time with hookers. Don't forget, in those days they had 'breach of promise' suits, and if you weren't careful you could be blackmailed or ruin your career with a paternity suit. A lot of stars and bigshots preferred hookers, only they kept it quiet.

"When I lived at the El Royale, there were two penthouse suites. Mack and I had one and Harry Cohn, the head of Columbia, had the other. He was separated from his wife at the time.

"Many times, as a gag, we both left our front doors open. I used to watch the stream of broads that went up to his place, and I found out later that he would check me out. Sometimes we would compare notes. I think between us we had every hooker in town. But if I ever saw a broad I had been with go to his suite—that would finish her with me.

"Even if I was at a restaurant or a party, and I saw a broad I had been with on someone else's arm, I would get jealous and feel hurt.

"Any girl I went to bed with was special to me when I was with her. I would consider her my private girl at that time."

At times his sex life seemed like a series of one-liners at a stage show. George recalled an incident that took place in his dressing room when he was waiting to go on for a personal appearance in San Francisco.

"This fantastic brunette, without knocking, walks into my dressing room. I told her I was busy. She didn't say a word, just came over, French-kissed me, and then smiling sensuously, she began to undress. I was so amazed I just sat and watched. First she took off her silk black dress. She wore black panties, bra, and a kind of chemise. She took each thing off slowly—in between coming over and kissing me. Then when she removes the last stitch she stretched out on this sofa. She had one of the greatest bodies I'd ever seen in my life.

"I had to go on stage in five minutes. I didn't know what the hell to do. Believe me, I wanted to follow my natural feelings. Mack comes in, looks surprised, and then he says, 'George, you can't. You have to get on stage.'

"The show almost didn't go on that night. I gave the girl the name of my hotel and room number and told her to come over later that night. She did and we did. It wasn't as good as it might have been in the dressing room that afternoon—but it wasn't bad, it never was in those days."

George Raft considered his sexual prowess merely that of an "average guy." The only difference between George and millions of other men, he believed, was that he was in a position to act out some "average guy's" fantasy. His most extraordinary performance in this regard took place in a Chicago hotel suite.

George was playing at a large theater, doing personal appearances. Part of his act included a dance with a chorus of beautiful girls. Naturally that night he took one back to his hotel after the show and made love to her. A friend's recollection of that evening in George's hotel suite assumed epic proportions:

"After she left, the theater manager waltzed in with seven girls from the chorus who were eager to meet Raft. They thought 'Georgie was adorable.' They all looked like beauty contest winners. I remember a statuesque redhead, with an unbelievable figure, wearing a white silk evening gown. You know, the kind Harlow wore. I also remember a little brunette who looked like Lupe Velez, you know, the Mexican spitfire type. She had on a tightfitting sheer dress, and there was obviously nothing on under it but a sensational body.

"George was their Latin lover, their Valentino, and they all seemed anxious to meet him. Picture this—we're in this plush ornate suite. Seven beautiful broads, all a little loaded and babbling away about how they simply 'had to meet George Raft.'

"The theater manager thought it was all too funny, since he was smashed himself. We called down and ordered food and more liquor. One of the girls turned on a radio and they're dancing around. One is doing a funny strip and they're getting more and more drunk. Meanwhile George is sacked out in the next room and I'm trying to keep the noise down. Finally the redhead says coyly, 'I'm going in to see my hero, Georgie.' Before I could stop her she floated into his bedroom.

"There's not a peep of protest from the room and the redhead is in there for maybe half an hour. She comes out with this big

171

satisfied grin on her face, her dress draped on her arm. She's dressed in the buff and her muff. She poses, then points to the door and cutely says, 'Next?' Like a shot, this little sexpot heads for the bedroom. While she was in there the others start kidding around and arguing about who's next. From that time on, in succession, each one of these broads sashayed into the room. By dawn, George had tagged all seven."

George vividly remembered the evening. "I was half-asleep at first and it was like a strange dream. They came in one after another, all beautiful and all very passionate. It was like a cascade of different bodies, shapes, and colors of dresses, chemises, panties, and perfume scents. They would walk in—very eager. I would kiss them and one thing always led to another. Somehow as the evening went on I became more and more passionate. I enjoyed every single minute of that night. The next day, my legs turned to rubber and I could hardly get out of bed. I guess I slept on and off for almost twenty-four hours."

Stardom often carries the assumption of Herculean attributes that in reality only reflect the vivid imagination of an agent. Few Hollywood stars probably even aspired to their aggrandized mass-media and screen images of dashing lovers, but Raft readily assumed the burden. In the Hollywood-American society of the 1940s, a man's sexual prowess was intrinsic to his identity Machismo implied admiration rather than derision, and George's off-stage sexual activities were the subject of considerable gossip. Were the seven showgirls magnetized by the screen image of the great star or were they putting a provocative he-man to the test? Whatever their motivation, George responded like a trouper and that night gave a stellar performance.

After leaving Warner Brothers, Raft was still very much in demand. He made several films at United Artists and RKO, including in 1943 *Stage Door Canteen* and in 1944 *Follow the Boys* (in which he partnered Vera Zorina), both popular star-studded army entertainment films; *Nob Hill* in 1945 with Joan Bennett and *Johnny Angel* with Claire Trevor; and in 1946 *Whistle Stop* with Ava Gardner; *Mr. Ace* with Sylvia Sydney, and *Nocturne.*

The Forties

These were not the prestigious films of former days . . . but it was true that "they didn't make them that way any more." Raft's film career continued; there were other roles to be played, however.

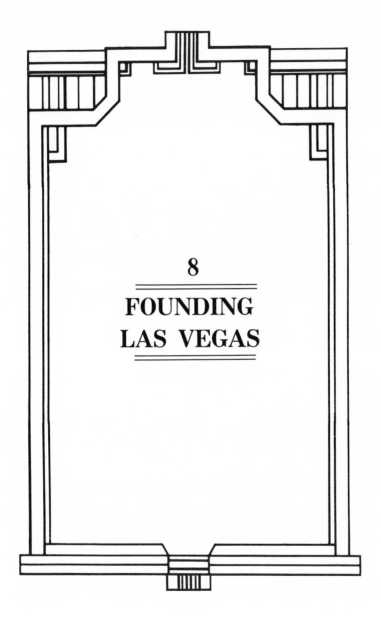

8
FOUNDING
LAS VEGAS

It was a hot summer day in 1954 at Santa Anita, and Walter Matthau was disturbed by more than the heat. Every starting bell automatically gave him another loser. And he was now broke, except for a $75 residual check from the Screen Actor's Guild for an old movie he'd rather forget. On his way to cash the check, a few scattered fans greeted him cheerily, "Hi, Walter, we loved you in *Season in the Sun.*" The man in the window assured him that their "No Checks Cashed" policy meant everyone, including Walter Matthau, and that it was pointless to see the manager.

"I was desperate. My luck had to turn; if only I could get the check cashed I knew I could get even. I went up to a few people I knew and got the cold shoulder. They were either losers themselves or didn't want to be bothered. A lousy seventy-five dollars. Christ, the week before I lost five thousand on one Yankee game.

"It must have been the heat. Anyway, I turned around in my box, looked up at the stands, and began to yell up at the crowd, 'Anyone here cash a check for seventy-five dollars? Where are all my fans? Who's going to cash a seventy-five-dollar check for Walter Matthau, the famous actor?'

"There were no takers. Then all of a sudden I heard this familiar voice, 'I'll cash it, sir!'

"'Sir? Sir?' I thought to myself. This has to be someone from the I.R.S. or the House Un-American Activities Committee. No one else ever called me 'sir.'

"I looked over a few boxes and there he was—right out of the late show. It was George Raft—hat, checked sports jacket, long roll collar—obviously a cool winner. He cashed my check by digging into a roll of bills as thick as my fist. His only problem was finding something smaller than a hundred."

Most of his adult life, Raft has been a familiar figure at racetracks around the country, making special effort to be at the great races at Saratoga or the Kentucky Derby. In the forties, he owned several race horses and gave horses as gifts to Virginia Pine and Betty Grable. He also owned and had a "piece" of several fighters, including World Champion Henry Armstrong. He has never thought of himself as a gambler, which is a fulltime and thoroughgoing lifestyle; but he did occasionally place bets. In the early New York days, he pitched pennies, played cards, shot a mean stick of pool, and, if the action was right, would bet "no" at the right crap game.

Betting is the "game" part of sportsmanship, and when affluence came he wagered substantial sums on racehorses. "I loved to go to the track, and I especially enjoyed it when one of my horses was an entry. I wasn't a heavy bettor. My biggest bet was $10,000 on a race."

Although George loved the races, his favorite sport was baseball, and of all the people he knew in baseball Raft's closest friend in the forties was Brooklyn Dodgers Manager Leo Durocher. Durocher had been a denizen of the very poolrooms where George and Billy Rose practiced their craft and they had known each other forever. Their friendship continued over the years, and they spent as much time together as their separate careers allowed. "We used each other's suits, ties, shirts, cars, girls, and for nine years when he was on the West Coast he always stayed at my house; and after the baseball season he'd move in for a couple of months. I still have the Dodger uniform he had made up for me, and I was proud to wear it around the ballpark or anywhere else. Those were great times, but then something happened between Leo and me that blew it."

In 1945, after Raft returned from a European USO tour, he made a personal appearance in New York at the premiere of the film, *Follow the Boys*. Afterward, Raft took some friends with their companions to Durocher's midtown New York apartment for a party. Leo was at the Dodgers' camp in Bear Mountain, New York, but he left George the key. As George recalls, he was playing gin with sportscaster Bill Stern when a stranger suggested a dice game. He seldom shot craps but, on a lark, after finding a pair of Stork Club souvenir dice, he began to play. When they quit in the early morning hours, George had won around $8000, mainly in checks.

Seven months later, when George was filming *Johnny Angel* in New York, the man who, according to George, had suggested the crap game and was its big loser, complained to Frank Hogan, District Attorney of New York, about the game. He claimed that he had been clipped by Raft, whom he accused of using loaded dice and taking, in cash, $18,500 from him in thirteen straight passes. The accusation leaked out and made newspaper headlines, and George became a target of several columnists.

178

Particularly damaging columns were written by Westbrook Pegler, whose usual victims were politicians considered liberal to any degree, especially President and Mrs. Roosevelt. It was one of Pegler's few attacks on a screen personality. His two articles in October 1946 on George Raft and Leo Durocher were a departure from the political preoccupations of his venomous pen, and they added fuel to publicity that had already burned George and Leo.

Martin Shurin, the chump of the evening, a young man with illusions about celebrities, particularly movie actors, is disenchanted now. He lost $18,500 to Raft in a few minutes and, in the ensuing notoriety, shot off his mouth, perhaps untruthfully, about his earnings as a sub-contractor in the war business of supplying airplane parts. He may have exaggerated. . . .

Shurin recalls that in the scramble for position at the crap table, he found himself alongside Raft. He would have preferred a place where he could retrieve the dice and count the spots as Raft ran up his 13 passes, all fours and tens, most of them the hard way. . . .

However, a spot next to the great man was a place of honor, so he did not scuffle and began to lay the conventional price against fours and tens. He says he gave Raft $1,500 in currency and a check for $1,000 that night and sent him ten $1,000 bills a few days later . . .

Durocher's choice of companions has been a matter of deep concern to Branch Rickey, the business manager of the Dodgers. The old practice of "whispering out" players and even managers "for the good of the game" could be revived. . . .

If the moving picture business knows that one of its stars prefers the underworld and doesn't care, that is one matter. For a time, and for a profit, Hollywood joined the newspapers and the department of justice in discrediting the Adonises and Little Augies, friends of George Raft. All that time, however, Hollywood was developing an underworld of her own, as evil and bold as the prohibition and union rackets, and without repudiation by the industry.

Nobody would bet on the outcome of a picture, but a few killings on fixed ball games would degrade something that the public, perhaps without realizing as much, has come to regard as an American ideal or treasure.

The moral "climate" of Durocher's circle and Raft's is ominously similar to that in which the corruption of 1919 occurred.

Durocher was about to catch a plane for Italy, where he was going to play exhibition baseball for American troops, when he read Pegler's columns. Dodger owner Branch Rickey phoned Durocher at the airport to lay down the law of what both he and the sport of baseball demanded of its players and managers. Then he made him promise that Raft would never again be permitted to use his apartment.

Unfortunately for George, who was also receiving a full share of Hollywood censure, the Sunday supplements wouldn't let the story fade away. One newspaper got John Scarne, the nationally known dice expert, to comment. He asserted that the odds against thirteen straight passes were 9851 to 1. A rival paper promptly had another expert conclude that the true odds were 25 trillion to 1. Meantime, no one attempted to interview George, who would have told them that he had not made thirteen passes, that he never collected all his winnings, and that his accuser was a liar who was later arrested for passing bad checks.

When the affair gave no evidence of passing away, the baseball commissioner, Happy Chandler, met secretly in Berkeley with Durocher on a fairway of the Claremont Country Club. There Chandler reputedly ordered Durocher to drop Raft and leave Raft's Coldwater Canyon home where he was staying. Arthur Mann, one of Branch Rickey's assistants, said that Chandler also forbade Durocher ever to see Joe Adonis and Benny Siegel again. If Durocher continued to see them or Raft, he would be asked to quit baseball.

Leo Durocher's life *was* baseball and nothing, even his close friendship with Raft, would prevent him from continuing in the sport.

When Durocher came to pick up his belongings, he had a painful parting with George. George vividly remembered it.

"Leo really felt terrible. For a guy with the nickname 'Leo the Lip' he was completely silent as he packed.

"'Go ahead, Leo, tell me what's up,' I said."

Reluctantly, Durocher explained his situation and the powerful pressure on him to break off his association with the notorious star. Raft understood Durocher's problem, but the loss of a close friend was not an easy thing. He felt, "Here I was, condemned by a lot of garbage written in the press."

Knowing that Leo had no choice he did not protest, but Durocher's behavior bitterly disappointed him.

Another acquaintance, though certainly not a close friend, Joe Adonis, gave Raft another sort of "brushoff." At a dinner in New York shortly after the Durocher episode, Adonis said, "George, I like you, so I'm going to give you some advice. We like each other, but it's no good for you to be seen with me. I'm in the rackets, and if the press connects you with me you'll get hurt."

Raft had thought people like Jack Warner and Durocher were friends he could trust, and he felt they had betrayed his trust. Certainly, though, his association with them had boosted his public reputation. However, another acquaintance, Benny Siegel, the notorious New York gangster, would cause Raft's career to suffer.

When in 1947 Benny Siegel was assassinated gangland style, newspapers were unsure of the correct spelling of his nickname. Variously, he was called Bugsy, Buggsy, Bugsie, and even Buggssy. The appelation in any spelling was unofficial, and its use forbidden in his presence. The label had been tacked on by his associates and the police and it characterized a murderous flash temper that bordered on the psychotic.

When the Countess Dorothy di Frasso was questioned by reporters about Siegel's death, she replied, "I don't know any Bugsy Siegel. Are you referring to Mr. Benjamin Siegel of Beverly Hills?" That a countess, albeit one born in the United States, would be questioned about a gangster's death indicates Siegel's social standings—and reflects on the Countess's as well.

Benny Siegel was a handsome, dapper, vain, and hot-tempered man who survived the gang slaughters of the twenties and thirties. A Hollywood gossip columnist once described his looks as "a cross between Rudolph Valentino and Tyrone Power." In the mid-thirties he moved to Los Angeles to open the West Coast territory and subsequently become its ranking executive. Reputedly he shared a slot on the syndicate board that included Meyer Lansky, Lucky Luciano, Frank Costello, Joe Adonis, and similar criminals. After his demise, those who knew him had diverse comments to make:

The circumstances surrounding Bugsy Siegel's career in crime tell the story better than words. Here was an individual whose life was a constant challenge to common decency. Yet he and his criminal scum were lionized and their favors sought after in so-called respectable social circles.

—J. Edgar Hoover

Maybe he did kill people. Maybe he had to. But he was like a father to me, and the best friend I ever had.

—Chick Hill, Virginia Hill's brother

Siegel was a brainy guy who might have made it big on the right side of the law. —Walter Winchell

Bugsy Siegel was officially an aristocrat of the new underworld . . . he had become one of the most formidable criminals of our time. —Westbrook Pegler

Countess Dorothy di Frasso naively believed Bugsy was an innocent overgrown boy, but he had a weird assortment of drifters, cutthroats, and confederates for friends.

—Elsa Maxwell

I didn't want Bugsy Siegel in my house. I wasn't going to wake up some morning and see the front page saying "Movie Tycoon Machinegunned by Opposition Mob," and then I wouldn't be able to read the paper anyway. But he got in.

—Jack L. Warner

Gossip columnists made much of Siegel's move into a Beverly Hills mansion when he came West in 1935. He rapidly became one of the most sought-after Hollywood figures and was a regular at parties given by Hollywood's upper crust. He counted among his friends Jack Warner, Cary Grant, Barbara Hutton, and the Countess Dorothy di Frasso. And though his background was common knowledge, his social conduct belied his tough and murderous history. It was this disreputable and mysterious aura that intrigued people and enhanced his public position.

No one seemed to care to examine his well-documented criminal record. In the pre-Prohibition gangland era, Siegel's partner was Meyer Lansky, a more sedate and methodical racketeer. During Prohibition Siegel, with Lansky, formed a tough gang that was well known in the underworld and to police as the "Bugs-Meyer Combine."

Among the services Lansky and Siegel provided was stealing cars on order and then selling them to other gangsters who were illegally transporting liquor. Stepping up to the next logical rung, they bought or hijacked whiskey and supplied it to speakeasies. In prohibition days "muscle" was important. Murder, like any other service, could be paid for, and Lansky and Siegel soon rose to power in an organization that became known as Murder, Inc.

Siegel, who in the twenties had frequented the clubs where Raft appeared, pressed their association when he arrived in Hollywood—for Raft was a "big star." Raft, though not a basically gregarious person, did not reject those who insisted and who seemed interesting. He knew Siegel was a "big man" in New York, and Siegel's attention was flattering. Moreover, Siegel spoke Raft's language and had acquired a Hollywood charm that was familiar and attractive to George. Raft, also, was quite at home in friendships where certain questions were never asked — these were a matter of discretion and not relevant to personal intimacies. Why shouldn't he become friends with Benny?

They went to the track or occasionally had dinner together, and, though Siegel was generally tight-lipped, he encouraged Raft's talk of acting and the movies. It even was reasonable to assume that Siegel secretly had ambitions to be a movie actor.

"Benny took a personal interest in motion pictures. He bought cameras, projectors, and other equipment and often came to the studios to watch the technical processes. He asked me to photograph him one day and I took some footage of him with his camera in my dressing room, and he later showed the film at home. I had a hunch that, like a lot of people, he was a frustrated actor and secretly wanted a movie career; but he never quite had nerve enough to ask for a part in one of my pictures."

Siegel emulated Raft's expensive manner of attire and wore his clothes well. Favoring embroidered shirts, houndstooth check jackets, and silk ties, he struck the correct Hollywood tone.

George Raft

Raft was never aware of the extent of Siegel's gangland connections, and since he frequently encountered him at tracks, hotels, clubs, and parties in the company of the respected, secure, and powerful, he assumed there was nothing reprehensible in their acquaintance. "If he was okay with producers, directors, even royalty, and other stars—there was no reason why I shouldn't get together with him once in a while."

Siegel had a relaxed amiability, an evident enthusiasm for the achievements of others and a flair for picking up tabs. Siegel often spoke of Raft as a great star, an actor whose gangster characterizations were so authentic they defied imitation and comparison; and Raft, by and large isolated from old friends with a like upbringing, took to Siegel because they could talk about Broadway and sports. "He was accepted by everyone because he was Broadway and Hollywood and he was interesting to be with."

Siegel participated in the exotic and freewheeling activities of Hollywood characteristic of the late thirties. For example, in 1938 he was invited on the voyage of the *Metha Nelson*, a vessel which had been used in the 1935 production of *Mutiny on the Bounty*. It was chartered by Marino Bello, Jean Harlow's stepfather, and others, who proposed to combine a pleasure trip with a shark-fishing expedition and a treasure hunt for ninety million dollars' worth of pirate gold supposedly buried on the Cocos Islands. Along also were Siegel's current girlfriend, Dorothy di Frasso, and Owney Madden's old partner, Champ Segal. Siegel enjoyed the trip, even though no treasure was found.

Siegel's life wasn't all pleasure, but the Hollywood crowd either didn't notice, or didn't care about his underworld activities.

Siegel's wife, Estelle, who shared with him a Lower East Side upbringing, did not circulate in Hollywood society. That Jean Harlow was godmother to one of her children meant very little to Estelle but a great deal to her husband; and she knew of her husband's playboy activities with many starlets and some stars. For a time Siegel dated Wendy Barrie, the British actress who had played with Charles Laughton in *The Private Life of Henry VIII* (1933), and Marie "the Body" McDonald, both good friends of Raft's. Estelle Siegel remained in New York while Siegel played in Hollywood. By 1946 she had had enough and they were divorced.

Benny's closest and later most notorious girlfriend, Virginia Hill, was an attractive woman who gave some of Hollywood's most extravagant parties. Virginia's income remained a mystery even to Senator Kefauver's subcommittee investigating organized crime, who questioned her about it in 1952.

Reputedly Siegel moved in on the offshore gambling fleets and the casinos in little resort towns like Redondo Beach and the dog track at Culver City. He also had an interest in the racetrack across the Mexican border, in Agua Caliente. These operations gave Siegel a favorable reputation among the East Coast bosses. Yet Siegel covered his criminal activities so well that after he had been in California a few years the newspapers seldom called him a gangster; he was generally referred to as a millionaire Hollywood playboy. But in 1939 Siegel moved from the social columns to the front-page headlines—as one of the alleged killers of a former New York hood, "Big Greenie" Greenberg.

The finger of guilt in Greenberg's assassination was pointed at Siegel by Abe "Kid Twist" Reles, who was given immunity and began to recite to then New York District Attorney William O'Dwyer (later mayor) the details of the history of Murder, Inc., including his own involvement in over eighty-five brutal gangland killings. "Big Greenie" was killed because the mob had good reason to believe that he was going to reveal the activities of the Bugs-Meyer Combine. "Greenie" was in hiding in Los Angeles. On the night of November 22, 1939, as he returned from a corner newsstand near his home, a car pulled alongside the curb and one of its occupants shot "Greenie" five times. Reles, when he talked, claimed to know that among the five assassins in the car were Allie Tannenbaum, Frankie Carbo, and Benny Siegel. Tannenbaum later confirmed that he went to California with two guns a few days before the killing, contacted Siegel, and was with Siegel and the others the night of the homicide. He told O'Dwyer that Siegel was the one who shot and killed "Big Greenie." Tannenbaum and Reles were flown to Los Angeles in 1940 under heavy guard to appear before a Grand Jury, and on the basis of their evidence Siegel and the others were indicted for killing Greenberg. Siegel, while lodged in the Los Angeles

County Jail, had innumerable "visits to his dentist" granted; and this later led to a great scandal in the Sheriff's Department. Presumably having his teeth fixed, he stayed at home for several days at a time and was often seen casually dining out in Beverly Hills restaurants with his many Hollywood friends.

While Siegel was supposed to be in jail awaiting trial, O'Dwyer was busily engaged in the prosecution of other members of Murder, Inc., including Louis "Lepke" Buchalter. He became hesitant about releasing Tannenbaum and Reles for another trip to Los Angeles when another potential Murder, Inc., informant, Whitey Krakower, was gunned down by unknown assailants on a New York streetcorner. O'Dwyer feared that Tannenbaum and Reles would not survive the trip to California to testify against Siegel, and he felt they were vital to the important homicide cases he was prosecuting in New York, especially against Buchalter.

Without Reles and Tannenbaum's testimony, the Los Angeles District Attorney, John Dockweiler, felt he had no case, and the indictment of Siegel and the others was dropped. Later on, Siegel was indicted again, but this case also fell apart when the State's star witness, Reles, under heavy guard at the Half Moon Hotel in Coney Island, mysteriously fell out of a tenth-floor window on November 12, 1941.

Siegel's Hollywood friends apparently did not pay much attention to the allegations, because when Siegel was released he easily re-entered the social whirl. In fact, in many quarters the headlines about his exploits had enhanced his prestige. He was often in Raft's special box at the racetrack with Raft and Betty Grable.

Their encounters were sporadic, for Raft was busy with his films, his "Cavalcade of Sports," and his European touring with the USO. When he returned to Los Angeles in June 1944, he had not seen Siegel for over a year, but he saw no reason to refuse Siegel's invitation to visit him at Allen Smiley's Sunset Towers apartment. "We would usually sit around, bullshit, and reminisce about the good old days in New York. Benny wasn't much of a drinker and neither was I. But, if it came to having a few broads up—that, of course, would be okay with me." When he arrived at Smiley's apartment, "they had the *Racing Form* and other racing sheets on the table, and were sitting around the living room making bets over the phone on horses at Churchill Downs in Kentucky. I took a look at the forms and picked a few likely winners myself."

Siegel was on the phone when the apartment door burst open; the unexpected callers were Captain William Deal and other members of the Los Angeles County Sheriff's Vice Squad. Captain Deal advised Siegel and Smiley that they were under arrest for bookmaking.

Raft's fierce loyalty was aroused, especially when he felt the activities had been perfectly innocent. "Look," he said, "if you're arresting them, arrest me, too." There was no reason to arrest Raft, since he was only a bettor and not part of the suspected bookie operation, so Deal declined the offer and clapped the cuffs on Siegel and Smiley, leaving Raft behind.

Siegel went to court before a Justice Cecil Holland and was represented by an eminent attorney, Isaac Pacht, a former Superior Court Judge and member of the State Parole Board. There were stormy scenes in the courtroom that morning, especially when Raft testified. Never a respecter of decorum, George deliberately baited Captain Deal from the witness stand, and he testified that neither Siegel nor Smiley were booking bets. As George was questioned he became so vehement in his defense of Siegel that he was cautioned several times by the judge that he was subject to contempt of court charge.

George had been warned by his movie employers to stay away from the trial on the grounds that an admitted friendship with Siegel could damage his screen career. But when subpoenaed he went without reluctance, because he was firmly convinced Siegel was innocent.

Producer Mark Hellinger also came to court, as described in the press, in his "uniform of a dark blue shirt and white necktie," and he said under oath that Bugsy was "a man of good moral character." Before the session ended, the prosecutor—who felt he did not have a solid case—offered a deal to drop the felony charges if Siegel and Smiley would plead guilty on one bookmaking count. They agreed and were fined $250.

Raft had made an impressive gesture when he stood up for Siegel, but he also risked his professional future. Whether or not it had anything to do with his court appearance, Raft's box-office appeal actually improved. Perhaps the public was now convinced more firmly than ever that George was really a gangster, off screen as well as on, especially when a photo taken at the trial with George's arm around Siegel was printed on newspaper front pages across the country.

As Siegel's interests on the West Coast solidified, he decided to emulate Raft and build a palatial home in Beverly Hills, not too far from George's Coldwater Canyon home. He sought Raft's advice on every aspect of his new project. George Raft and Benny Siegel were a pair of incongruous suburban home builders as they met occasionally to observe the progress of the project. Hot tempered, Siegel often badgered the contractors, carpenters, and plumbers to make sure they were following the blueprints.

So involved was he in his emerging dream house that Siegel went there after dark and occasionally coaxed George into coming along. They toured the rooms, sometimes lighting wooden matches or using flashlights to see how things were progressing. When the house was near completion, Siegel took Raft to the master bedroom on the second floor and showed him a sliding panel controlled by a concealed button. George could not figure out why Siegel needed the secret exit until Siegel explained, "It will come in handy one of these days when I gotta get out in a hurry."

Siegel had a number of neurotic habits and obsessions, and one was his concern with his hair. He combed it every five minutes and tried without success to stop its thinning with every known lotion, medicine, and treatment. Two years after Siegel's death while making *Red Light* (1949) with Virginia Mayo, Raft tried to capitalize on Bugsy's habit. "I remembered Benny's hair-combing compulsion and thought it a good mannerism, like the *Scarface* coin-tossing." But the director wasn't interested. "He told me, 'You'll never convince an audience that a guy would really do that.'"

Raft remembered being at a club with Mack Grey and Siegel one evening. "Siegel began to badger Mack Grey about his thick head of hair. It bothered him so much that he finally offered Mack one thousand dollars cash if he would cut it off."

Mack Grey saw the intensity of Siegel's desire to do this and felt he had no choice except to "go along with the gag." "I told Siegel okay. Then the son-of-a-bitch got a pair of scissors and butchered my hair. He must of got some kicks out of it."

Once, Raft seriously underestimated Siegel's hair fixation. As a gag, he sent him a toupee on his birthday. Furious, Siegel drove to George's house and it took almost an hour for George to calm him down. From then on he avoided kidding Siegel on any personal matters. He never mentioned Siegel's use of face creams, eye shades, and other things to improve his looks and maintain a youthful appearance.

Siegel, like George, was a ladies' man and attempted to balance several affairs at one time. George, without any desire for the role of Siegel's counselor, often found himself reluctantly involved in Siegel's lovelife.

One evening when he was depressed and would rather have been left alone a distraught Dorothy di Frasso appeared. Mack Grey showed her into the living room and Raft could see she had been crying. After a long, convoluted explanation, it appeared she was disturbed because Siegel was running around with other girls. Also, she was angry with Raft. "I thought you were my friend, George. You know I'm crazy about Benny—and you know he's running around with other girls. Why didn't you tell me?" George tried to console her and said that the next time he saw Siegel he'd talk to him. She answered, "Tell him if I catch him with anyone else, I'll kill her."

The Countess's behavior was hard to fathom. "I took her to the door, eased her out, and watched her go down the walk toward her Rolls-Royce. Here she was—a wealthy, attractive woman who had everything money could buy—wasting her tears on a guy like Benny, who couldn't care less."

George had other unwanted problems concerning Siegel's romances. He had warned Wendy Barrie, who had also fallen for Siegel's dubious charms, that she was "playing with fire" by going out with Siegel. George's good advice backfired, for Wendy promptly passed on George's "warning" to Siegel.

Mack Grey recalls, "This Sunday morning I saw Ben pull up to the house. When he got out of his car he looked mad as hell. He didn't even knock on the door. 'Where is he?' I told him, 'Take it easy, Ben. George had a big night and he's still sleeping.' That didn't stop him, he ran up the stairs to George's bedroom. It scared the hell out of me. I knew Siegel's reputation as a killer and he looked like one that morning.

"I was right behind Siegel when he busted into George's room.

189

He pulled out a gun and told George, 'You dirty son-of-a-bitch. I thought you were my friend and you told Wendy all that crap about me. I'm going to wipe you out.'"

Raft knew something of Siegel's reputation and that the threat was no idle one, but he kept his cool. "Okay, pal, just settle down. You're liable to do something neither of us would like." George kept the conversation going for a half-hour, reminding Benny of their friendship; and finally he said, "Let's forget it. Come on, Baby Blue Eyes." Miraculously, George had hit on the right approach to Siegel.

George recalled, "Somehow that remark got to Benny. He settled down. He even smiled and said, 'It's okay this time, Georgie. But you shouldn't have told all that stuff to her.' Now that he was calmed down, I said, 'You know you're not doing her any good. Right?' He agreed that maybe I was right. We shook hands, went downstairs, and had breakfast." From that day, whenever George saw Siegel in a rage and a violent quarrel seemed imminent, Raft called him "Baby Blue Eyes." It was the inexplicable key to calming Siegel's anger.

Siegel took advantage of Raft's well-known generosity and, when in need, borrowed from him several times. His first loan was a modest one and may very well have been a trial balloon for the later increasingly heavier loans. A local hood had conceived the daring idea of running a gambling ship anchored off the Santa Monica shore. Siegel became involved and asked George for a loan of $20,000 so that he could buy a "piece of the action." Raft would share in any dividends from the venture. "I haven't got that much cash, Ben," Raft said, but Siegel persisted and finally somehow Raft agreed to get the money.

"Early next morning I drove a hundred and forty miles to Arrowhead Springs and borrowed the money from my agent, Myron Selznick, as an advance against a future picture I was going to do. I took his check, turned around, and barreled back to Los Angeles in time to get to my bank and take it in cash over to Siegel. To this day I don't know why I did it. Except I just hate to turn a guy down and Benny acted like he needed the money bad." A few months later, George heard through the grapevine that the gambling ship venture was making big money. He figured that he was entitled to some of it from his $20,000 investment. Besides, he had accumulated debts from his past and present courtships and the expenses on his big home.

When they met, Siegel fielded Raft's questions about repayment of the loan. It was not George's style to pressure anyone, but finally he wrote Siegel politely requesting the $20,000. A few days after, Siegel pulled up to Raft's car as they were both driving down Sunset Boulevard and motioned George to pull over. They got out of their cars and Siegel handed George a check for $2000. "Here's two on account, George. I'll get the rest to you when I can. I'm pulling out of the ship deal." Over the next several months, in lots of $500 or $1000 in cash, Siegel repaid his debt to Raft. George was puzzled because he had heard that his "pal" was betting $2000 to $5000 a day on horseraces, fights, and ballgames. It was long past the time when one would ask for a logical explanation of Siegel's behavior; and Raft finally concluded that it would be hopeless to ever expect one.

In 1945, Siegel had a brainstorm. A luxury hotel and casino on the outskirts of Las Vegas would be a goldmine. Siegel, of course, was right and is now credited as being "the man who invented Las Vegas."

When Siegel conceived the idea, despite his loan from Raft, he was far from broke. The borrowed money was probably petty cash he used for personal pet projects that were not related to syndicate activity. In December 1945, after getting the approval of Lansky and others and with substantial backing by the Eastern mob, Siegel began building the Las Vegas Flamingo Hotel. Estimates vary, but the initial investment must have been in the area of one-and-a-half million dollars.

Siegel was like a man possessed, for the Las Vegas Flamingo was to be his monument to the world. From his viewpoint, it was one of the few truly legitimate activities he had been involved in. He used whatever "muscle" he could muster to get building materials during the postwar period when there were great shortages and harassed the workmen and building foremen. Del Webb, the project's main contractor, told Siegel that he should "lighten up" his attacks on the workers, for they knew Siegel's New York reputation and many of them were frightened. Siegel responded to Webb with his most charming and pleasant demeanor, even though in their ensuing conversation he admitted that he had personally killed twelve men. When he saw Webb's shocked expression, he quickly assured him, "Don't worry, nothing will happen to you. We only kill each other."

The project was by no means complete when the original one-and-a-half million ran out. Through every ounce of influence Siegel could muster, and with Lansky's less than enthusiastic support, Siegel acquired more money—but not before being denounced as a "psycho wasting money" by wiser, more conservative, mob leaders. Lansky was told to keep a sharp eye on Siegel and the project.

Siegel was driven to make a great financial success of the project as soon as possible. In the fall of 1946, Siegel and Virginia Hill had quietly slipped off to Mexico and were married. He was in serious debt to the Flamingo stockholders, and now, like every newlywed husband, he was anxious to prove his mettle as a successful breadwinner.

Siegel was a tough guy, if not a potential killer. But with Virginia he was an old-fashioned lover. He wrote her love poems addressed, "To My Sweetheart." Virginia Hill, who had long since lost count of the intimate relationships in her life, had a special love for Siegel. Their "love Bible" was *Forever*, a book by Mildred Cram which told a romantic fantasy about a modern Romeo and Juliet, who, unable to be together in life, assure each other that after death they will be reborn to consummate their love. Virginia and Ben read the book together many times— and they circled passages of dialogue that had special meaning. In the novel, Julie says to Colin, "If you should go first . . . and then what if I could never find you again? Or you me?" He answers, "We'll find each other. Somewhere. Somehow. You'll be born knowing about me, wanting me. And some day we'll come back here." Virginia heavily underscored a particular line: "Julie lifted her head. 'This is forever,' she said."

Siegel felt that the Flamingo would solve all of his problems and consequently, unwisely and prematurely, opened the hotel's gambling facility, even though the rest of the hotel was not ready. He used every public relations device he could to assure the success of the opening. There was to be a galaxy of stars present, but his public relations man gave him bad news: most of the actors and actresses who had been invited had not accepted.

Siegel phoned his friend George Raft for help. "'I'm in a spot, pal,' he pleaded with me. 'Can't you get some of your friends up to the opening? What about Joan Crawford and Greer Garson? And Spencer Tracy and Gary Cooper? Don't they want to come?'"

"I don't like to tell you this, Ben"—and Raft filled him in on the refusals. He told Siegel that William Randolph Hearst had passed the word around the front offices of every lot that he was against the whole idea (he meant gambling and mobs). "Everybody was told by their studio to stay away. Benny exploded over the phone. I felt sorry for him—why I don't know. I tried to cheer him up. I said he could count on me, Georgie Jessel was coming and so was Charlie Coburn. I told him I would try to get some other top names."

The planes Siegel had chartered couldn't get off the ground in Los Angeles because of a storm, and the few big names at the ringside tables weren't the ones he really wanted. George drove alone to Vegas. Monocled Charles Coburn, then almost seventy, went by train. Sonny Tufts and George Sanders arrived with Jessel; and Jimmy Durante was the Flamingo's first headline act.

To top off the awful drive to Las Vegas, Raft had a run of incredibly bad luck. Everyone seemed to win that first week except Raft. He lost $65,000 cash in a chemin-de-fer game. But even Raft's contribution wasn't enough to balance the disastrous gambling losses of the Flamingo. By late January 1947, they approached half a million dollars. Siegel had no alternative but to close down until the hotel section could be opened.

With Eastern money sources dried up—for the syndicate was prepared to write Siegel and his "mad plan" off the books—Siegel was in terrible trouble. Around the hotel he was belligerant and unnecessarily abusive to many employees. The only positive thing in his life was his marriage with Virginia Hill. He thought of taking whatever money was left and running off to Europe. Relentlessly pursuing the chance to make the Flamingo work—and with monumental chutzpah—Siegel flew from Las Vegas to Los Angeles to meet with Raft about his problems. He told Raft he desperately needed $100,000 cash not only to save the Flamingo but also his own life. Shocked, Raft told him, "I don't have that kind of dough, especially now; things are tight." But Siegel, a fast talker, knew how to deal with Raft, ever a soft touch to a friend in need. George raised the money by borrowing on his remaining resources, a substantial annuity fund he had maintained. There was no collateral put up by Siegel, and Raft received no receipt of any kind. (In 1965, when George was indicted for income tax evasion, he told the judge with a wry understatement, "I was never a good business man. I've always been a little careless with my money.")

With the bankroll acquired from Raft and other wealthy Hollywood people, Siegel planned to reopen the Flamingo. It was his last effort in every sense. He had planned to get the hotel into the black, take a percentage of the profits, and then retire in Europe. When Lansky heard of Siegel's plan over the phone, he flew expressly to Las Vegas to impress some facts on him. Although Lansky might approve this plan, no one else would. The two quarreled bitterly, for Siegel now had become defiant, even with Lansky.

The Flamingo was reopened in March 1947 with some rooms ready for occupancy, and by May the hotel and casino began to show a modest profit. New information, however, came to Lansky's attention about his errant partner, and an emergency meeting of the Flamingo stockholders was called at New York's Waldorf Astoria. Lansky, who kept tabs on Siegel, reported to the group that Virginia Hill had flown to Paris and that Siegel had put together a bankroll of $600,000 from hotel funds and was planning to join her. Albert Anastasia, who harbored a longtime dislike for Siegel, bluntly concluded *farlo fuori*—"Kill him." Siegel had exhausted whatever tolerance or good will his associates had allowed, including that of his former partner. Lansky agreed that Siegel could no longer be allowed to continue his activities.

By now, the Flamingo was operating on its own momentum. Siegel often visited Los Angeles and on the morning of June 21, 1947, showed up at Raft's house while Raft was having breakfast.

"He looked awful. He told me he hadn't slept for days, and that he was having a lot of trouble with the hotel and the investors from the East Coast. He invited me to have dinner with him that night at Jack's at the Beach. He seemed serious, like he had something to tell me. But I had a meeting planned with a producer, Sam Bischoff, to discuss a three-picture deal we were putting together.

"When I told him I couldn't make it, he said, 'Okay, Georgie.

194

I'm going to be at the house later on, so why not come by when you've finished whatever you're doing? Virginia's in Europe and we can talk there with no interruptions.'"

George finished his meeting with Sam Bischoff about nine at night. "In those days I was a bridge fiend. I used to play bridge every night I could at this club over in Beverly Hills. Since Benny probably wouldn't be home 'til maybe eleven o'clock, I figured I could get in a few games and then I would go over and see him later on.

"It must have been around ten-thirty or so when this actor, Dewey Roberts, comes busting into the room all excited and he says to me, 'Did you hear? It just came over the radio. Benny Siegel got killed in his house.'

"I was stunned. I didn't know what the hell to do. In a way, it wasn't my business, but I got in my car and found myself driving over to the house on Linden Drive. The police and photographers were all over the joint. So I turned around and went home."

Siegel had gone to dinner at Jack's at the Beach with his friend Allen Smiley, and they returned to Siegel's Beverly Hills mansion around ten o'clock. Siegel and Smiley sat side by side on the living room sofa, their backs to a large window that opened on to the garden. As they talked, Siegel spread a newspaper he had picked up at Jack's across his lap. The killer (or killers) arrived in the garden and balanced a 30-30 carbine on the windowsill. The first bullet blasted the window glass, went into Siegel's skull, and drove his right eye across the room. Another crashed into his head and seven more peppered the room.

One slug went through Smiley's sleeve. He fell to the floor and, apart from being unable to stop shaking for an hour, was unharmed. When the police arrived they found the bloody remains of Siegel, half of his head gone, sprawled on the couch. The newspaper spread on his lap had a stamped advertisement on the front page that read, "Good-night. Sleep well with the compliments of Jack's."

Virginia Hill was at a party in Paris when she heard the news of her husband's death. Frightened and in a state of shock, she went into seclusion. Several days later she went to Monaco, where she attempted suicide by taking an overdose of pills. She never told all she knew, not even when she was called as a star witness before Kefauver's Senate Crime Committee in 1951.

Several years later, after a number of attempts, she finally succeeded in committing suicide.

Twenty minutes after Siegel was gunned down in Beverly Hills, three men—Gus Greenbaum, Moe Sedway, and Morris Rosen—walked into the Flamingo Hotel and took over its management on behalf of its Eastern stockholders. Soon after that Siegel's wild dream became a reality and the Flamingo prospered. Gus Greenbaum successfully managed the hotel for seven years. It was then sold several times and succeeding owners all made enormous profits. The hotel was owned by a number of corporate bodies; however, as late as 1960, Meyer Lansky was known to receive income from the hotel. Las Vegas has become a wide fantasy town far beyond anyone's most extravagant imaginings—including those of its luckless founder, Ben Siegel.

After Raft arrived home the night of Siegel's death, representatives from the District Attorney's Office came to question him. "They asked me, 'What do you know about the killing?'

"'I don't know anything,' I said. 'But I can tell you this: when they shot Benny they shot me.'

"If my remark seemed mysterious to them at the time, they know what I meant by now. They say you can't take it with you, but Benny did. My hundred thousand dollars, I mean."

George's cryptic remark at that time masked his real sorrow over Siegel's death.

"As far as I'm concerned, he was a wonderful guy. Everyone I knew liked him. Benny had a temper—but who doesn't? As far as all those things about his past, they were probably true; but in those days in New York a lot of people were into the rackets. He was serious about the Flamingo. If he had lived it would have been fine. I think Benny and Virginia loved each other and it could have worked out.

"As for me, I might have been sitting there in that living room that night, right next to Benny. I guess it was fate, or just not my time to go."

Why would Raft—who had by the early forties clearly extricated himself from any contact with hoods and gangsters—maintain an association with a Benny Siegel? Certainly Raft better than anyone else could see beneath the thin veneer of Siegel's flashy Hollywood playboy polish to the psychopathic killer. Of course, he knew Siegel for the kind of man he was. At times erratic and dangerous, Siegel had a kind of personal style comfortably familiar to Raft, a style of talking, of being together, of shared interests—and of specified limitations. In different ways, they were against the system and the odds were against them. They shared a way of being fiercely independent, self-styled loners—and yet they were always trying to break through. They were adept at playing their luck. Siegel was not a common thug: he was a high-class hood with a first-rate reputation not only among his gangster associates but in Hollywood society. The Bugs–Meyer Combine was feared and respected in New York, and the charming, mysterious Benny Siegel was a popular Los Angeles figure.

By 1946 Raft had been earning several hundred thousand dollars a year for almost fifteen years. Having had the ability to command $100,000 for a few months' work on a picture, he felt that a loan of that amount was not impossible. And, when Siegel came to Raft for the loan of $100,000, Siegel was fighting for his life.

Another element that accounts for Raft's relationship to Siegel was George's film image. It was a double-edged sword: he wrestled furiously with his tough guy–gangster casting, yet he knew that it was crucial to his success. It had made him what he was, and there was no denying it. The redeeming facets he tried to insist on, the kinds of roles he refused were ways of tempering but not destroying the image. His acting depended crucially on what he observed, and he didn't realize the value of his knowledge of the gangster world until he came to Hollywood.

In the late forties with the film industry's waning power and the dismantling of the star system, film actors like George Raft no longer had their previous security. Moreover, Raft was older now, no longer physically convincing in the rough-guy roles that had made him famous.

In his fifties, in a declining industry, Raft was no longer in a position to gamble his career with people like Bugsy Siegel. His extravagant generosity and large expenditures had come to an end. If he was to continue in the movie industry, he would have to become less flamboyant and less ferociously independent. But this might entail not being "George Raft," and with his stubborn adherence to his personal ethics, and a degree of personal rigidity, it was unlikely that he would or could make such a transition.

197

9

THIS IS NO MOVIE

There is a brutal apocryphal story that circulates in Hollywood about the rise and fall of a star.

> Producer to his assistant:
> Phase I: Who is Rock Lamont?
> Phase II: Get me Rock Lamont.
> Phase III: Get me a Rock Lamont type.
> Phase IV: Get me Rock Lamont, but younger.
> Phase V: Who is Rock Lamont?

By 1950 George Raft was still well remembered—his name had become part of the American language—but his film career was headed for a back-page story. He was fifty-five now, and good roles suited to his particular gifts were scarce. It seemed as though movie marquee lights were growing dim all over Hollywood and across the nation. Television had made inroads and the major studios cut back to about twenty percent of the production they had maintained during the war years. In the ensuing years they retrenched by selling off their backlots to real-estate developers and their props to antique dealers and wreckers. They entered into co-production and distribution deals with independent companies and, finally, turned toward television, producing various series based on a property they owned—and whose production did not require established stars and expensive overhead. Actors were no longer given long-term contracts; now they worked on an independent basis. These were financially thin years for Raft and, within reason, he took whatever jobs were available.

He made several films in association with Sam Bischoff and other independent producers, including in 1947 *Christmas Eve* and *Intrigue*, in 1948 *Race Street*, and in 1949 *Johnny Allegro, A Dangerous Profession, Outpost in Morocco*, and *Red Light*. The reception and return from these films was unhappy proof that they lacked the box-office appeal of Raft's earlier films. Nevertheless, because Raft was willing to cut his salary without cutting his professional approach to the assignment, he continued to work in the United States and Europe: *Nous Irons à Paris* (1949) in France; *Lucky Nick Cain* (1951) in Hollywood. These films, however, proved to be vain efforts both on screen and at the box office. Back home, he starred in *Loan Shark* in 1952 and subsequently left for Italy to star in *The Man from Cairo* in 1953. His career appeared to be on the upswing again in 1954 when he co-starred with Ginger Rogers, Gene Tierney, Van Heflin, and Peggy Ann Garner in Nunnally Johnson's *Black Widow* and with Robert Taylor in *Rogue Cop:* To Raft's further delight, he was signed in 1955 to appear with Edward G. Robinson and Claire Trevor in *A Bullet for Joey*. His delight, however, was ill advised. Unfortunately for everyone connected with this movie it was poorly received. Raft, who was cast as an aging gangster, emerged on screen as a caricature of his former smooth, tough image, and a role that had originally seemed to be a great opportunity became an ironic disappointment. At the film's conclusion Raft helps Robinson stop a Communist pilot. After the death of the character played by Raft, Robinson says of him, "He died a hero and never knew it." The line was an ego boost for George, but it was probably the only satisfaction he got from the film; it did nothing for his career.

In 1952, it was apparent to George Raft and Mack Grey that Raft's present state no longer required the services Mack had provided. They were reluctant to separate after over twenty years, and Mack even offered to stay on for room and board; but honesty and practicality forced them to accept the facts: the good years had passed. Mack went to work for Dean Martin.

Now that he was approaching sixty, and having to accept second billing in B pictures, the last thing he needed was a "bad press." At this most vulnerable time, Raft was involved in another damaging incident.

The headline in the September 30, 1953, *Los Angeles Times* read "RAFT FREES CAPONE." The story under this caption was:

> Actor George Raft today helped his "old pal," John Capone, 49, brother of the late mobster, "Scarface" Al Capone, get out of jail here.
>
> The coin-flipping film star was in Capone's Beverly Hills Hotel room last night when the police burst in to arrest the Chicagoan and a friend, Joe Laino, 42, on suspicion of robbery, the customary "roust" booking. . . .
>
> Capone, who had $5,362 in cash with him, said he was in Los Angeles "to collect some dough I loaned a guy — and then drop a little in Las Vegas on the way home. . . ."

Today, Raft interceded, asking Police Chief C. H. Anderson to release the pair and guaranteeing they would "take the first plane out of here."

Raft offered another version of this story, one that radically clashed with the newspaper's. "As a favor to Jimmy Durante, I went to the Beverly Hills Hotel to pick up Lou Cohn, a friend of his. When I went upstairs, I found Cohn with Al Capone's brother, John. As far as I knew, this Capone had never done anything wrong. He was a gambler, and he used the name John Martin because he was embarrassed at the family connection.

"The minute I got inside, two Beverly Hills cops banged on the door. They walked in like *Dragnet* characters and gave Capone a ride to the station. I called my attorney Cyril Moss. Capone had committed no crime and he was released. The next day the newspapers screamed: RAFT FREES CAPONE. Of course Al Capone had been out of Alcatraz for some time—in fact he was dead—but I'm sure the public thought I had brought him back to Los Angeles to start something."

Such publicity, which gave Raft awkward notices at a critical time in his career, made him look harder for roles that would move him to the right side of the law. In *Black Widow*, he had played a police officer, and another chance to continue as a man of the law came when he was offered the lead in a short-lived television series, *I Am the Law*. In this he was a cool, determined detective who always got his man. "I feel badly about this series because once again I didn't use my head to reason out business or people. Lou Costello was bankrolling the project. Now I'd known Lou ever since I was in vaudeville and worked on the same bill with his brother, who was in a band. In fact, Lou used to carry his brother's saxophone case.

"I learned fast that television isn't movies—I mean the speed with which it's done. We went in high gear from eight in the morning and quit at six at night. A quarter of seven I'd be in bed —alone. The pace was knocking me out. I thought the series was lousy; yet we had some good reviews. Jules Levy and Charles Feldman were my agents at this time, and they wanted to buy three of these thirty-minute episodes and tie them together into a picture. They wanted to give me a hundred and twenty-five thousand and that much to Costello. Like an idiot, I said no. To this day I can't explain why.

"They finally 'did me,' like they say Owney Madden did Carnera. I was supposed to get ninety thousand for doing the *Law* series. By the time they were finished deducting expenses like office space, telephones, and stuff like that, I wound up with practically nothing. Later on they had reruns on the series, and called it *Briefcase* here and in England—but I was also cut out of those profits."

By the mid-fifties George Raft was a career in search of a vehicle. No one was beating at his door with offers—yet the high cost of maintaining the George Raft image was becoming unmanageable.

"Sometimes I wouldn't bother getting out of bed because as soon as my feet hit the carpet I needed a grand. Sometimes I needed a grand and a buck—and only had the buck. So I got back into bed. But the next day I needed two grand—one for the day I'd spent in bed. Maybe I was going to end up as the classiest bankrupt in Hollywood. It seemed that way. On top of everything else, I was in every high-class callgirl's black book. I mean those in town. And somehow they all thought George Raft should pay more than anyone else.

"One day this gorgeous young broad was over. For the hell of it, when she went to take a shower, I snuck a look in her little black book. I laughed to myself as I read 'Cohn $25, So-and-So $20, and Raft $50.'"

By making a few pictures a year, even with second billing, George made enough to maintain most of his expensive habits, and he continued to live in relative comfort. He did not capitulate to his declining income or resources. He was still the fastest man in town with a five- or ten-dollar bill, as any maître d', waiter, or carhop would attest. He also remained a soft touch for old "friends." The classic George Raft bankroll, however, was not supported by an appropriate bank balance.

One of his part-time jobs at this time was connected with Benny Siegel's Flamingo Hotel. After Siegel's demise, the hotel had been a big moneymaker for eight years under Gus Greenbaum's management. But by 1955, through skimming of profits by Eastern investors, large investments in redecorating, and the growing competition of other hotels, the Flamingo—on paper, at least—was verging on bankruptcy. At this time Al Parvin, a very successful Beverly Hills interior decorator and owner of a carpeting business, was owed a large amount of money by the Flamingo. A deal was arranged, very favorable to the Flamingo stockholders. Parvin and several other financially stable business men pooled their resources and took over the Flamingo. They began to manage the hotel effectively and brought it back into the black.

They began to vastly improve the quality of the entertainment, bringing in more top entertainers. Parvin, who had known and admired George Raft for many years, asked him to be an entertainment consultant on a part-time basis. Some of George's major booking contributions to the Flamingo included the garnering of Pearl Bailey, Dean Martin, and Frank Sinatra.

Pearl Bailey had had a personal success in the Harold Arlen–Truman Capote Broadway musical *House of Flowers* and was at this time performing in London; and Raft flew there to secure her services. Through George's efforts she was one of the first featured black entertainers in Las Vegas. She received a fat three-year contract involving $15,000 a week for eight weeks each year. In grateful high spirits she labeled him "the Abraham Lincoln of show business." For his efforts, he was offered, as partial payment, the opportunity to buy a share in the hotel.

"To buy into the Flamingo, I had to pay $65,000 for two points. I wasn't working regularly and I was kind of desperate. In order to raise the $65,000 I sold my house in Coldwater Canyon. Although it had originally cost me over $200,000 to build, I sold it for a lot less. That was how bad I was doing. I auctioned off the furniture, and I think I got something like $30,000 for the furnishings. My wife Grayce of course got half of everything."

In order to acquire the Flamingo stock, Raft was required to file an application with the Nevada State Gaming Control Board. This was to be the first in a series of disastrous setbacks.

"I was driving home from Santa Anita this one afternoon in the spring of 1955. The freeway was full of cars and my wallet was full of nothing after a bad day at the track. I had a lot of bad afternoons like that. I've dropped a fortune on the horses, and I kept on telling myself that I'd get even. I was driving alone that day, and I flipped on the radio just to hear some human voices. I heard a news broadcaster saying:

"'George Raft, the movie star who made his reputation playing gangster roles, had his past catch up with him today. The
205

Nevada State Tax Commission denied Raft a gambling casino stockholder's permit because he was friendly with such underworld figures as Owney "the Killer" Madden, Joe Adonis, Lucky Luciano, and Bugsy Siegel.'"

The news was a terrible blow. He had an appointment for dinner that night with a pal, producer Jack Dietz, who assured Raft that it would straighten itself out. While waiting for dinner, they watched television with Dietz's ten-year-old son, Jack Junior, whom George was very fond of.

"I sat in a chair in front of the set and little Jackie Dietz crawled up on my lap. I had known and loved the kid since he was a baby, and he always called me 'Pal.' We watched the baseball scores on one station, and then I switched to another channel to hear George Putnam, the TV newsman. That was a mistake, because here it came again: Putnam had a grim look like a judge on his face, and I felt that he was staring straight at me.

"He told how I had applied for a permit to buy $65,000 worth of stock in the Flamingo Hotel at Las Vegas, and how the tax commission had turned me down. He mentioned my association with Luciano, Siegel, Madden, and even Mickey Cohen, and said the commission figured I was a gangster on the screen and off.

"I flipped off the set and started to say something to Jackie. The kid looked embarrassed. I didn't know how to explain it to him, because I didn't understand it myself. I knew I couldn't eat any dinner. I grabbed my hat, and said good-bye. As I went out the door I could feel the kid's eyes following me. I felt like a criminal."

Despite all of those unfortunate associations, which he never denied, Raft's record was clean. As Raft has pointed out, he numbered many major sports figures among his acquaintances and friends and "That didn't make me a famous athlete, did it?" He did have a bad temper and he had been in many fights; but so had Bogart and McLaglen and many other screen tough guys. Yes, he had helped run some booze, which high society had no qualms in buying. Yes, he had defended the personal rights of men who had criminal records. Yes, he rented the services of women, but so did large corporations and even governments. Raft was learning the hard way that people know you by the company you keep; and if that company happens to be notorious the most fragile connecting thread can become a steel band in the public eye.

Many influential and respected personalities interceded on his behalf with the Nevada Gaming Commission. The commission spent six months making a meticulous appraisal of Raft's background and then concluded that nothing in his record could properly deny him a license.

Justice had triumphed, but with trying slowness. An article in the *Los Angeles Times* (December 20, 1955) reported the commission's conclusion:

> GEORGE RAFT WINS O.K. ON HOTEL INTEREST
> *Neveda Gambling Board Lifts Ban, Approves Actor*
> Nevada's new gambling agency switched signals today and recommended Movie Actor George Raft for an interest in the Flamingo Hotel at Las Vegas. . . .
>
> The action came after Raft was questioned for an hour about underworld figures with whom his name had been linked in a previous investigation made by the Tax Commission last spring.
>
> . . . Of slain gangster Bugsy Siegel, the actor said he knew him—"like everyone else in Hollywood." He added that he was on speaking terms with Virginia Hill, at whose home Bugsy was slain, and that he knew Joe Adonis. . . .
>
> John Capone, brother of gangster Al Capone, was linked with Raft once when he went to Capone's hotel to aid an inebriated friend, the actor said. . . .
>
> Before the board voted unanimously to recommend Raft's application, Chairman Robbins Cahill observed that many early-day entertainers had associations with hoodlums because most establishments presenting entertainment were run by bootleggers.
>
> He added, however, that he was satisfied that none of Raft's early connections exist today. . . .

Shortly after this painful encounter with the gaming commission, he had to sell his two percent in the Flamingo, with considerable loss on his original investment, because he had an urgent need of cash. If he could have held onto his investment, he might once again be living on Coldwater Canyon and be sitting poolside in a silk robe. Parvin confirmed that if Raft could have held on to his interest until 1960, when Parvin and his partners sold the Hotel-Casino, Raft's $65,000 investment would have been worth close to half a million dollars.

In 1956 Raft was intensively interviewed by writer Dean Jennings for a series of articles on his life "as told to Dean Jennings" that appeared in 1957 in *The Saturday Evening Post.* Raft contends that he was not given a chance to see the articles before they appeared, and he was extremely disappointed with the results. "They were shooting for sensationalism rather than my real life story. They had gory pictures of Benny Siegel shot to death, and other gangsters plastered all over the pages." Little attention was paid to his lengthy show business career and his real personal life.

Because of the series, several studios made offers to film Raft's biography, among them Paramount and 20th Century-Fox. Actors considered for the lead were Tony Curtis, Dean Martin, and Robert Evans. Evans recalls, "There was serious talk about my playing George Raft. One day I met with George and a long-time friend of his and mine, Sidney Korshak, about the possibility. I wasn't sure whether George really liked the idea of using me—but he knew Sidney approved and consequently was agreeable. The contrast between George's screen image and the man in person was remarkable. He was very polite and kind and told me that he would be pleased to have me play him in the proposed film. You know how movie deals are. For some reason the film drifted away, and I became involved in other movie projects."

Steven Brody, a producer for Allied Artists which had made a number of Raft's later films, finally acquired the rights. Raft saw several shooting scripts and found them—at the least—unsatisfactory. Finally, he dissociated himself from the project and resisted efforts to involve him as an advisor.

His misgivings about the film proved correct. *The George Raft Story,* containing as little accuracy as the typical movie biography, was released in 1961 and starred Ray Danton as Raft and Jayne Mansfield and Julie London as his girlfriends. The women had no real-life counterparts. The film received mostly negative notices. It seems, though, to be one of the more frequently shown late night television movies.

In 1956, producer Mike Todd gave George a cameo role in *Around the World in 80 Days,* a film that included Hollywood's

208

top stars. But other than this nothing of interest came his way. His involuntary leisure time was spent often in the company of 20th Century-Fox producer Darryl F. Zanuck, whom he had known since the making of *The Bowery* in 1933. Darryl, his wife Virginia, and his son Dick welcomed George as a member of the family. Richard Zanuck, for a time the inheritor of his father's position at 20th Century, later recalled his fondness for Raft. "George was always terrific to me when I was a kid, he took me to ballgames; and later on he was nice to me when I was in the army. He went out of his way to visit me on the base in New Jersey and took me out to dinner a few times. I always thought he was a fine actor and enjoyed seeing him in movies.

"When I say he was a good friend to my father, you have to understand my father is a complicated and rather distant person, a loner. But of the men my father was close to and had great affection for, I would put George Raft in the top ten."

Raft recalls his friendship with Darryl Zanuck. "There were sometimes months where he and I went out almost every night. I'd hang out with him when he was cutting a film. I'd go see him after I finished my work, say about ten at night, and we'd talk and look at his dailies. Then, before we left, he'd write notes for every producer under him who was shooting. What he thought of the rushes, what should be highlighted or chopped, what he thought was good or bad about pace, things like that. No question, he was a genius in cutting a picture.

"In the mid-fifties Darryl'd broken up with his wife and was seeing a European actress, Bella Darvi. Now few guys spy on their wives; girlfriends are something else—ask me. So once, while I was in New York, as a favor to *him*—he asked me to spy on Bella Darvi. He was insanely jealous of Bella and he'd heard a rumor that she was having an affair with a black fighter, someone I knew, in New York. Since I'd never asked anyone to do that for me, I hesitated to do this for anyone, even a best friend. But he kept after me until I finally thought—he's a pal, why not?

"So I did it, feeling all the while like a rat, and the only bright spot for me was—after I spent almost a week hanging out with this fighter all over New York and especially Harlem—that we had a few laughs and some fun in the uptown clubs. When Zanuck would call me next morning from Hollywood about the 'manuscript,' I was always able to tell him that the 'script'—which meant Bella—was clean and he ought to forget it; there was no reason to worry."

Since Raft was no longer in great demand, he often sought Zanuck's advice about working in some other capacity in the business. He knew enough about the Hollywood hierarchy to understand that in diminishing order respect was always accorded studio heads, producers, directors, writers, stars, ex-stars, and actors. Being just another out-of-work actor was a position that his tenuous self-esteem could not sustain for long. Therefore, he made an effort to become a director. This was not merely a desperate try, for he always had a great interest in working on the other side of the camera. After all, he had worked steadily in films for over twenty-five years and had a good eye for stories with wide audience appeal. And he knew a great deal about camera angles, lighting, and handling actors.

Recalling George's interest in directing, Zanuck said recently, "If I could have helped him I would have. But around that time I was in England and had less control at the studio. I recommended him a few times—but no one picked up the ball.

"I've always considered George a fine actor. He was a personality first, but he listened, moved well, and had a certain gracefulness on the screen.

"I've always like George a great deal and considered him one of my best friends."

Although, at the time, Zanuck tended to avoid making any direct statement about Raft's suggestions, in January 1957 he had written to Raft from London.

> . . . I know that more than anything else you want to keep busy and have some sort of continual activity. It basically gets down to this. You face exactly the same problem that 90% of the actors face when they try to get out of acting and go into another branch of the business. Everyone looks upon you as actors and nothing else. I bet there are at least a dozen actors who can direct as well as Kazan if they got the chance. After all, Kazan was an actor, but he had the sense to quit before he ever played a big part or before he became established as an actor; so he had no difficulty in living down the fact he was a "dumb actor."
>
> Dick Powell made the grade because he had sufficient

dough to buy a couple of stories and develop them with top writers. He sold himself as the director as well as the actor.

As an example, I know that —— has been trying for years to talk M.G.M. into letting him direct. I think he would be good at it. Frankly, I don't want to tell you of the headaches I had trying to get you in creative work at the studio as well as in our TV outfit. The only time I almost had you set was before the economy wave came along and that killed it. It always came to the same thing, "We like Georgie. He is my personal friend, but what experience has he had as a director or as a producer? How can I put him on when I am laying off experienced people? etc. etc."

This is why last year I urged you to try to find a story and develop it on your own. When a man comes into a studio as the owner of a finished script they are inclined to at least listen to him. . . .

Zanuck's letter, though somewhat evasive, was encouraging. When a few months later Raft received a call from Zanuck's production chief in London, Robert Goldstein, about a role in a film that was to be shot there, he assumed that this was a more concrete expression of help. It turned out to be what Raft later called "a swift kick in the ass."

With evident distress Raft recalled the misadventure: "In March 1957, while I was at the Fairmont Hotel in San Francisco on some business, I got this call from Goldstein. I'd never met him, but he sounded like a nice guy and he asked me, 'George, will you do a picture with Bella Darvi in London?' I said, 'Of course.' Zanuck knew I needed the work. And I thought, with the warmest feelings, this was really nice of Darryl. Goldstein told me someone I didn't know in L.A. would deliver $5000 to me as an advance on doing the film. A few days later I got the money at home. In those days international flights were brutal—or maybe my age made me feel like they were. I had a short layover in New York and arrived in London on a Friday morning, totally exhausted. The press was there, which was nice, and I told them I'd come over to make a movie for Fox, which Zanuck was producing.

"Two guys who said they worked for Goldstein met me at the airport and took me to the Dorchester Hotel, where there was

211

more press to ask me about the picture, its name, and so on. I
told them I didn't really know, although these two guys had told
me it was a script about a detective who's on his way home from
a case. At the airport he gets a call to go back where he's just
been, to work on a new case. I didn't really know what it was
all about. Later on, after I read the script, I still didn't know
what it was all about because it was so jumbled, very loose, no
direction, and less continuity. But most scripts are written to be
rewritten." George asked the two men about Zanuck's participation and received a lot of Hollywood doubletalk about how
"Zanuck wanted him for the part," George Raft was a "natural,"
but no straight answers. He was ready to quit and go home
because of the script, the confusion, and the mystery of "Where's
Zanuck?" The two men prevailed on George to stay put at the
Dorchester, and they assured him that Zanuck would phone
later.

"I unpacked, took a bath, had some food sent up, and was rest-
ing—when the telephone rang. It's Darryl, calling me from his
hotel. He says, 'Glad you're here, baby.' I said, 'What's this picture all about?' He doesn't answer me straight. He says, 'I'll
call you back later.' He calls me back, and says, 'George, talk to
Bella, she's upset.' I don't know what the hell he's talking about,
it's just a jumble, even worse than the script, but I told him to
put her on.

"So Bella Darvi gets on the phone and she is crying how much
she hates me! Finally she told me that Darryl had told her I
didn't want to do the picture because she's in it! How's that for
an opener? I calmed her down and assured her I wanted to be in
the movie with her by saying something that made sense. 'Bella,
listen,' I began, 'why would I come all the way over here if I
didn't?'

"Finally Bella calmed down, so I asked her to put Darryl back.
He gets on, very pleasant, and I asked him what exactly was he
trying to do to me? Why was I here in the first place? Was he producing this project?

"'Calm down,' is his reply. Calm down, I almost hemorrhaged
when he told me that this wasn't a Fox production but only a
project he was sponsoring for Bella.

"By this time I'm confused and mad as a son-of-a-bitch at him
and myself. I still couldn't get anything sensible from Zanuck on
212

the phone, so I told him that I was coming directly over to his place. By the time I got there, exhausted and upset, he'd gone out, his secretary didn't know where. I went to club after club looking for him, which took all night. Fortunately for him, I can say now, I didn't find him because the way I felt I would've choked out of him why he'd brought me to London to screw me around like that.

"It was morning by the time I got back to the Dorchester for about three hours' sleep. At about ten the director, the writer, and the production manager all arrive at my hotel for a story conference. But even if I'd slept for a hundred hours the biggest mystery in all this would've been the terrible script. If Bella'd cried about the script, I'd've been happy to join her. Still, I knew that movies make for a hard life, so I asked this very nervous writer if he'd seen me in pictures. 'Yes,' he said, 'I've seen all your films.' 'Good,' I said. 'Now do you think this is the right part for me?' He was honest and said, no, he didn't think so. And the director now chimed in that he'd seen all my pictures and knew I'd made pictures in Europe, but this wasn't my kind of a role. However, they were going to rewrite the entire script by Monday, when we were scheduled to begin shooting. This wasn't for real, I reminded them. This was Saturday morning, so how could a script be entirely rewritten by the day after tomorrow? But I heard what I heard, and I heard the production manager's assistant say, 'We must start Monday. We have everything set.'

"'Now look, honey,' I was polite, 'that's your life, to start Monday. But this is my life and it's not gonna last to Monday if I don't take care of myself. And one thing I've gotta follow now, at this stage of my life, is to take care of myself because no one else will. And nobody's shown me how you can have a new script by Monday.'

"Suddenly, some smart-ass producer, dressed like a clown in a beret, leather jacket, and leather gloves, barges into my suite, walks over to me, and in the snottiest way possible asks me, 'What is this I hear? You're not going to do this movie?' I jumped up. 'Hold it, you son-of-a-bitch. Go outside, knock on the door, and then — if I decide to let you in — be sure you come in like a gentleman.'

"He saw I was mad, ready to climb all over him, so he went out, did as he'd been told, and acted a lot nicer after I let him in.

213

Finally I just had to tell them I wasn't going to do the picture, period. Now would they please leave? I went to bed and didn't leave my room until Monday, when I caught up with Zanuck at his hotel and called him everything under the sun for bringing me across the world for nothing. A man, any man, would've hit me for even the least of what I said to him. Finally I told him I was willing to return the five grand they'd advanced, either to him or whoever was responsible for this mess. He said, 'George, calm down. I have appointments all day. Give me a call tomorrow and we'll straighten the whole thing out.'

"Next day, when I called the hotel and got his secretary on the phone, she said, 'Oh, Mr. Raft, I'm so tickled to death to talk to you because of the way you yelled at him. Nobody ever yells at him that way. It was a pleasure to hear someone finally stand up to him.' Then she told me that Zanuck had left the night before for New York. I was furious. I left for home on the first available flight."

It took months for Raft to learn what role had been assigned to him in this grotesque farce. Zanuck, it turned out, had to leave London, where he was then living, on business. Still insecure and suspicious of Bella Darvi, he had concocted a phony movie production to keep her busy while he was away, with George Raft flown in from Hollywood as the star to give the film project an air of reality. In short, the project was a cover to make Raft a high-priced chaperone for Zanuck's girlfriend. His humiliation and anger were such that for sometime Raft avoided going anywhere in Hollywood where he might run into Zanuck.

Raft's hostility toward Zanuck for what he considered to be "the shaft" almost exploded one evening two years later in New York's Little Club. He was having dinner with the owner when he saw Zanuck, and a party of Gregory Ratoff, Charles Feldman, Leland Hayward, and Zanuck's latest girlfriend, Juliette Greco, enter the club. Raft avoided Zanuck's eyes and Zanuck's apparent desire to greet him. When Zanuck and his party were seated, George told the owner of the Little Club, "I'm going to make your joint famous tonight." Then Raft rose from the table and approached Zanuck. Before Raft could get to Zanuck, Feldman, a good friend of Raft's, took him aside and tried to settle the matter peaceably. Zanuck joined them and said, "Look, George, we've been friends too long to let this thing stand between us. I was all wrong." George looked away and whispered, "I still can't figure out why you did that to me." They both finally decided to let the matter drop and shook hands.

When asked for confirmation of the story, Zanuck said, "You know, it may have been exactly the way George told it to you. But frankly I was so busy in those days with a variety of deals that I just don't remember that happening. George and I have been friends for over forty years and I'm sure we have had a few misunderstandings in our time."

Whatever the precise details, the whole business had a profoundly negative effect on Raft's interest in continuing his acting career. He was an ex-star, and people in that position are no better than, to use Zanuck's term, any other "dumb actor." In a recent interview, Jack Lemmon commented feelingly on Raft's situation:

"Everyone adulates a star and then, boom—all of a sudden—they stop. No matter how well adjusted you are, you're bound to take it personally. It has to be a shock to your ego. For George, I'm sure it meant far more than not being offered good parts. That was a loss I feel he could accept. However, he lost something terribly special—an exalted position in the world. One day you're a superstar as George Raft was. Then, pow, suddenly it's over. Emotionally that must be a terrible blow to a person."

Raft had seen enough of the chicanery and doubledealing that went on in Hollywood to know that this experience was only the beginning for him—if he permitted himself to be further victimized. In the new Hollywood, where jobs were scarce, each interview was an emotionally traumatic event. An actor might be told, "You're *in* the picture—we'll be in touch with you." Sometimes this meant the actor was hired; too often, it was a Hollywood-type message that meant, "Sorry, pal, you're a nice guy, but we can't use you. I don't have the courage to give you a flat no because I know how desperately you need the job. Let's just pleasantly shake hands, and don't let the doorknob hit you in the ass on your way out." If the actor had straightforwardly asked, "Please tell me the truth—am I in or out?" he would have been guilty of violating a basic rule of the double-message game—don't mess with evasiveness—and next time out the producer might not even call him in for a tryout.

In his weakened position Raft might have to grovel before the

powerful—a posture he detested and would not assume for anyone. Consequently, when an offer came to work in another area
of show business he was eager to accept. He would still accept
what he thought were appropriate film jobs; but he needed income from another source that would allow him to maintain his
independence as well as his integrity.

His association with the Flamingo had given him substantial
reputation as a man with a good eye for talent. People in all
branches of show business had enormous respect and affection
for George, and a call from Raft to entertainers like Frank Sinatra or Dean Martin would command attention.

In the spring 1958, Jerry Brooks, another crony from Broadway days when he owned a nightclub called the Famous Door
phoned Raft from Havana and offered him the position of entertainment director for the new Capri Hotel which Brooks was
managing. The Del Capri was a large, luxurious 300-room hotel
equipped with a posh gambling casino. Brooks felt that with Raft
on board he could edge out the keen competition from the other
Havana gambling casinos and hotels. Raft's name would draw not
only visiting Americans, but big-name entertainers.

During the few weeks in the spring of 1958 that George Raft
hosted at the Capri, it did phenomenal business. He booked Tony
Martin, Jose Greco, and Mexico's most popular singer, Pedro
Vargas, into the club. When the heat reduced tourism in June,
Raft requested and received a leave of absence.

On his return to Los Angeles, Billy Wilder offered him a feature role in his forthcoming comedy, *Some Like It Hot* (1959). The
picture had a sixteen-week shooting schedule, and after completion Raft planned to return to his post at the Capri.

Hot, which starred Marilyn Monroe, Tony Curtis, Jack Lemmon, Pat O'Brien, Joe E. Brown, and Raft, opens in the mid-
twenties of Al Capone's Chicago. By coincidence, two musicians,
Lemmon and Curtis, witness a St. Valentine's Day-type gangland massacre committed by Spats Colombo, played by Raft, and
his mob. Lemmon and Curtis escape from Spats by joining—in
drag—an all-girl band that features singer Sugar (Marilyn Monroe). The band heads for an engagement in a palatial beachfront
hotel in Miami.

Most of the shooting was at Universal Studios and La Jolla,
where the behind-the-scenes activities of the principals provided

events even more complex than the film's antic plot. Arthur Miller was constantly in attendance on the set to patiently care for his wife, Marilyn, who, in addition to her debilitating insecurity, was also pregnant. Their marriage was never an easy one and at this particular time Miller felt he had to be with Marilyn every possible minute. George remembered how Miller would sometimes hold her arm as he led her on and off the set.

On the set and after hours, Pat O'Brien, Joe E. Brown, and Raft reminisced about the old days. According to Raft, O'Brien, Brown, and himself were Wilder's "utility infielders." Whenever Marilyn would not or could not be on the set because of a crisis, physical or psychological, they would be called upon to film scenes that were to occur later in the schedule.

"Her life as a star was hell. I can imagine what it must have been for her. Everywhere she looked, some photographer or reporter wanted to get at her. She seldom had a chance to relax or concentrate on her acting. Whenever she appeared on the set, some photographer was there trying to take a picture of her for *Look* or *Life*, while a reporter was begging for just the smallest interview. Wouldn't she please answer just *one* question?

"Even at night, when a person likes to take it easy, the studio forced her to do publicity things. Here was a sex symbol who'd become a slave to her career and what the public wanted. "I only talked with her a few times, but she was always friendly, someone who'd go out of her way to say hello. It was Marilyn's suggestion that the picture end with Sugar and Spats together, tangoing into the sunset. Billy Wilder liked the idea at first, but then decided to end the movie on a comedic note with Joe E. Brown and Jack Lemmon—maybe because Marilyn wasn't always available.

"Strange thing. I knew her long before the movie, since Joe DiMaggio and I were very good friends. While I was making that television dog, *I Am the Law*, he was on the set with me almost every day. Marilyn was working then and I can't tell you how many times a day, after I finished a setup, he'd call Marilyn. I remember saying to him, 'I'm seeing some girl, so why don't all of us have dinner tonight?' He'd answer, 'I'd like to, but Marilyn is usually knocked out by evening and we don't go out at night.'

"Joe was madly in love with her and followed her whenever he could. I know he quit a good job he had, toward the end of her
217

life, because there was some chance they'd get back together again. Once he went up to Canada, where she was filming. He didn't live at her hotel but stayed at another place just to be near her. During those last years of her life, when she was so depressed, he'd come to see her. He would have done anything to help her. If only she could have told him or somebody what she needed. A lot of people loved that sweet, beautiful woman.

"The last time I saw Marilyn I was driving down Sunset, near the Beverly Hills Hotel, and had to stop for a light alongside a big, chauffeur-driven black Caddy with the shades down. All of a sudden, Marilyn, who was in the limousine, saw me. The shade went up and there she was, with her big smile, waving hello. She looked pale, but gorgeous as ever. I cried when I heard what finally happened to her."

Except for the delays and temperamental flareups caused by Monroe, the filming of *Some Like It Hot* went relatively smoothly. There was one incident, though, where Billy Wilder was the culprit. In the opening scene Raft, as Colombo, and his boys rub out his arch-rival, Toothpick Charley played by George Stone, with a tommy gun. Spats, as a final act of contempt, was to kick Charley's trademark, a toothpick, out of the dead man's mouth. Charley had a real toothpick in his mouth. Raft feared that he would hurt the man lying on the ground, an old actor friend, and when he kicked at the toothpick he was too far from the mark.

After ten unsuccessful takes, Billy Wilder exhorted Raft to "please, please, George, kick the toothpick." To no avail. Finally Wilder, in his frustration, volunteered to prove how simple it all was. But when he kicked at the toothpick, he missed by an inch, the toe of his shoe struck the man in the face, and he had to be hospitalized. At Raft's suggestion, the scene was made safe by substituting a painted metal nail for the toothpick. This enabled Raft to take careful aim and do the scene on the next take.

Jack Lemmon had fond memories of the film—one of his early starring roles—and he smiled as he remembered another funny incident. Lemmon, disguised as a woman, was forced by the situation to accept the attentions of Joe E. Brown, who played an eccentric millionaire. Lemmon and Brown were to do a tango that involved passing a rose from mouth to mouth.

"The studio had hired this young guy to teach Joe E. Brown

and me the tango. But it developed that the kid really didn't know the dance. For a time we were stuck; then George came to the rescue. You know he was a sensational dancer—especially the tango—and he gave us lessons for hours. It was the most outrageous, funniest real scene on the set. Just visualize George Raft, Joe E. Brown, and Jack Lemmon seriously engaged in doing the tango together. Somehow Billy should've worked the three of us dancing together into the film."

A long-time fan of Raft's, Lemmon became impressed with him personally and professionally during their work together. "The first time I really met George was on the set of *Some Like It Hot*. I must say I was bowled over by how different he actually was from the tough guy I had expected. You'd think I would know better being in the business myself, but I was truly surprised.

"I was struck by his courteous behavior and generosity. He was a gentleman, a terribly likable man, almost shy. He gave no evidence of the star syndrome. Maybe he did in days when he was one of the biggest stars in this town—but I doubt it. He was self-effacing, a total pro, and just a terribly sweet guy. I don't know anybody in my experience who knew George then or now who doesn't share my opinion of him.

"George and Pat O'Brien were terrific guys on the set. They were very patient, very cool, very calm, very professional. They never gave anyone trouble. I never saw George unpleasant. All of us have a right to be in a grumpy mood or be upset by something; but I never saw George in that kind of a mood. Also, he was never pushy, never coming on with the good-old-days crap or any of that stuff. He was terrific.

"George is a different kind of actor than I am. I've spent all my life purely trying to be an actor and to be the best I can in playing a variety of parts. I try as much as possible to completely get away from, let's say, a Jack Lemmon personality.

"I don't think that George ever had that kind of desire in his work. George is a bright man and what he did with his career was very wise, since he took whatever acting talent he had and those aspects of his personality that were the most unique and used them to the fullest. Humphrey Bogart did the same thing. Ninety percent of the time Bogart played himself. George is in that genre of actor.

"There are so many strong, identifiable personal traits and mannerisms that there's no escaping them. I don't think that Bogart could have talked differently if he had to. George used certain mannerisms that were perfect for him, and fit like a glove.

"If George believed that he was playing himself in a role, he identified more and more strongly with that part. And he was not willing to accept parts where he behaved in a way he wouldn't want to act in his personal life. I believe that during his career George's concern to play only sympathetic roles was certainly more justified than it is today. The audiences in the thirties and forties might have really blamed George Raft for playing that type of role. In those days there was more interest in an actor's personal life. Being a movie star was different. People identified with the man behind the mask—with the actor as a person."

There are fewer personality-stars today, partly because no major studio has sufficient interest in a single star to persistently devote their efforts to build them up. They may have a star for only a one-picture deal. This is in contrast with the 1930–1946 star system: then, one star could keep an entire studio in the black. The dominant number of film stars today are first-rate actors and the general public is much less involved with their personal off-screen lives. This specific difference is partially revealed by, among other factors, the tremendous decline in audience attendance from around eighty-five million per week to eighteen million.

When George completed his work in *Some Like It Hot*, he was exhausted. Although he did not look it, he was sixty-three years old, and he had begun to develop an aggravated and debilitory respiratory ailment. Smoking, and the local smog, had taken their toll. In fall and winter 1958, he rested and spent most of his time in the company of his Hollywood friends.

Jerry Brooks eventually telephoned Raft from Havana to learn when he intended to return to the Capri, where his presence was sorely missed. Could he at least return for the two weeks of Christmas and New Year, when business was at its crest? Raft was reluctant to leave Beverly Hills, and, although he had never pretended to be religious, he was sentimental about Christmas and did not care to spend that holiday in Havana. Also, revolutionary fervor was at a feverish pitch in Cuba. Castro had made

220

vital thrusts into Batista's Havana stronghold and the country was steeped in violence. In the end it was Raft's financial situation and ongoing obligations that compelled him to return to the Capri.

He landed in Havana the day before Christmas 1958, and he was pleased with the suite he was given. In every way, his job was easy and familiar. Evenings he would dress—in this tropical city a silk tuxedo was in order—then take the elevator to the casino, his new set, where he starred in the role that no one else could duplicate: George Raft, manager of a posh gambling casino. Days passed pleasantly, uneventfully, until a report circulated that Castro and his troops were but a day's march from Havana.

On New Year's Eve George was in the club, holding a soft drink for the sake of appearances and enjoying the happy people around him. There was lively music, good food, and, obviously, expensive liquor. Everybody was animated with the holiday spirit, and Raft pushed his way through the boisterous crowd wishing everyone a Happy New Year. He was accompanied by a girl who had recently won a Miss Cuba contest.

"About three-thirty in the morning, my girlfriend was a little tight, so I gave her the key to my room and suggested she go up and rest, since I planned to join her shortly. There was a swimming pool near the suite. A perfect set up with a tropical moon.

"I'd done my job, greeted everyone, wished them all Happy New Year and all that. Around six in the morning I headed for my suite. There she was, asleep in my bed, but I noticed how she'd opened one eye when I came in the room. Now she's half-awake and amorous. 'Feliz Año Nuevo,' I said as I got between my special silk sheets, alongside this fantastic girl. In the middle of this beautiful scene—suddenly—machinegun fire! And what sounds like cannons! These made me put things in neutral while I phoned down to the desk. 'This is Mr. Raft,' I said. 'What's going on down there?' The operator answered but I could hardly hear her—there was so much commotion. Finally I made out what she was saying. 'Mr. Raft, the revolution is here. Fidel Castro has taken over everything. He's in Havana! Batista has left the country!'

"I started out of bed, but my girlfriend, still a little tight, thinks it's all great fun and very affectionately tries to pull me back. Yet I have to find out what the shooting's all about. So I

221

grab the nearest shirt and pants, a pair of slippers, no socks, and head for the lobby.

"Everybody working for the hotel is yelling and screaming, 'Bandits are coming! Hide everything!' It was mass confusion. People running back and forth. I realize no one's in charge at this time except maybe me, since people are asking me what to do. Then I remembered the old gag about how to be a weatherman — first look out the window. Which is what I do — to see people running, soldiers shooting in the streets. I actually saw people being killed! But along with this — there are all these civilian kids — mostly teenagers, throwing rocks and bottles through store windows and houses. Then some of them began to aim at the hotel."

A group of revolutionaries, according to Raft's count about 100, charged into the lobby, yelling and screaming in Spanish. They began to demolish the place. A few of the *locos* sprayed the bar with machineguns, and glasses broke as if in a scene from *Scarface*. Luckily, nobody was hit by the gunfire.

"I wasn't sure what the hell to do, even though, without knowing it, I'd become the director and star. So I got on this table — in the middle of all this mayhem — and began to shout something like 'Calm down! For Chrissake, calm down!' I was surprised as hell when all of the yelling, shouting, and smashing stopped dead.

"The leader of these armed hoods, this girl, pointed and yelled in English, 'It's George Raft, the movie star!' Now I had their attention, but I didn't really know what the hell to say. I had no script, no lines, but I managed some kind of a speech about how I was an American citizen and neutral. That if they cooperated they could have food and things like that. It worked! They calmed down, did some lightweight looting, and most of them left. The others just sat around drinking Cokes. So while the shooting and all that continued in the streets, the Capri was saved, at least for the moment.

"But we couldn't get out of the hotel. It was dangerous to go into the streets. Remember, people were being killed. Some tough Cubans came into the hotel and sold protection for big figures, and some of the guests went for it."

George attempted to call J. Edgar Hoover, who had been helpful to him years ago at President Roosevelt's Birthday Ball, but he couldn't get a line to Washington. People were not allowed to leave the hotel—not because of any orders but because even with protection the streets were too dangerous and the shooting was heavier and wilder. The next day no maids came to make up the rooms, and the rest of the staff disappeared. Luckily, the hotel had a substantial storeroom full of food. Because of his position, and probably because of his screen image, people assumed George could help them. After all, in a dozen or more films he had been in tougher spots than this and always came through.

"Guests are begging, 'Mr. Raft, get us out of here.' One little guy got to me about four or five times, but I couldn't help him, or anyone else, including the former Miss Cuba who was still in my suite suffering from a lack of attention.

"I tried to get the American ambassador on the phone but had to settle for someone in his office, who said, 'The only thing I can tell you is that Mr. Smith is very busy with the States about the problem.' Then he hung up. Now what could I say to our guests except that they oughta stay in their rooms and keep off the streets? We had a P.A. system at the pool and I used it to tell our guests that I'd just talked to Mr. Smith, *himself,* and he'd given me a message for them. We'd all have to stay put a little longer. So lots of guests went to the roof—since the building was tall—to look down into the streets to see a real war where people were actually lined up and shot!

"One fellow kept buttonholing me with dialogue, like, 'George Raft, you're a big man, get me out of here.' To which I'd say that I couldn't get myself out. Well, this went on for days, until there came a morning when Castro's regular army came marching into town and some soldiers came to our hotel for rooms, which I politely gave them. For reasons I'll never understand, they preferred sleeping on the floors to using beds."

During the following week, George was asked by some official to go on Cuban TV, where in English, with a Spanish translation, he made a plea for peace. He told people that they could have some food from the hotel and they could use it any way they wanted. His main message was that the Americans were neutrals and should be treated decently. He was now considered a hero at the hotel by the trapped guests and even by the former hotel staff, who had now become part of Castro's army. "One kid, who used to bring me breakfast every morning, now was a bigshot, and said to me, 'George, give me some cigarettes.' Since he carried a cannon I never argued with him about anything he wanted."

One night George was on the phone with the wife of a congressman that he knew. She asked, 'How's it going?' and he replied, 'Fine, fine.' Suddenly shooting broke out. Raft dropped to the rug because bullets were ricocheting around the room. He made it to the elevator and the suite of a Mr. Shepard, one of the hotel's managers, where about forty guests were hiding out. They put out the lights and hugged the floor because revolutionaries were shooting at the Capri from the National Hotel, formerly owned by Meyer Lansky and now Castro's main headquarters in Havana. George never learned why Castro's troops suddenly decided to take pot-shots at the Capri. Perhaps they were just drunk and thought they'd have some fun with the Yankees there.

"This confusion went on for about two weeks. By the fifteenth day we're out of food, the place is ransacked and in a shambles. Everyone left, including me, is frantic, at the end of our ropes. Suddenly I get word from another official—all of their names sound the same to me—to get ready. They tell me a plane's ready at the airport and we're cleared to leave for the States. That's all swell, but I'm thinking how the hell are we going to make it to the airport? Finally, on this sixteenth day, the manager of the casino and I were driven to the airport by two tough Cuban soldiers, in a no-class old Chevy painted like an army tank. I hoped we were going to the airport because we were in their hands and helpless. At the airport we sat, waited, and passed time by looking out at the plane on which we're supposed to leave.

"Some airport. Armed troops all over it. Everything in the terminal torn up and vandalized. Yet, in the middle of all this mess, on the wall there's this sharp picture of me in an ad, welcoming people to the Capri. Frankly at that moment it seemed to me it was the only civilized thing left in that crummy terminal.

"Finally I go through immigration with the casino manager. While officers talked to him, I smoked two cigarettes. At last he came back and I asked what'd taken so long. And he said, 'They were talking about you.' I said, 'About me? What were they talking about me for?'

"Before he could answer, four guys with guns and an airport official came up to tell me, 'Mr. Raft, these men want you.' That was obvious, because they surrounded me, all with little machine-guns, and they marched me into an office. It was hot there, sticky, so I take my hat off. Some son-of-a-bitch grabbed it and I never saw it again.

"Next this guy—I guess he was the leader—asked me in broken English if I had a passport. I said 'Yeah, I'm an American. Here it is.'

"That over, they began to argue with each other in Spanish, while they ate sloppy cheese sandwiches. Then this one guy searched me and took all the money I had on me, twenty-eight hundred in cash. After they took my money the three of them slammed me up against the wall. They stepped back like they were a firing squad and these three goons pointed their guns at my head. I said to myself, 'This is no movie.'

"Beads of perspiration broke out all over me. At last I had voice enough to ask why they were picking on me. I'd put up every soldier who'd come into the Capri. One guy said, in broken English, 'We no know what you did or didn't do, Señor Raft.' He looked toward his leader, still eating his cheese sandwich, while I'm against the wall with the three guns still aimed at my head.

"Finally the leader says, 'Where's the money?' I said, 'Look, you got the twenty-eight hundred I had on me. Your men searched me. That's all I have.' I could tell he didn't believe me.

"I was absolutely petrified, my clothes soaked with sweat, I was ready to ask for a priest. They kept on chattering in Spanish when they weren't laughing. This went on for what seemed like eternity, but it was only around twenty minutes.

"In the movie *Background to Danger* about three times in the script I was in a similar situation, with guns pointed at me by Sydney Greenstreet and Peter Lorre. Instead of 'Where's the money?' Greenstreet always wanted to know, 'Do you have the plans?' Before I always had a script to help me figure some way to break loose, and I usually made a fool out of guys like Lorre, Greenstreet, and other tougher characters. God knows how many times on the set I broke out of prison or away from cops in a hail of bullets. But this was the real McCoy. These were real guns, real bullets, and these guys meant business. I couldn't think of anything—except I figured this was it.

"Around then, a big, fat captain walked in—and I hoped like in a movie the guy came from the Governor with a reprieve. He looked at me as if he knew what I was thinking. Finally, he freezed me with a smile and invited me and the boys with their choppers to follow him. At that moment I would have followed the Devil to get out of that room. Then I was facing a bigger officer, someone who looked like a Spanish general right out of Central Casting. He's big, mean, and red-faced. Funny, it crossed my mind that the head of wardrobe at Paramount would never've put him in a uniform as crummy as the one he was wearing.

"Yet, since it looked like I was going to get a reprieve from my execution, I began to feel much better. I was taken to the plane and ordered to pick out my suitcases from the pile near the gangwalk. It finally dawned on me. Now I knew what they were after. You see, the twenty-eight hundred they'd robbed me of in the little room was chicken feed, since they suspected that I was smuggling a few hundred grand, maybe even a million dollars, of the Capri's casino bankroll out of the country.

"They tore into my luggage, looking for cash! But all they found was my clothes, a few bottles of cologne, and some pictures of me—publicity glossies I'd give away to fans.

"Now that I was a little out of the range of their guns pointed at my head, I began to get mad as hell. My clothes were scattered all over the ground, and they didn't care how dirty anything got. When they jammed my clothes and things back into the suitcases, they had no feelings about how they stuffed my good suits and shirts—they even left some of my clothes hanging out. I was furious but kept it to myself.

"Then came the final insult. This captain, with a big shiteating grin on his face, comes up to me with one of my publicity photos. He holds it out with a pen and asks for my autograph! While I smiled and autographed the picture, I called him every kind of son-of-a-bitch, but under my breath—because his soldiers were still around the airplane. Finally I got clearance and boarded the airplane for Miami. It's corny but after we landed in the States— I got down on my shaky knees and kissed the ground.

"I had many regrets after I gave Bogart the role of Rick, the slick casino owner, in *Casablanca;* but the part caught up with me in Cuba. The Havana movie I starred in was more exciting than *Casablanca*—it had a live revolution as a background, and the bullets in the machineguns pointed at my head were real."

Returning from his Cuban ordeal, he found Hollywood life dull and uneventful. He had bright memories of the days he lived on top of the Hollywood hills, but adjusting to the reality of his present existence was a painful experience.

Life in the sixties would deal further blows, but a man who gives Jack Warner $10,000 when the movie cobra, admittedly, was about to give *him* $10,000 is destined to wind up on the short end of any business deal.

George Raft handled most of his business arrangements on his own. A few friends gave advice, but they seldom had the time to provide the followup required to convert propositions, even good ones, into profit.

Most of his income came from a string of undistinguished supporting roles, cameos and even slapstick burlesques of his old image. In 1960, when he returned from his Cuban ordeal, Frank Sinatra and his friends in the Rat Pack made *Ocean's Eleven*, a picture about war veterans who plan and execute the robbery of a Las Vegas casino. Major parts were played by Dean Martin, Joey Bishop, Sammy Davis, and Richard Conte. George Raft did a cameo as a Las Vegas hotel manager. Somewhat damaging to his self-esteem were two pictures he made with Jerry Lewis, *The Ladies' Man* (1961) and *The Patsy* (1964), even though he was grateful to Lewis for giving him a break. In a French film, *Rififi in Paris* (1965), he played, opposite Jean Gabin, an aged gangster; both men walked through and read the lines that gave neither they or the audiences who saw the film much pleasure.

During this period, he lived in a trim, mortgage-free $70,000 modern house with pool on Beverly Estates Drive, a home still congruent with his former star status. About George's patent-leather image, Milton Berle perceptively commented, "I've known George for over forty years—going back to Broadway. There's one thing about George Raft, no one ever knew if he had a dime in his pocket or ten grand. He was never a *schnorrer*—you know, someone who had his hand out. He always had pride and great dignity. And there isn't a person in show business who has a bad word to say about him. Whether he was up or down, he's always been a real man. But that kind of extreme pride and image can kill you."

His posture was often that of a man wearing a general's uniform, without the financial support of the army. "You know, you go to a hotel and you get a room. When George Raft checks in they automatically set up a $100-a-day suite. I can't afford it any more; but yet I can't not afford it. What am I going to do? Tell the room clerk it's too expensive for George Raft?"

Although his film career was minimal, his reputation was as great as ever. The name George Raft still had cash value, a fact that was not lost on his friends. In 1960, a businessman named Bud Kiley, who was a Raft buff for many years, along with several other financial adventurers hit upon the idea of setting up a chain of consumer discount stores called Consumer Marts of America with George Raft as the front man. In his capacity as C.M.A.'s "Public Relations Director" George appeared at store openings and made personal appearances and gave "pep talks" to the stores' employees.

When Raft appeared at the first store's opening in Chicago, he greeted a mob of over 6000 fans, all potential customers. The C.M.A. in a three-year period expanded to twelve stores with locations in Miami, Phoenix, San Francisco, and Tampa. To complement his appearances, Raft was able to garner such co-stars as Jerry Lewis, Martha Raye, Red Skelton, and Jayne Mansfield. They appeared as a favor to Raft, without compensation.

The C.M.A., at least on paper, seemed a profitable venture, and George was promised that, in addition to the modest fees he received for openings and $150 a week for use of his name in promotion and advertisements, he would share in the company's stock when the organization went public.

After a year, Kiley and his grateful partners made Raft a vice president of the firm, a role he was to later regret more than any ever foisted on him by Jack Warner or Adolph Zukor. He signed papers which gave him status and financial responsibility—but no more salary than he was already receiving. George paid little attention to the business's operation until a Jarvis Weiss, the corporate accountant he had met once or twice, called him one evening in 1964 and told him that the firm had gone into "chapter eleven." George told me, "I never knew they were writing a book on C.M.A., and when I found out that chapter eleven meant bankruptcy, I said, so what? When I talked to Stern later that night I found out how serious the thing was to me."

Raft, along with the others, was financially responsible for

C.M.A.—and when the bankruptcy was sorted out Raft's tangible assets, including the Beverly Estates house, were lost in the tangle of high finance and court action. For the first time in his Hollywood career, George had the ego-battering experience of moving from a home into an apartment.

But the move was only the tip of the arrow aimed at his pierced ego. In 1965 the Internal Revenue Service undertook an investigation of the poorly financed firm. Its agents discovered that no withholding taxes had been deducted from the sums paid to Raft.

"I really had no decent business management, tax man, or legal advice at that time. I didn't think I needed it. I wasn't making much money. Then all of a sudden I hear from this I.R.S. guy. I didn't remember it clearly, but I guess I told the guy who did my taxes in those years that C.M.A. had made the deductions.

"I don't know how many things got fouled up. But I was called in and he told me, 'You owe us.' I said, 'What do I owe you?' And he said, 'We're not supposed to tell you, you're supposed to tell us.' I said, 'I really don't know what this is all about,' and I didn't.

"Then the guy said, 'You had an interest in these discount stores?' 'That's right.' They paid me a hundred-and-a-half a week as a public relations consultant. But would a man that made the money I did go to work for that kind of dough? Then he said the company had me down as vice president, they were using my name, and weren't paying my taxes as they said they were supposed to. Do you remember a 1941 picture called *Strawberry Blonde* with Cagney, Rita Hayworth, Olivia de Havilland, and Jack Carson? Well, in this picture Cagney is a shnook who's always being given papers to sign by his good friend Carson, who finally gets Cagney signed right into the pen. Now I saw this happening to me, because now, finally, I'd really go to the can—not for knowing or associating with hoods, but with businessmen."

Raft's finances were so bad he couldn't cover the amount he owed in taxes. The case might have been quashed at that point if it weren't for his pride, for he could have borrowed the money. Later, when the case became public, he received offers of financial aid from wealthy friends, most notably Frank Sinatra, but by then the judicial processes were in motion.

The case went to a grand jury, which indicted him for "falsifying" his income taxes by more than $85,000 for the five-year period from 1958 to 1963. The *Los Angeles Times* (September 29, 1965) offers an account of this humiliating experience:

> Former movie tough guy George Raft stood before the bar of justice Tuesday clutching his grandmother's rosary and weeping unashamedly as he awaited sentencing for income tax evasion.
>
> But his tears of fear and sorrow quickly turned to tears of joy.
>
> "I sentence you to a fine of $2,500," decreed U.S. District Judge Pierson M. Hall.
>
> Raft could have gotten a maximum sentence of three years in prison and a $5,000 fine or both. . . .
>
> Outside the courtroom, Raft told reporters:
>
> "I am very happy with the court decision. It was most fair. The judge was wonderful. . . ."
>
> Raft's attorney, Jerome Weber, said that a host of Raft's friends had written the judge pleading for leniency. They included Sinatra, Bob Hope, Lucille Ball, Jimmy Durante, General Manager Buzzy Bavasi of the Dodgers and Senator George Murphy (R-Calif.). . . .

"Today, when people in our business get into trouble, Sinatra is the guy who helps out. He's right there, not as a grandstand play, but behind the scenes. The first one to call was Frank, who said, 'George, it's Frank. What do you need?' He then asked me if I had an attorney or if there was anything at all he could do to help. At that time I was so destroyed by the whole thing I didn't know what to say.

"Then next day, something happened that I'll never forget as long as I live because it's an example of friendship that doesn't happen very often in this world. My lawyer called me and said, 'You have one of the greatest friends that ever lived.' I said, 'What do you mean?' He told me that Sinatra's business manager had just called and informed him that Frank would give anything necessary to help. Frank gave me a blank check. He offered to give me anything up to one million dollars to help my case!"

The whole matter might have been avoided if Raft had called Sinatra or any of his affluent friends. That would have allowed them to return Raft's previous generosity; but Raft had great

230

pride, an unbending stance of independence, and, perhaps most crucially, a built-in resistance to place himself in the path of any possibility of rejection. Regardless of how desperate his condition, he was unable to ask even his closest friends for minimal assistance. These offers would be acknowledged with appreciation, but to ask or accept—that could not be done.

After his 1965 bout with the I.R.S., Raft received a number of offers of "help"—and some of them he would prefer to forget. "In the early days I did many favors for—let's call him Joe Smith. I thought he was my pal. I bumped into him one day, he was running a studio then. He asked how I was doing, and I told him not so hot. He invited me over to his office and there we talked for quite a while. He offered me a job as a talent scout, something I thought I'd be good at—it wasn't charity." After all, he had helped Mae West get her first film role and had recommended Ava Gardner for *Whistle Stop*. He had promoted, among others, Janet Blair, Frances Drake, Ida Lupino, and Marlene Dietrich into good roles.

The morning he arrived to start his new position, he was disappointed when "Smith" did not meet him at the front office. Instead, he was greeted by a pleasant and polite assistant's assistant. And when the young man took him to his office George really felt despondent.

"We walked and walked and walked. Finally we got to the very end of the lot to an old, rundown building. We went into it and he said, 'Here's your office, George.' Completely disgusted, I looked at this hole-in-the-wall, then told the guy that he wasn't to blame, but if I couldn't go first class I wasn't going at all. No secretary. No nothing. I was really pissed off. I told him as I was leaving, 'Tell Smith to shove the whole deal up his ass.' Those were my last words.

"Smith called the next day. Couldn't understand why I was mad. So I gave him a little education about how I'd taken his offer seriously because I sincerely wanted the job and would've worked hard to do it right; but what he'd offered me was a handout, a dump of an office and no help. So he'd best forget it. Then I hung up.

"Some time later I met him in Chasen's and he said he was sorry. I said, 'Look, if I come to see somebody, if I can't see the top guy, I don't want to see anyone.' He said, 'Well, it's my fault.'

I should have talked to you but I was busy.' I said, 'Believe this if you don't believe anything else about me: that I never would've treated you, or anyone, the way you treated me.'"

In January 1966, still haunted by his mythic screen image and past associations, Raft was subpoenaed to testify before a New York Grand Jury engaged in an investigation of Scopeatone, a business firm whose executives had been threatened by gangsters. He contributed nothing because he knew nothing. After his brief and blank testimony, he was dismissed with a thank-you that did not assuage his feelings of being exploited for no good reason.

If George was beginning to feel like a reluctant witness to a hostile past, the future was to be more troublesome yet.

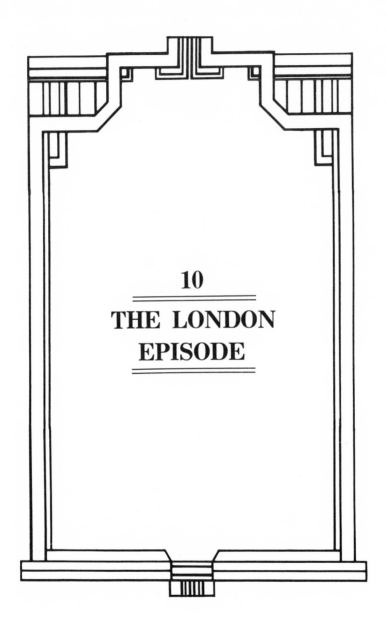

10
THE LONDON
EPISODE

The London Episode

The scenario—too perfect, too complete in its melodrama—
might have been lifted from one of his 1930s movies; but it was
now January 1967. George Raft was doing his best to fall asleep,
but the Los Angeles smog had aggravated his asthma and filled
his chest with rales and whistles. Fortunately, he thought, he'd
taken care of business at home and could fly back to London
in a couple of days.

His modest Beverly Hills house, seldom used now, still reflected George's penchant for a contemporary design dominated
by red and gold. Above the bed were photographic studies of
three of his favorite women, all images from the past: Marlene
Dietrich in a rakish sailor suit with a cryptic comment—"Love
Me! Marlene"; Carole Lombard, in a diaphanous white silk gown
from their film *Bolero;* Virginia Pine, with the coquettish in-
scription, "I'm trying to decide whether I love you."

Restless and uncomfortable, George slipped his G.R.-mono-
gramed robe over silk pajamas and padded into his bathroom,
past a wall of 100 perfume bottles, for several sleeping pills that
he knew would not work. Then back to bed to try again for
sleep. It wasn't only the smog that affected him physically;
mentally and emotionally, the city triggered a thousand bitter-
sweet memories. There had been a twenty-five-year reign as
one of Hollywood's movie kings. In one year he had given away
or spent more money than many people earn in a lifetime.

Then had come hard times and lean years when the producers
were always out to lunch unless they had some bit part they
called a cameo for him. Now, in England, after twenty years
of hard scuffling, once again he had star billing at "George Raft's
Colony Club"—the most successful gambling casino in London.
His enactment of a suave, debonair, cool boss was perfect. All
that was required of him at the Colony Club was to play the
role of George Raft—a role that he had lived for many, many
years.

As the suave host of the Colony Club, a part which he lived
and breathed, Raft enjoyed a part that surpassed all of his
comparable screen roles. He had a $35,000 maroon Rolls-Royce
with a liveried chauffeur, a flat in Mayfair with appropriate
help, a lovely twenty-five-year-old British girlfriend, the respect
of everyone he met, and a pen that signed all tabs. He was back

on top, and understandably restless to return to his new kingdom.

The phone rang. George sat up in bed and noted that it was one in the morning. Who would be calling him at this ridiculous hour? Not his pals; they knew better. Maybe, he smiled, it was some aggressive hooker who'd found his name in an old black book and wanted to drum up some trade.

"Is this Mr. George Raft?"

"Yeah. Who is this?"

"I'm a reporter with *The New York Times.* Have you read today's *Manchester Guardian?*"

"*The Manchester* what?"

"*Guardian.* There's a front-page story with a headline 'GEORGE RAFT BARRED FROM ENGLAND.'"

"You got some very wrong facts, mister. I'm due back in London in a few days."

"The story says you have been declared an undesirable alien. It says that Roy Jenkins of the Home Office declared you persona non grata in England. . . . . Mr. Raft? Are you still there? Do you have any statement on the story, Mr. Raft?"

His voice was just above a whisper, but polite. "As far as I know none of what you've told me is true. I have nothing more to say."

Head spinning, Raft hung up and began to cough until he was limp. At last his head cleared and he felt strong enough to phone Joel Tarlo, the attorney of the Colony Club, in London. Tarlo expressed surprise and assured George that the story was a hoax. Take his word for it, there was no problem. He felt somewhat relieved; then, just as suddenly, he was overcome with depression. "Everything," he thought to himself, "everything was fine in England. But now this. What the hell went wrong?"

The next twenty-four hours were a nightmare as calls poured in from reporters all over the world. Their papers and magazines in France, Germany, Japan—all wanted to know why he was barred from England. Was it because George was involved with the international underworld? Would he care to sell them an exclusive to the big story?

For several days George appeared on some of the local television stations to tell his interviewers what he had been told by his London solicitor: that the story was unfounded. And this was what he chose to believe until he received a call from Tarlo informing him that the story was true. They were doing everything legally possible to reverse the government's decision. It looked hopeless, however.

That day George was cornered by a group of reporters and TV cameramen who demanded the "real story" behind the government's action. Was it true he was affiliated with the Mafia? Did Meyer Lansky really own George Raft's Colony Club? It was a cameo role for the six o'clock news and George played it smoothly. "What did I do? You tell me."

But the part became more difficult: whether George knew it or not, alleged mob boss Meyer Lansky, through his associate Dino Cellini, owned a substantial piece of George Raft's Colony Club. Years later, in June 1972, Lansky was indicted by a federal Grand Jury for failing to declare in his 1967 and 1968 tax returns $200,000 in debts he had collected in the United States from American gamblers who had lost money at the Colony Club.

Raft retreated from the heat of the inquiry about the British insult into his small, immaculate Beverly Hills house. This seemed to Raft the most painful and unwarranted rejection of his life. He was George Raft. He was a star. He was seventy-one years old.

He had had many setbacks during his top Hollywood days, but in retrospect they were minor problems; he had been younger then and more resilient. There had been more arguments than he cared to remember over bad and out-of-character roles. There had been suspensions at Paramount and Warner Brothers, ego battles with guys like Jack Warner, Darryl Zanuck, Wallace Beery, Eddie Robinson. But, in most respects, the mood of those early years had been one of optimism and triumph. When the roles and scripts offered him began to dwindle in the fifties, he still had a strong name in Hollywood and throughout the world. George Raft could still command a reasonable living from supporting roles, cameos, and sharp bit parts. When his role as an actor faded, his reputation as a ladies' man, sharp dresser, and *bon vivant* led him into other areas of employment. The George Raft image was still negotiable currency. A stint as a part-time entertainment consultant to the Flamingo

Hotel in Las Vegas led to a bigger and better part, that of playing himself as nightclub manager at the Hotel Del Capri in Havana, until he was bombed out of that role.

The international image George had created in films, together with his work in gambling casinos, made him a most eligible candidate for employment to a group that owned the Colony Club in London. The Colony was attractive, well located, and well financed, but it lacked the atmosphere of excitement and aura of class its owners felt George Raft could bring to the establishment. At that time, George was visiting a friend in Florida. A call came from a man named Andy Neatrour, a British businessman who represented the Colony Club and its interests. Would Raft be interested in joining the club as host? "I was nervous," he recalled. "Suppose they put my name out there, 'George Raft's Colony Club,' and no one comes? A bad box office would reflect directly on me."

He had made many personal appearances in Europe over the years. In 1926, in London, he had been a great success as a dancer. The Duke of Windsor had been an ardent fan and a sponsor of George Raft. And the consummate dancer, Fred Astaire, who considered Raft to be one of the best dancers in America, had recommended him for the tour. In 1941 Raft was too old to enlist in the service, but a few years later he was among the first Americans to entertain Allied troops in Europe. Later on he entertained British soldiers in Europe and in the Near East. He spent more than $50,000 of his personal funds to bring his Cavalcade of Sports boxing shows and entertainment to the troops.

It took a number of phone calls to convince Raft, but he finally agreed to a London meeting with the owners of the Colony Club. Concurrently, he agreed to appear on the most popular television show in England, the Eamon Andrews program. Before a live audience, Raft reminisced about the golden years of Hollywood, then did the dances that made him famous on Broadway during the twenties. This television success led to his being signed by Charles Tucker, Julie Andrews' former manager, and Jimmy Tarbuck, master of ceremonies at the London Palladium, for a Sunday night TV spectacular. London was treated to an imported stylization of "Mr. Cool."

"It was a gimmick. An old 1920 car rolls onstage surrounded

by gangsters—Chicago in the twenties. I get out of the car. There's a guy on the fender. I just touch him and he falls over. And the master of ceremonies says to the audience, 'Why, this is like a George Raft picture.' And then, as if he's very surprised, 'Why, it *is* George Raft!'

"I'm in a black overcoat and spats, and wear a black hat pulled down over one eye. We talk and do a little shtick. I tell him about my problems, my tax case. You know, I never pulled any punches about things like that.

"Finally Tarbuck says, 'Well, gee, my mother told me you were a great dancer.' I say, 'In 1926 I worked here, and I did a dance called the Charleston. I'd like to have the pleasure of doing it now.'"

London was impressed. This performance led to another special, a British TV version of *This Is Your Life* carried from the Grosvenor House hotel. In the audience were British celebrities from all walks of life: politicians, entertainers, government officials, royalty, and business men. George recalled for them his deep affection for England and other speakers reminisced about George's participation in British life.

"While all this hoopla is going on I had a few more meetings with Andy Neatrour and a man named Dino Cellini. This was the first time I met Cellini, although I'd heard of him in Cuba and the Bahamas as a guy who trained British dealers for the islands. Later I heard he was somehow connected with Meyer Lansky, but that wasn't important to me."

Lansky, at this time in more legitimate operations, was a large property owner in Miami, the Bahamas, and Las Vegas. He reputedly owned or controlled the Eden Roc and the Desert Inn hotels and Las Vegas gambling casinos. He formerly owned the Riviera and Hotel National in Havana. He was a large contributor to Nixon's presidential campaign and a variety of charities. Hank Messick, in his definitive biography *Lansky*, concluded that Lansky was the brains behind organized crime in America and had amassed a personal fortune of $300 million.

Raft presented his conditions to Neatrour and Cellini for taking the Colony Club job. The Colony was not merely employing a man, it was importing an image. The club had to carry his name. A regal flat with servants was essential. He had "to travel around in class"—in a proper Rolls-Royce. His personal attire was part of the package. "I need my clothes pressed every day. I told them a good wardrobe would add a feeling of class to me and to the place."

Emphatically, he did not want to be involved with hiring, firing, or finances. The details of management were not his concern. He also asked for "a small salary, around $200 a week, and a few points in the club.

"They agreed to everything. They gave me the salary, five points in the club, a chauffeured Rolls-Royce, a two-bedroom flat at the Belton Towers, 55 Park Lane in Marble Arch, with a fulltime maid. Everything was taken care of, including my meals. It was a perfect setup."

His role at the Colony was almost a recap of his role in *Night After Night*. It was a new cast in a new setting but the script and the props were essentially the same.

Five points made George a small partner in the club. The other American part-owner, but with a larger piece, was Dino Cellini, who ran the gambling. Fourteen Englishmen were the other stockholders. But Raft was the official host, the man out front, and he delighted in the role. A newfound hero of the jet set, he loved his home, his car, and the respect that for so long had escaped him.

The Colony became the "in" place of London, *the* place to see and be seen. Frequent guests were Elizabeth Taylor and Richard Burton; Ari Onassis and Jackie Kennedy; former Supreme Court Justice Earl Warren; and Charlie Chaplin. To the dismay and envy of the other club owners the Colony was crowded every night.

The club's advertising highlighted its special features:

Samuel Pepys, the seventeenth-century diarist, described my club, the Colony, pretty well about 300 years ago. He said that a true club is a group of people getting together to enjoy sociability, conviviality, and sportsmanship with appetizing food and wine. There is very little to add to Pepys's recipe, which sums up a twentieth-century definition of the Colony. There's a cocktail lounge, an elegant restaurant with excellent cuisine, dancing from 9 P.M. to 3 A.M. to a live band, and, of course, in the casino there are games to suit all players.

—George Raft

George's presence as host was the club's most valuable asset, but he made other contributions. Everyone, from busboys to dealers, dressed in the sartorial style associated with George Raft and wore his trademark, red handkerchiefs, in their breast-pockets. The club was decorated in George's favorite colors, lush red velvet and gold. The chandeliers were gold and the red carpeting was thickly luxurious. On a more functional level Raft saw to it that the food was superb. Mervyn LeRoy, the famous Hollywood producer, said, "George was probably responsible for upgrading the cuisine all over London. George's club was a pace-setter and had the best food in England." George further saw to it that the entertainment was excellent, but subdued. "After all, the main business of the club was gambling, and I didn't want to distract people."

Visitors to the casino generally wore elegant evening dress; wealthy women patrons used the club as a setting for their dia-monds and furs. The Colony flourished and everyone was pleased. Time passed quickly and pleasantly for Raft. Even the climate was more compatible than Los Angeles. He felt a certain freedom about walking around his neighborhood at night. A friend ran an allnight horseroom and George would drop by regularly after work for the sort of talk he enjoyed: sports, the old days, good times, bigtime action, and beautiful women.

George's love life was rather calm and conservative for him during his year in London and quite different from what it had been in Hollywood during the thirties and forties. Then he was considered by many to be a swordsman whose sexual adventures and prowess rivaled—even eclipsed—the amorous adventures of John Barrymore and Errol Flynn. Perhaps it was the conserva-tive climate, perhaps the demands of the job, but in London, at the age of seventy, he had only one girlfriend. She was twenty-five and beautiful, and a constant companion to Raft during most of his British sojourn.

In contrast to his hectic years in film-making, evenings at the Colony had a pleasant rhythm. Generally, he arrived at the club about eight-thirty to check the kitchen, bar, entertainers, and tables. George was a meticulous host; nothing, from napkins to chips, was neglected. Satisfied that all was well, he would order his own dinner. Most often he dined in typical American fashion on a fine cut of steak and a baked potato carefully prepared by a chef informed of George's culinary preferences.

Dinner over, he would check the reservation list to make sure that he personally greeted whatever celebrities were coming. As guests arrived he gave personal attention to longtime patrons and firsttime visitors. He congratulated the winners and consoled the losers, whose loans and markers he approved. One of his responsibilities was to settle the overdrawn accounts of delinquent gamblers. Among these were Hollywood executives and stars and politicians who paid their debts promptly when they were presented by Raft.

"One night," George remembered, "Darryl Zanuck came into the club with Charlie Feldman, the producer, John Huston, and Dino DiLaurentis. Darryl is a good gambler. He lost a sizable chunk of dough and wound up owing around $8000. He was a little late in paying. I made a personal visit to his hotel to see him, in case he had a beef of some kind. He assured me that nothing was wrong and took care of the eight grand immediately."

In addition, he did a cameo spot in *Casino Royale* (1967), the disastrous film extravaganza spoof of James Bond, produced by Feldman. In one scene he flipped his famous coin and shot himself with a gun that fired backwards. His films played regularly on British television. There was even talk of starring Raft in a new feature, *The Midnight Man*.

The Colony Club hosted many English charities, and Raft's popularity continued to soar as he was sought after to headline sporting events. One of these was billed as "The George Raft Colony Sporting Club Trophy Meeting," an affair sponsored in June 1966 by the British Automobile Club.

Although he loved London, George wanted to be home in the States for Christmas. He arranged for a three-week holiday and returned to his Los Angeles home. A few days before he was to return to London he received the phone call that dramatically affected his life. An article in the *Los Angeles Herald-Examiner* (March 30, 1967) offered George a forum for his analysis of the situation.

Somebody put the finger on me. They haven't accused me of anything; they've just barred me from the country without charges, without a trial or anything. And just when I was about to start participating in the profits of the Colony. All I got was an apartment, the use of a car and a small salary until the investors were paid off. Now that they have been, I won't be there to collect.

I suppose the British had some information on me, and it must have come from the FBI. I'm going to New York this week to see about a job, and I plan to drop down to Washington and wait in Hoover's office until he sees me. I knew him; once I introduced him to Aly Khan at the Del Mar race track.

I'm not a member of any mob, never was. Sure, I know some guys that are, but I know a lot of people. What am I supposed to do when those guys say hello to me—tell them to get lost?

What have I got to do to clear myself? I lead a quiet life. I don't ask for any trouble. I have never taken a drink. I don't get in any fights. If broads are an offense, then I plead guilty.

In a poignant report on the banning from England, Pete Hamill, the brilliant columnist for *The New York Post*, on March 4, 1967, wrote a premature obituary for George Raft entitled "The Last Caper":

. . . He was the last one left, the only true survivor of that gaudy mob that had marched so boldly through the land of Warner Brothers. They were the best film actors America had produced, and with the pearl gray hats and the sub-machine guns, the tight coats and polished shoes, the glittering blondes and black limousines, they showed a whole generation of big city kids a style that would allow them to last. But with Bogart, Lorre, Greenstreet dead, and the best of them all—Mr. Cagney —in retirement, all we had left was George Raft. . . .

. . . We always knew that the heroes of gangster pictures were part of our secret mind, the cowboys working the big town; the British thought they were documentaries.

... At 71, Raft is not about to make any more movies. A few years ago he was bankrupt. They probably won't put him to work in Las Vegas, because he has had a cup of coffee from time to time with the wrong guys. So he will sit around the ruins of Hollywood, serving the last years òf the longest bit there is, and I for one only wish that someone would give him a long coat and a machine gun, a pair of spats and a blonde, and let him flip a silver dollar in the air, before shooting it out with the cops. George Raft, of all people, should be allowed to go out in style.

Through Walter Winchell, a friend of Hoover's, Raft was able to communicate with the FBI. He received the following bureaucratic response dated April 4, 1967, and signed personally by J. Edgar Hoover.

Dear Mr. Raft:
This will acknowledge your letter of March 28, 1967, concerning the actions of the British Government in excluding you from the United Kingdom. I am certain you realize that the FBI has no jurisdiction in England and has no control over governmental action taken by a foreign country.
In the event you desire to supplement your letter with additional data, you may be certain that such will be made a matter of permanent record upon receipt at this Bureau.

Raft had been tried and convicted without being given the chance to defend himself. "The least they should have done was to call me in and confront me with the problem." Several people in British government came to his defense. Bessie Braddock, then a colorful Labor M.P. from Liverpool, spoke out on behalf of Raft; but the Home Office remained adamant. As far as Jenkins was concerned, the case was closed.
A total of eight Americans had been barred from England that year, all of them without a hearing. In addition to George, they included Meyer Lansky; Dino Cellini; Charles (Charlie the Blade) Tourine; Angelo Bruno, a Philadelphia rackets figure; Anthony (Tony Ducks) Carollo; Morris Lansburgh, then owner of the

Flamingo Hotel; and Lansburgh's son Leonard. The fact that Raft's barring was done so publicly, while he was out of the country, raised the speculation that Raft was being used as a flagrant example to other Americans who might get interested in London's gambling industry.

The notion that Raft was really a victim of the scramble for the big business of gambling in London may have some truth. In 1965 there were 4000 gambling houses in England and one London club alone cleared $4.2 million. For all the clubs, the total take that year—in London alone—was two-and-a-half billion dollars!

In a column in July 1967, Walter Winchell made an indictment of his own:

> George Raft Story: George Raft, still in a daze trying to find out why Britain rates him persona non grata, may be interested in the buzz making the London night life rounds. . . . The film star's name still is headlined in lights at the gambling casino where he was employed as an attraction. . . . If the "buzz" is true, some people in London may wind up as defendents in a lawsuit. . . . One of the many gambling places there, enjoying robust prosperity, allegedly used influence with certain people close to the British government to get rid of Raft. . . . Because his place was packing them in. . . . A certain competitor feared his business would suffer. . . . The latter, the story alleges, paid $12,000 for Raft's ban. . . . He has been unemployed in the U.S. ever since.

Raft's bitterness had a sharp edge. "I don't live in a palatial home. I don't go out much, I'm home most of the time. I go out to dinner, wait for the paper, come home and take a sleeping pill. I live the life of a hermit. If, as some of them say, the FBI is really watching me all the time, those guys must be leading an awfully dull life.

"The only reason I believe I was barred is guilt by association. Sure, I say 'hello' to everyone who says 'hello' to me. When I first went into the motion picture business, I wasn't too brilliant; I was called into the front office by the publicity department and told, 'Look, be nice to everybody, say hello to people. This is part of the image you create.'

245

"Sure, I knew Benny Siegel; he was a guy who tried to imitate me. He dressed like me and tried to copy my style. I met Meyer Lansky, but I never associated with him. I knew lots of people. In London, a guy from Bobby Kennedy's office came into the club and gave me a PT 109 tie clip. He said that when Bobby Kennedy became President this was my ticket to the inauguration.

"George Murphy, the senator, called the State Department for me. They told him as far as they knew I was clean, but that they couldn't interfere in England's business. I wrote to J. Edgar Hoover and he said the same thing."

Being barred from England in 1967 has remained one of the most painful experiences of his life. "I'll never forget what happened to me in England. I look back at my life and wonder what the hell I had done to deserve that kind of a kick in the balls. Sure, I was a rough kid, but you had to be in those days—or you wouldn't have survived.

"In the twenties, the worst thing I could be accused of was being a guy who loved to dance. That was my life. I liked nothing better. And I made a pretty big success of it."

"Sure I worked the speakeasies, the clubs, and anyplace else I could. So the clubs were owned by bootleggers and even a few killers. That didn't bother the patrons, who were some of the biggest names around. And Jimmy Durante, Ruby Keeler, Milton Berle, Georgie Jessel, Al Jolson—all of them worked the same places. Most entertainers in those days got their start in the New York clubs, and I'm grateful for those years. The clubs were fun and a proving ground for talent. They're part of the history of this country.

"In my time I knew or met them all. Al Capone, Joe Adonis, Frank Costello, Vito Genovese, Dutch Schultz, Machinegun Jack McGurn, Lucky Luciano, Vinnie Coll—most of them were around when I was a young guy. I'll tell you the truth: I admired them. They became names, top people in the country. And when you talked with them as I did you learned a lot. The really big guys—not the punks—were interesting company. Over dinner at a good restaurant or club, they were more fun and laughs than any business man or studio head I met. What they did in their work was their business, not mine.

"Sure, I admired Owney Madden. He was a big hero in our

neighborhood. He ran things in New York and even the mayor and the governor of New York liked him.

"The worst thing I ever did for Owney was help his boys move some booze from one place to another. In those days no one saw that as crime. It was a service. The main crimes I committed were on the silver screen."

When asked what was the peak experience of his life, without hesitation Raft replied firmly, "The thirties and forties, those twenty years."

"What about them?"

"Everything. Everything. I loved and enjoyed every single minute."

Six months after his English experience, in June 1967, George was honored once again at a special Friar's Roast, produced by George's long-time friend, now an executive with the Los Angeles Dodgers, Danny Goodman. Gathered to pay tribute on the dais were Red Buttons, Pat Buttram, Sammy Cahn, Richard Conte, Jackie Cooper, Billy Daniels, Bobby Darin, Andy Devine, Henry Fonda, Glenn Ford, Mike Frankovitch, Robert Goulet, Jack Haley, Pat Henry, George Jessel, Dean Martin, Bobby Morse, Carl Reiner, Don Rickles, Johnny Rivers, Edward G. Robinson, Willie Shoemaker, Frank Sinatra, Barry Sullivan, Robert Wagner, Jack L. Warner, Walter Winchell, and Richard Zanuck.

Several celebrated singers offered their versions of popular songs to honor Raft. One, a parody of *My Favorite Things*, gives something of the flavor of the evening:

Silk ties from Sulka, and hankies to weep in;
Lounging pajamas a fag wouldn't sleep in;
Ten-dollar hookers who bounce off the springs —
These are a few of his favorite things . . .
When his luck fails, like in London,
When they said, You're through,
He simply remembered his favorite things
And said to the Queen, "— —!"

But, jokes aside, all of them — Sinatra, Martin, Zanuck, Robinson, Warner, Fonda, Jessel, Winchell — extolled Raft. He was a fine actor; a generous friend to many people; a person who helped to build the film industry; and a man who would always hold a legendary position in Hollywood.

George Raft is one of a handful of great stars left from Hollywood's decades of the thirties and the forties, when Cary Grant, Katharine Hepburn, Joan Crawford, Bette Davis, Fred Astaire, Marlene Dietrich, Mae West, and Jimmy Cagney graced the screen and made their significant contributions to the social and mythic history of America.

As we draw further away in time from those glorious years of film history, they seem grander, more romantic, of greater achievement and value. The American films of the thirties do not represent the "greatest movies ever made." The transformation of film into art was more convincingly achieved by others—like Eisenstein and Pudovkin in Russia; the early work of Lang and Pabst in Germany; Chaplin and von Stroheim in Hollywood (*Citizen Kane* seems to be America's only undisputed sound masterpiece); Clair and Renoir in France, Italy after the war with Rossellini; de Sica, Fellini; Kurosawa in Japan; and Ingmar Bergman in Sweden. The cult and promotion of American masters of the thirties is another affair, concerned almost with a different kind of movie-making. The films of John Ford, William Wyler, Frank Capra, Raoul Walsh, William Wellman, Howard Hawks, George Cukor, Henry Hathaway, and George Stevens have another sort of vitality, one so specifically American that it is difficult to conceive of them as "classic." They are distinctly products of their times, so imbued with the particular values of the period that seeing them today requires an enormous adjustment of perspective. But this sort of shift, this real suspension of time, this entrance into an Oz without witches, enhances their enchantment.

In interviews American directors and actors of that time are constantly asked about their "art," and they answer that they were craftsmen, doing a job, providing entertainment. It seems difficult to some to accept great entertainment as an art of its own: we press it to mean more than it intends, we embroider social fact with intellectual nuance where none was necessary.

Yet the depression films of the thirties and the war films of the forties, however overdrawn in plot or character, embodied the unconscious assumptions of their time. And the personal identification of the audience with the screen image reflected these assumptions. Thus the great box office stars, Raft among them, became very personal heroes and friends to millions. The private lives of the stars merged with their screen roles in the public consciousness. Films in those two decades became a personal extension of people's lives. It is in this aspect of popular film entertainment, rather than in the accuracy of the films' social reporting, that their deepest social meaning is to be found. For the most part, those films were not meticulously made in the manner of an Eisenstein movie; in character they had none of the depth the French films had already achieved. But in liveliness, vigor, interest, fun, excitement, glamour, a relaxed sense of improvisation, sharpness, sentimentality, real affection, and a zest for existence—these films were unsurpassed. These films are indeed glorious and golden, as engaging today as they were at birth.

The gods bestow their gifts at random, and with odd combinations of good and bad luck. Those people, like Raft, who were stars in the thirties, were granted immortality. Certainly there were earlier and also different transcendent film stars—Pickford, Fairbanks, the Gish sisters, Garbo, Chaplin, Keaton—but for the popular audience there was an additional personal investment in the screen lives of Bette Davis, Humphrey Bogart, James Cagney, Mae West, Clark Gable, W. C. Fields, the Marx brothers, Edward G. Robinson, Marlene Dietrich, Gary Cooper, Henry Fonda, James Stewart, and many more—Raft among them. Their films do much to explain who we are today; we are the children of those films and those stars. Audiences loved that consistent and indelible character George Raft in *Scarface, Souls at Sea, They Drive by Night, Each Dawn I Die, Manpower* and *Bolero.* Raft shares with his fellow craftsmen of that time our gratitude, our admiration, and our love.

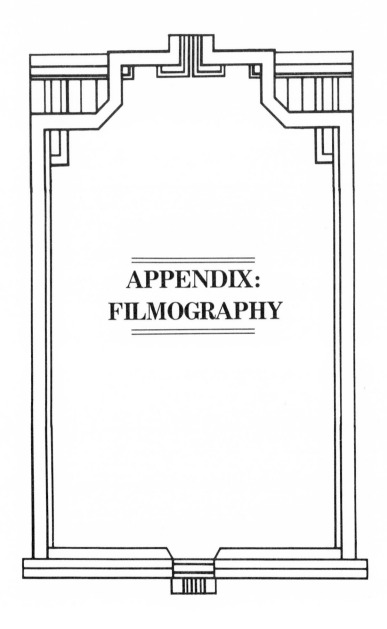

APPENDIX:
FILMOGRAPHY

Appendix: The films of George Raft

The following filmography does not attempt to be exhaustive or complete; it is intended to provide a quick reference to the films of George Raft. I have included, where available, the name of the producer as well as the director but have for the most part listed only the principal actors. In a few instances actors in minor roles were included for historical interest.

1929

Queen of the Night Clubs (Warner Brothers)

Director:
BRYAN FOY

Cast:
TEXAS GUINAN
JOHN DAVIDSON
LILA LEE
EDDIE FOY, JR.
ARTHUR HOUSMAN

1931

Hush Money (Fox)

Director:
SIDNEY LANFIELD

Cast:
JOAN BENNETT
MYRNA LOY
OWEN MOORE
HARDIE ALBRIGHT
C. HENRY GORDON
SALLY EILERS

1931

Palmy Days (United Artists)

Producer:
SAMUEL GOLDWYN

Director:
EDWARD SUTHERLAND

Cast:
EDDIE CANTOR
BARBARA WEEKS
CHARLOTTE GREENWOOD
SPENCER CHARTERS

1931

Quick Millions (Fox)

Director:
ROWLAND BROWN

Cast:
SPENCER TRACY
SALLY EILERS
ROBERT BURNS
LEON AMES
DIXIE LEE CROSBY
MARGUERITE CHURCHILL

1932

Scarface (United Artists)

Producer:
HOWARD HUGHES

Director:
HOWARD HAWKS

Cast:
PAUL MUNI
BORIS KARLOFF
ANN DVORAK
KAREN MORLEY
OSGOOD PERKINS
C. HENRY GORDON

1932

Taxi (Warner Brothers)

Director:
ROY DEL RUTH

Cast:
JAMES CAGNEY
LORETTA YOUNG
GUY KIBBEE
GEORGE E. STONE
DAVID LANDAU

George Raft

1932

Dancers in the Dark (Paramount)

Director:
DAVID BURTON

Cast:
MIRIAM HOPKINS
JACK OAKIE
LYDA ROBERTI
WILLIAM COLLIER, JR.

1932

Madame Racketeer (Paramount)

Directors:
ALEXANDER HALL
HARRY WAGSTAFF GRIBBLE

Cast:
ALISON SKIPWORTH
RICHARD BENNETT
EVALYN KNAPP
JOHN BREEDEN
ROBERT McWADE

1932

Night after Night (Paramount)

Director:
ARCHIE MAYO

Cast:
MAE WEST
ALISON SKIPWORTH
CONSTANCE CUMMINGS
WYNNE GIBSON
ROSCOE KARNS

1932

Undercover Man (Paramount)

Director:
JAMES FLOOD

Cast:
NANCY CARROLL
CLYDE BROOK
HELEN VINSON
GREGORY RATOFF
LEW CODY
NOEL FRANCIS

1932

If I Had a Million (Paramount)

Producer:
LOUIS LIGHTON

Directors:
H. BRUCE HUMBERSTONE
ERNST LUBITSCH
NORMAN TAUROG
NORMAN McLEON
JAMES CRUZE
STEPHEN ROBERTS
WILLIAM A. SEITER

Cast:
W. C. FIELDS
GARY COOPER
CHARLES LAUGHTON
CHARLES RUGGLES
JACK OAKIE
FRANCIS DEE
RICHARD BENNETT

1932

Night World (Universal)

Director:
HOBART HENLEY

Cast:
LEW AYRES
MAE CLARK
BORIS KARLOFF
RUSSELL HOPTON
DOROTHY REVIER

1932

Love Is a Racket
(Warner Brothers)

Director:
WILLIAM WELLMAN

Cast:
DOUGLAS FAIRBANKS, JR.
FRANCES DEE
ANN DVORAK
LEE TRACY

Appendix: The films of George Raft

1933

Pick Up (Paramount)

Producer:
B. P. SCHULBERG

Director:
MARION GERING

Cast:
SYLVIA SIDNEY
LILLIAN BOND
GEORGE MEEKER
WILLIAM HARRIGAN
CLARENCE WILSON

1933

Midnight Club (Paramount)

Directors:
AL HALL
GEORGE SOMES

Cast:
CLIVE BROOK
HELEN VINSON
ALISON SKIPWORTH
ALAN MOWBRAY

1933

The Bowery (United Artists)

Director:
RAOUL WALSH

Cast:
WALLACE BEERY
JACKIE COOPER

1934

All of Me (Paramount)

Director:
FRITZ LANG

Cast:
FREDRIC MARCH
MIRIAM HOPKINS
HELEN MACK

1934

Bolero (Paramount)

Director:
WESLEY RUGGLES

Cast:
CAROLE LOMBARD
SALLY RAND
WILLIAM FRAWLEY

1934

The Trumpet Blows (Paramount)

Director:
STEVEN ROBERTS

Cast:
FRANCES DRAKE
ADOLPH MENJOU

1934

Limehouse Blues (Paramount)

Director:
ALEXANDER HALL

Cast:
JEAN PARKER
ANNA MAY WONG
KENT TAYLOR
MONTAGU LOVE

1935

Rumba (Paramount)

Producer:
WILLIAM LeBARON

Director:
MARION GERING

Cast:
DENNIS O'KEEFE
CAROLE LOMBARD
MARGO
LYNNE OVERMAN
MONROE OWSLEY
MACK GREY

George Raft

1935

Stolen Harmony (Paramount)

Producer:
ALBERT LEWIS

Director:
ALFRED WERKER

Cast:
BEN BERNIE
LLOYD NOLAN
GRACE BRADLEY
GOODEE MONTGOMERY

1935

She Couldn't Take It (Columbia)

Producer:
B. P. SHULBERG

Director:
TAY GARNETT

Cast:
JOAN BENNETT
WALTER CONNOLLY
BILLIE BURKE
WALLACE FORD
JAMES BLAKELEY

1935

The Glass Key (Paramount)

Producer:
E. LLOYD SHELDON

Director:
FRANK TUTTLE

Cast:
EDWARD ARNOLD
CLAIRE DODD
RAY MILLAND
ROSALIND KEITH
CHARLES RICHMAN

1936

It Had to Happen (20th Century-Fox)

Producer:
DARRYL F. ZANUCK

Director:
ROY DEL RUTH

Cast:
ROSALIND RUSSELL
LEO CARILLO
ARLENE JUDGE
ALAN DINEHART
ARTHUR HOHL

1935

Every Night at Eight (Paramount)

Producer:
WALTER WAGNER
Director:
RAOUL WALSH

Cast:
ALICE FAYE
FRANCES LANGFORD
PATSY KELLY
LOUISE PLATT

1936

Yours for the Asking (Paramount)

Producer:
LEWIS E. GENSLER

Director:
ALEXANDER HALL

Cast:
DOLORES COSTELLO BARRYMORE
IDA LUPINO
REGINALD OWEN
JAMES GLEASON
EDGAR KENNEDY

Appendix: The films of George Raft

1937

Souls at Sea (Paramount)

Director:
HENRY HATHAWAY

Cast:
GARY COOPER
FRANCES DEE
HENRY WILCOXON
HARRY CAREY
ROBERT CUMMINGS
OLYMPE BRADNA

=======

1938

You and Me (Paramount)

Producer/Director:
FRITZ LANG

Cast:
SYLVIA SIDNEY
ROBERT CUMMINGS
LLOYD NOLAN
HARRY CAREY
ROSCOE KARNES
BARTON MacLANE

=======

1938

Spawn of the North (Paramount)

Producer:
ALBERT LEWIN

Director:
HENRY HATHAWAY

Cast:
HENRY FONDA
DOROTHY LAMOUR
JOHN BARRYMORE
AKIM TAMIROFF
LOUISE PLATT

1939

The Lady's from Kentucky (Paramount)

Producer:
JEFF LAZARUS

Director:
ALEXANDER HALL

Cast:
ELLEN DREW
ZASU PITTS
HUGH HERBERT
LOUISE BEAVERS
LOU PAYTON

=======

1939

Each Dawn I Die (Warner Brothers)

Associate Producer:
DAVID LEWIS

Director:
WILLIAM KEIGHLEY

Cast:
JAMES CAGNEY
GEORGE BANCROFT
JANE BRYAN
VICTOR JORY
MAXIE ROSENBLOOM
STANLEY RIDGES

=======

1939

Invisible Stripes (Warner Brothers)

Executive Producer:
HAL B. WALLIS

Director:
LLOYD BACON

Cast:
HUMPHREY BOGART
WILLIAM HOLDEN
JANE BRYAN
FLORA ROBSON
PAUL KELLY

George Raft

1939

I Stole a Million (Universal)

Associate Producer:
BURT KELLY

Director:
FRANK TUTTLE

Cast:
CLAIRE TREVOR
DICK FORAN
VICTOR JORY
HENRY ARMETTA
JOSEPH SAWYER

1940

The House across the Bay (United Artists)

Director:
ARCHIE MAYO

Cast:
JOAN BENNETT
LLOYD NOLAN
WALTER PIGEON
GLADYS GEORGE
WILLIAM "BILLY" WAYNE

1940

They Drive by Night (Warner Brothers)

Executive Producer:
HAL B. WALLIS

Associate Producer:
MARK HELLINGER

Director:
RAOUL WALSH

Cast:
HUMPHREY BOGART
ANN SHERIDAN
IDA LUPINO
ALAN HALE
GALE PAGE

1941

Manpower (Warner Brothers)

Executive Producer:
HAL B. WALLIS

Producer:
MARK HELLINGER

Director:
RAOUL WALSH

Cast:
MARLENE DIETRICH
EDWARD G. ROBINSON
FRANK McHUGH
BARTON MacLANE
ALAN HALE
WARD BOND
EVE ARDEN

1942

Broadway (Universal)

Producer:
BRUCE MANNING

Director:
WILLIAM A. SEITER

Cast:
PAT O'BRIEN
JANET BLAIR
JANIS PAIGE
BRODERICK CRAWFORD
EDWARD BROPHY
MARJORIE RAMBEAU
MACK GREY

1943

Stage Door Canteen (United Artists)

Producer:
SOL LESSER

Director:
FRANK BORZAGE

Cast:
CHERYL WALDER
WILLIAM TERRY
MERLE OBERON
TALLULAH BANKHEAD
RALPH BELLAMY
KATHARINE CORNELL
KATHARINE HEPBURN
BENNY GOODMAN
HARPO MARX
RAY BOLGER

1943

Background to Danger (Warner Brothers)

Producer:
JERRY WALD

Director:
RAOUL WALSH

Cast:
SYDNEY GREENSTREET
PETER LORRE
BRENDA MARSHALL
OSA MASSEN
TURHAN BEY

1944

Follow the Boys (Universal)

Producer:
CHARLES K. FELDMAN

Director:
EDWARD SUTHERLAND

Cast:
VERA ZORINA
CHARLES GRAPEWIN
Guest Stars:
CHARLES BOYER
W. C. FIELDS
DONALD O'CONNOR
ORSON WELLES
JEANETTE MacDONALD
SOPHIE TUCKER

1945

Nob Hill (20th Century-Fox)

Producer:
ANDRÉ DAVEN

Director:
HENRY HATHAWAY

Cast:
JOAN BENNETT
VIVIAN BLAINE
PEGGY ANN GARNER
ALAN REED

1945

Johnny Angel (RKO)

Producer:
WILLIAM L. PERIERA

Director:
EDWIN L. MARIN

Cast:
CLAIRE TREVOR
MARVIN MILLER
SIGNE HASSO
HOAGY CARMICHAEL
LOWELL BILMORE

1946

Mr. Ace (United Artists)

Producer:
BENEDICT BOGEAUS

Director:
EDWIN L. MARIN

Cast:
SYLVIA SIDNEY
STANLEY RIDGES
JEROME COWAN
SARA HADEN

1946

Nocturne (RKO)

Executive Producer:
JACK GROSS

Director:
EDWIN L. MARIN

Cast:
LYNN BARI
VIRGINIA HUSTON
JOSEPH PEVNEY
MYRNA DELL
EDWARD ASHLEY

George Raft

1946

Whistle Stop (United Artists)

Producer:
SEYMOUR NEBENZA

Director:
LEONIDE MOGUY

Cast:
AVA GARDNER
VICTOR McLAGLEN
TOM CONWAY
FLORENCE BATES

1947

Intrigue (United Artists)

Producer:
SAM BISCHOFF

Director:
EDWIN L. MARIN

Cast:
JUNE HAVOC
HELENA CARTER
TOM TULLY
MARVIN MILLER

1947

Christmas Eve (United Artists)

Producer:
BENEDICT BOGEAUS

Director:
EDWIN L. MARIN

Cast:
GEORGE BRENT
JOAN BLONDELL
RANDOLPH SCOTT
ANN HARDING
VIRGINIA FIELD

1948

Race Street (RKO)

Executive Producer:
JACK GROSS

Director:
EDWIN L. MARIN

Cast:
WILLIAM BENDIX
MARILYN MAXWELL
HENRY MORGAN
GALE ROBBINS

1949

Johnny Allegro (Columbia)

Producer:
IRVING STARR

Director:
TED TETZLAFF

Cast:
NINA FOCH
GEORGE MACREADY
WILL GEES
GLORIA HENRY

1949

Red Light (United Artists)

Producer/Director:
ROY DEL RUTH

Cast:
RAYMOND BURR
GENE LOCKHART
VIRGINIA MAYO
BARTON MacLANE
HENRY MORGAN

Appendix: The films of George Raft

1949

A Dangerous Profession (RKO)

Executive Producer:
SID ROGELL

Director:
TED TETZLAFF

Cast:
ELLA RAINES
PAT O'BRIEN
JIM BACKUS
BILL WILLIAMS

1949

Outpost in Morocco (United Artists)

Producer:
SAMUEL BISCHOFF

Director:
ROBERT FLOREY

Cast:
MARIE WINDSOR
AKIM TAMIROFF
JOHN LITEL
EDUARD FRANZ

1949

Nous Irons à Paris (Unidex)

Director:
JEAN BOYER

Cast:
PHILIPPE LEMAIRE
FRANCOISE AMOUL
CHRISTIAN DUVALLOIX
HENRI GENES

1951

Lucky Nick Cain (20th Century-Fox)

Producer:
JOSEPH KAUFMAN

Director:
JOSEPH M. NEWMAN

Cast:
COLLEEN GRAY
CHARLES GOLDNER
ENZO STAIOLA
GRETA GYNT
WALTER RILLA

1952

Loan Shark (Lippert Productions, Inc., England)

Producer:
BERNARD LUBER

Director:
SEYMOUR MARK FRIEDMAN

Cast:
DOROTHY HART
PAUL STEWART
JOHN HOYT
HENRY SLATE

1953

I'll Get You (Lippert Productions, Inc., England)

Producer:
BERNARD LUBER

Director:
SEYMOUR MARK FRIEDMAN

Cast:
SALLY GRAY
CLIFFORD EVANS
REGINALD TATE

261

George Raft

1953

The Man from Cairo
(Lippert Productions, Inc., England)

Producer:
BERNARD LUBER

Director:
RAY H. ENRIGHT

Cast:
MASSIMO SERATO
GIANNA MARIA CANALE
GUIDO CELANO
IRENE PAPAS

1955

A Bullet for Joey
(United Artists)

Producer:
SAMUEL BISCHOFF, DAVID DIAMOND

Director:
LEWIS ALLEN

Cast:
EDWARD G. ROBINSON
AUDREY TOTTER
PETER VAN EYCK
GEORGE DOLENZ

1954

Rogue Cop (MGM)

Producer:
NICHOLAS NAYFACK

Director:
ROY ROWLAND

Cast:
ROBERT TAYLOR
JANET LEIGH
ANN FRANCIS
ROBERT ELLENSTEIN
STEVE FOREST

1956

Around the World in 80 Days
(United Artists)

Producer:
MICHAEL TODD

Director:
MICHAEL ANDERSON

Cast:
DAVID NIVEN
CANTINFLAS
MARLENE DIETRICH
AND GUEST STARS

1954

Black Widow (20th Century-Fox)

Producer/Director:
NUNNALY JOHNSON

Cast:
GINGER ROGERS
VAN HEFLIN
GENE TIERNEY
PEGGY ANN GARNER

1959

Some Like It Hot
(United Artists)

Producer/Director:
BILLY WILDER

Cast:
MARILYN MONROE
JACK LEMMON
TONY CURTIS
JOE E. BROWN
PAT O'BRIEN

Appendix: The films of George Raft

1960

Jet over the Atlantic
(Intercontinent)

Producer:
BENEDICT BOGEAUS

Director:
BYRON HASKIN

Cast:
VIRGINIA MAYO
ILONA MASSEY
GUY MADISON
GEORGE MACREADY

1960

Ocean's Eleven
(Warner Brothers)

Producer/Director:
LEWIS MILESTONE

Cast:
FRANK SINATRA
PETER LAWFORD
DEAN MARTIN
ANGIE DICKINSON
SAMMY DAVIS, JR.
RICHARD CONTE

1961

The Ladies' Man (Paramount)

Producer/Director:
JERRY LEWIS

Cast:
JERRY LEWIS
KATHLEEN FREEMAN
PAT STANLEY
HELEN TRAUBEL

1962

Two Guys Abroad
(Summit, London) (Not released)

Producer:
IAN WARREN

Director:
DON SHARP

Cast:
MAXIE ROSENBLOOM
DIANE TODD
DIANA DECKER
DAVID LAWTON

1964

For Those Who Think Young
(United Artists)

Executive Producer:
HOWARD W. KOCH

Director:
LESLIE H. MARTINSON

Cast:
JAMES DARREN
PAMELA TIFFIN
NANCY SINATRA
JACK LaRUE
WOODY WOODBURY
TINA LOUISE

1964

The Patsy (Paramount)

Producer:
ERNEST D. GLUCKMAN

Director:
JERRY LEWIS

Cast:
JERRY LEWIS
INA BALIN
EVERETT SLOANE
PETER LORRE
KEENAN WYNN
PHIL HARRIS

1967

Five Golden Dragons
(Blansfilm Productions)

Producer:
HARRY ALAN TOWERS

Director:
JEREMY SUMMERS

Cast:
ROBERT CUMMINGS
BRIAN DONLEVEY
DAN DURYEA
MARGARET LEE
RUPERT DAVIES

1967

The Upper Hand (Paramount)
(U.S. release of *Riffifi*
in *Panama-Comacio*)

Executive Producer:
RAYMOND DANON

Director:
DENYS DE LA PATELLIERE

Cast:
JEAN GABIN
GERT FROBE
NADIA TILLER
MIREILLE DARC

1967

Casino Royale (Columbia)

Producer:
CHARLES FELDMAN

Directors:
JOHN HUSTON
KENNETH HUGHS
VAL GUEST
ROBERT PARRISH
JOE McGRATH

Cast:
DAVID NIVEN
ORSON WELLES
WOODY ALLEN
PETER SELLERS
WILLIAM HOLDEN
URSULA ANDRESS

1968

Skidoo (Paramount)

Producer/Director:
OTTO PREMINGER

Cast:
JACKIE GLEASON
CAROL CHANNING
FRANKIE AVALON
FRED CLARK
GROUCHO MARX

1971

Deadhead Miles
(Paramount) (not released)

Producers:
TONY BILL
VERNON ZIMMERMAN

Director:
VERNON ZIMMERMAN

Cast:
ALAN ARKIN
PAUL BENEDICT
AVERY SCHREIBER
OLIVER CLARK
IDA LUPINO

1972

Hammersmith Is Out
(United Artists)

Executive Producer:
FRANK BEETSON

Director:
PETER USTINOV

Cast:
RICHARD BURTON
ELIZABETH TAYLOR
PETER USTINOV
BEAU BRIDGES

SELECTED BIBLIOGRAPHY

Asbury, Herbert: *The Gangs of New York*, Alfred A. Knopf, Inc., New York, 1927.

Bergman, Andrew: *We're in the Money: Depression America and Its Films*, New York University Press, 1971.

Boulart, Ron: *Line Up the Tough Guys*, Sherbourne Press, Inc., Los Angeles, 1966.

Churchill, Allen: *The Great White Way: A Re-creation of Broadway's Golden Era of Theatrical Entertainment*, E. P. Dutton & Co., Inc., New York, 1962.

Day, Beth: *This Was Hollywood*, Doubleday & Co., Inc., Garden City, New York, 1960.

Gilbert, Douglas: *American Vaudeville: Its Life and Times*, McGraw-Hill Book Company, Inc., New York, 1940.

Goodman, Ezra: *The Fifty Year Decline and Fall of Hollywood*, Simon and Schuster, New York, 1961.

Gottlieb, Polly Rose: *The Nine Lives of Billy Rose*, Crown Publishers, Inc., New York, 1968.

Graham, Sheilah: *The Garden of Allah*, Crown Publishers, Inc., New York, 1970.

Green, Abel, and Laurie, Joe, Jr.: *Show Biz: From Vaudeville to Video*, Henry Holt and Co., New York, 1951.

Gussow, Mel: *Don't Say Yes until I Finish Talking: A Biography of Darryl F. Zanuck*, Doubleday & Co., Inc., Garden City, New York, 1971.

Jennings, Dean: *We Only Kill Each Other*, Prentice-Hall, Inc., Englewood Cliffs, New Jersey, 1967.

Knight, Arthur: *The Liveliest Art*, The Macmillan Company, New York, 1957.

Laurie, Joe, Jr.: *Vaudeville: From the Honky Tonks to the Palace*, Henry Holt and Co., New York, 1953.

Messick, Hank: *Lansky*, G. P. Putnam's Sons, New York, 1971.

Rivkin, Allen, and Kerr, Laura: *Hello Hollywood!*, Doubleday & Co., Inc., Garden City, New York, 1962.

Sadoul, Georges: *Dictionary of Film Makers*, University of California Press, Berkeley, 1972.

George Raft

Seldes, Gilbert: *The Great Audience*, The Viking Press, Inc., New York, 1950.

Shipman, David: *The Great Movie Stars*, Bonanza, a division of Crown Publishers, New York, 1970.

Shulman, Irving: *Valentino*, Trident Press, New York, 1967.

Wagenknecht, Edward: *The Movies in the Age of Innocence*, University of Oklahoma Press, 1962.

Warner, Jack, and Jennings, Dean: *My First Hundred Years in Hollywood: An Autobiography*, Random House, Inc., New York, 1964.

West, Mae: *Goodness Had Nothing to Do with It*, Prentice-Hall, Inc., Englewood Cliffs, New Jersey, 1959.

Zierold, Norman: *The Moguls*, Coward-McCann, Inc., New York, 1969.

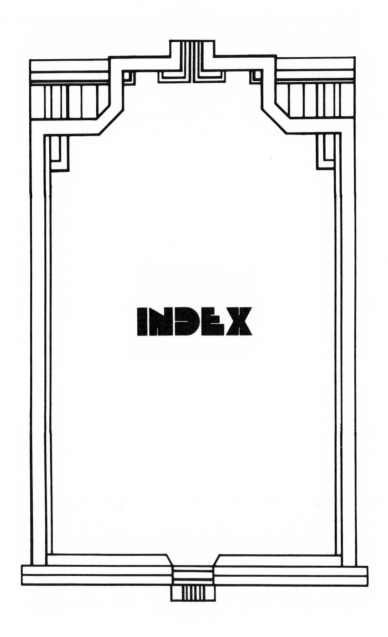

INDEX

INDEX

Index

Index

Index

Index

Index

Index

Index

Index

Index

Index

Index

Index

Index

Index

Index

Index

Index

Index

Index

ABOUT THE AUTHOR

Lewis Yablonsky was born and grew up in Newark, New Jersey, and was graduated from Rutgers University in 1948. He received his Ph.D. in Sociology from New York University in 1958. Yablonsky has taught sociology and criminology at the University of Massachusetts, CCNY, Columbia, Harvard, and UCLA. In 1965 he became President of the California Institute of Psychodrama, an educational institute devoted to the theory and practice of psychodrama and group psychotherapy. He is currently Professor of Sociology at California State University at Northridge. His books include *The Violent Gang* (1962), *Synanon: The Tunnel Back* (1965), *The Hippie Trip* (1968) and *The Robopaths* (1972). Professor Yablonsky lives with his wife and young son in Los Angeles.